The Hunny Bunny: A Memoir

The Hunny Bunny: A Memoir

A YOUNG GIRL'S LIFE WITH A CONGENITAL HEART DEFECT

Jack Murtha

ISBN-13: 9781544630571
ISBN-10: 1544630573
Library of Congress Control Number: 2017904434
CreateSpace Independent Publishing Platform
North Charleston, South Carolina

For Katie.

The day will come when even this ordeal
will be a sweet thing to remember.

—Virgil, *The Aeneid*

Table of Contents

Note to Readers

Medical information included in this book represents my understanding of my daughter's complex heart defect and treatment. Short of watching an occasional episode of *MASH*, I have no medical training. Anyone suffering from, or caring for someone with, similar or other serious conditions should seek guidance from a medical professional.

This book originated in the extensive notes I kept throughout Katie's life. I built upon this framework using hospital records, correspondence, recollections of family members and staff, and, invaluably, the medical log my mother kept. Quotations come from my own memory and contemporaneous notes. I tried to characterize conversations herein accurately. Any fault in so doing is entirely mine.

I used no composite characters in this book. Due to space constraints, I included but a fraction of Katie's caregivers. I hope those omitted feel no slight. Filling a library with expressions of thanks would not begin to capture the depth of my gratitude, let alone a single memoir.

I did take poetic license in one regard: I am much thinner in the book.

Introduction

My tenure as a biology major lasted three days. Fifty-three hours to be exact. As I struggled to stay awake during the second lecture of Bio 101, I observed how the course material enthralled my pre-med classmates. After the lecture, I proceeded to the Registrar's Office to change my major. My exposure to the life sciences ended and, with it, any formal preparation for the ordeal that lay ahead. Little did I know that, years later, physicians would expect me to make critical decisions regarding my infant daughter's medical treatment. When I walked out of that classroom almost twenty years ago, I thought I had forever left the world of medicine. I was wrong.

Life has many cruel realities. That some kids are born sick is one of them. I am not referring to tummy aches and runny noses, but the very adult conditions of heart defects, lung disease, and neurological disorders, just to name a few. Some kids lose the genetic lottery, while others are stricken by pure chance. I managed to live almost four decades shielded from that reality. I would never have a sick kid, for that only happens to other people. I was wrong.

My daughter, Katie, suffered from a rare congenital heart defect known as Ebstein's Anomaly. A heart valve smaller than the diameter of a pencil failed to develop properly. Her deformity was even rarer by its severity. Less than one percent of Ebstein patients are so afflicted. Moreover, Katie's diagnosing cardiologist had never encountered a more profound case of Ebstein's. After receiving her diagnosis, I saw nothing in our little family's future but sadness and despair. I was wrong.

Katie lived a life of triumphant inspiration and joy. I am not sugarcoating the adversity she faced or the trials of parenting a critically ill baby. Despite a difficult and brutal road, the joy of the exquisite good times far exceeded the sadness. From her little hospital bed, Katie brought out the very best in those who knew her. That is quite an accomplishment for an infant who did not live to see her first birthday.

Katie's illness opened my eyes to a world I never knew existed, a world populated by an army of doctors, nurses, therapists, and professionals dedicated to saving the most innocent among us. Many children with conditions constituting a death sentence just years ago now have a fighting chance not only to survive, but to thrive. While we sleep in after a night out, they take care of our kids. While we catch a ballgame, they take care of our kids. While we celebrate holidays, they take care of our kids. They are blessings to our community.

A congenital heart defect does not bring the world to a grinding halt. The stressors of normal life remain. Family and staff alike occasionally buckled under the pressure. Neglecting this aspect of those involved in Katie's life would undermine her ultimate triumph. Our human imperfection makes her story all the more remarkable.

For you parents currently fighting on behalf of your sick child, I offer you my prayers. We thought we were running a marathon, and, even though our race ended all too soon, the experience left us drained and exhausted. For those battling year after year, you have my admiration. To those who know parents in such circumstances, I ask you to continue your prayers and support. I cannot tell you how many nights I sat in the hospital scrolling through text messages and rereading e-mails and cards. I found great solace in those words of comfort, and I doubt I am alone in this. You never know when your simple token of support will provide the one glimmer of light in an otherwise dark day.

In this writing, I chronicle Katie's story as I experienced it. This is not, however, a book about me, my wife and family, or Katie's caregivers and supporters. This book is ultimately about Katie. Dennis Wilson once said of his brother, "Brian Wilson is The Beach Boys. We are his messengers." Those of us privileged to know Katie are her messengers. I hope that, in the course of reading this book, you become a messenger, too.

I invite you now to follow Katie on her journey and thank you for the honor of introducing you to The Hunny Bunny.

CHAPTER 1

Hubris

"How BAD COULD THIS BE?" The thought reverberated in my mind. "How bad could this be?" Little did I know.

My wife, Krista, and I pensively awaited the arrival of our first baby following an emergency C-Section. A nurse practitioner, Shea, had whisked our daughter to another floor for testing while the doctor closed Krista's incision. Shea, suspecting the newborn had fluid in her lungs, explained this was standard procedure and promised to return the baby in roughly forty-five minutes. An hour passed and then some before Shea returned alone.

"The cardiologist wants to speak with you," she said.

Shea had entered Krista's room without turning on the light and stood ramrod straight with hands clasped at her abdomen. The darkness of night partially obscured her face. Ambient light from monitors and the hallway at 3:00 a.m. served more to cast shadows than illuminate. Her features betrayed no hint of concern; her voice lacked all inflection. She crossed the room in silence to hand me my phone. Krista had not seen her child during the chaos of the delivery, so I had given the device to a nurse and asked her to take a few photos for the new mom. Her message delivered and task complete, Shea left us literally and figuratively in the dark.

I approached my wife's bedside and brought up five pictures of Katherine on my phone's small screen. Her color appeared normal. She was alert, her eyes scanning the room. Her head was in focus in every shot, but her hands blurred in a few, indicating motion. Katherine sported a diaper and a white band on her left wrist. Dark, matted hair covered her scalp. Two white, nickel-size discs adhered to her upper chest, connected to a machine by two wires. Two pieces of taupe tape ran ear-to-ear across her face, holding a white, flat piece of plastic shaped like an elongated "X" over her mouth. The plastic device anchored a clear tube, the significance of which I did not recognize.

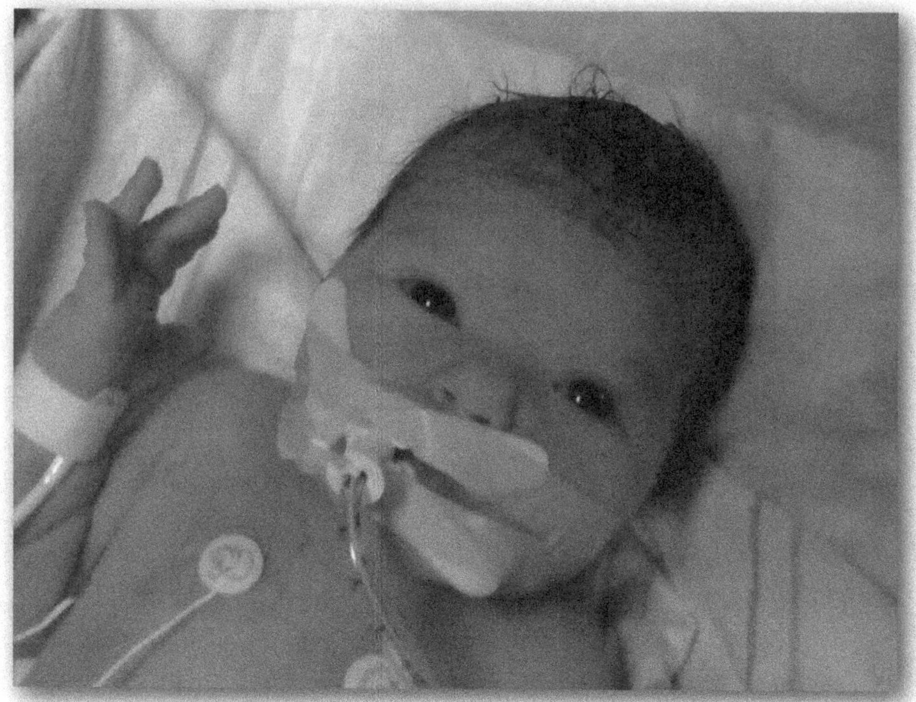

An alert Katherine within an hour of her birth.

Tears overcame my wife as she gazed at the photos. If she were clear headed enough to recognize the tube, she did not express alarm. I passed the phone to my mom standing on the other side of Krista's bed. She smiled and remarked that her new granddaughter was beautiful before returning the phone. With almost forty years of nursing experience, many of them in intensive care, she recognized the tube instantly: The baby was on a ventilator. Oblivious, I returned to my chair when Krista closed her eyes to rest.

My mind started the mantra again as I scrolled through the pictures, "How bad could this be?" In the operating room, the nurse practitioner suspected

Katherine might have fluid in her lungs. The cardiologist's impending visit suggested a much more serious issue.

"How bad could this be?" It was 2013. We had done everything right. Krista, a pharmacist, had maintained a good diet and abstained from alcohol. She had all the recommended tests. If something were seriously wrong with Katherine, someone, somewhere would have detected it long ago. We saw Katherine's heart beating when she was the size of a grape. Surely, someone would have caught a major problem. Replaying Shea's message in my mind, I wondered if I missed something in her delivery, perhaps a tell indicating something terribly amiss.

The sparse light from the hallway flittered as someone entered the room. I surmised she was a physician by the confidence in her movements. Although nicely dressed in dark slacks and a button-down shirt, her tousled brown hair betrayed that someone had roused her from sleep. Katherine's problem, whatever it was, could not wait until the morning shift arrived or be resolved over the phone. It required the doctor's presence despite the early hour.

The hallway light flickered again. Six nameless staff members clad in scrubs silently entered and formed a phalanx ten feet behind the doctor. They moved slowly, dejectedly, without making eye contact.

The cardiologist broke the silence. "Krista?"

"Yes," my wife replied weakly.

"My name is Dr. Ginnie Abarbanell. I'm a pediatric cardiologist."

Dr. Abarbanell pulled an empty chair alongside Krista's bed. She took Krista's right elbow in her right hand, allowing her forearm to rest on that of Krista. I recognized this sign of intimacy and my heart sank. I did not need to hear anymore. I knew.

"I am so very, very sorry."

Dr. Abarbanell maintained contact with Krista in silence as the new mother absorbed the message. After a long pause, she placed a piece of blank printer paper against a clipboard and began to draw.

Katherine's story began in the college town of Fort Collins, Colorado. Krista, a junior at Colorado State University, and I met at a swing dance class in the final months of my first Air Force assignment. Our budding friendship was short-lived. I transferred from F.E. Warren Air Force Base (AFB) in Cheyenne, Wyoming to Hanscom AFB, a stone's throw from Boston, four months later. We lost touch as our paths diverged. She eventually enrolled in pharmacy school at the University of Colorado while I remained in the service. We began e-mailing two years later. E-mails gave way to phone calls. By the fall of 2004, we were officially a couple, albeit geographically separated.

After I volunteered to deploy for more than two years, the Department of Defense finally granted my request. With war raging in Iraq and Afghanistan, the Air Force sent me to Cuba. While not exactly the opportunity I envisioned, it was a deployment nonetheless. Assigned to the organization conducting tribunals for detainees captured during post 9/11 operations, I spent the majority of my time in a support role while the military attorneys did the heavy lifting. Working with the JAGs inspired me to attend law school upon returning to the States.

Location was the most significant consideration in selecting a school. Eight years had passed since I left my hometown for the Air Force. Nestled in the heart of the Appalachian Mountains on the meandering Youghiogheny River about sixty miles southeast of Pittsburgh, the small hamlet of Connellsville will always be home. Once known as the "Coal and Coke Capital of the World," Connellsville's fortunes waned in correlation with the demand for its cheap coal. My mother, maternal grandmother, aunts, uncles, and a large extended family remained. My grandmother still lived in the stone house my grandfather built in the Forties. My only sibling, Susan, however, had left the Pennsylvania years earlier to work for a major pharmaceutical company in Indianapolis, and my dad retired to Florida with his wife. Wanting to be closer to family, I applied to schools close to family in multiple states and crossed my fingers.

I cannot name the patron saint of school loans, but I know he has a soft spot for Notre Dame. The Notre Dame Law School offered me a seat in the class of 2009. As a Catholic from a working class family who attended twelve years of parochial school and served 494 masses, this accomplishment is second only to curing cancer, presuming the football team is having a rough year.[1] Moreover, only a three-hour drive separated the university from Indianapolis, where my sister lived and my mom planned to relocate upon retirement. After Krista gave her blessing, I set out for South Bend.

The economy collapsed as graduation approached, leaving Krista and me amongst the masses scrambling for employment. With enormous school debt and not even two nickels to rub together, we could not afford for either of us to remain unemployed. I fortunately received an offer from an insurance defense firm in northwest Indiana. Krista received two offers, both in Indianapolis, and accepted a position as a hospice pharmacist with St. Vincent Hospital. We decided to live apart for yet another year before one of us would relocate after our wedding in October of 2010.

In accordance with the plan, I resigned my position with the firm in the weeks before our wedding and packed my bags for Indianapolis. Krista and I moved into our first apartment on November 1, 2010. Although I had not yet found permanent employment, I finally lived in the same town as my wife, sister, and my sister's family. Five years of planning and sacrificing had finally paid off … for seven months. After accepting a position with The Hershey Company in Pennsylvania, my sister left Indiana with her husband and kids the following July.

Marooned in a city with neither family nor attachments, Krista and I never established roots. We sought opportunities to relocate to either Colorado or Pennsylvania without luck. Odious licensing requirements, enormous school loan debt, and a terrible job market frustrated our efforts at every turn. I struggled to find steady employment. Having transferred into the Air National Guard as a military attorney, I volunteered for every exercise and training opportunity that came my way. I occasionally found work augmenting the legal office at Wright-Patterson AFB outside of Dayton, Ohio. As I crossed the bucolic plains of Ohio in route to Wright-Patterson in September of 2012, Krista called to announce she was pregnant.

1 Max Reidman, who administered my church's alter boy program, kept statistics as if he worked for Major League Baseball.

We entered 2013 with the wind at our backs and clear skies ahead. Aside from some heartburn and nausea, Krista experienced an uneventful pregnancy with no sign of any problems. I had accepted a position with the U.S. Army at the Rock Island Arsenal in Rock Island, Illinois, approximately five hours from Indianapolis. Starting in March, 2013, I commuted to Illinois during the week and spent my weekends back in Indianapolis. We anticipated this arrangement lasting until July when Krista and the baby would join me.

Krista had her second sonogram in the seventeenth week of her pregnancy. I tagged along for moral support. The technician positioned the screen so that Krista could not see the images from the gurney. Sitting on the other side of the room, I had a great view. Playing John Madden, I called the images as I saw them only for the technician to correct me. I stopped talking after exclaiming, "I see her spine!" and the technician replied dryly, "That's her jaw." The technician thereafter identified the baby's various body parts as she worked through a checklist without my commentary. She gave no indication of anything amiss.

A doctor met with us briefly afterward to discuss the test results. He was not Krista's primary obstetrician, and we would never see him again. He entered the room carrying a strip of ultrasound pictures, briskly introduced himself, and said that everything looked fine. He asked Krista for her due date. She responded June 1. He quickly measured and listened to her belly before heading for the door. As the doctor turned the handle, Krista reported that her blood pressure was uncharacteristically high. The doctor stopped, turned to me, and said half-jokingly, "Does she always complain like this?" He did not wait for an answer and told Krista it did not warrant concern. With that, he disappeared. Our elation that the baby was healthy overshadowed the doctor's unorthodox bedside manner.

Both the doctor and the technician failed to identify the heart defect. In the days immediately following the birth, Krista and I asked many doctors how such a large problem could escape detection. Opinions amongst physicians willing to answer varied. No one would affirm whether one could detect the anomaly that early in the pregnancy. I sensed at least some professional deference if not doctors circling the wagons. Discovering the defect in utero would not have changed the prognosis, so I considered the failed diagnosis little more than an academic curiosity. On the positive side, it saved us five months of worry.

I settled into my new job at the Rock Island Arsenal as the due date approached. The Arsenal is, as the name suggests, an island in the Mississippi River between the Illinois cities of Rock Island and Moline to the south and Iowa's Davenport and Bettendorf to the north. Better known as "The Quad Cities," the area has a small town, Midwestern feel – a perfect place to raise kids. I found the ideal house for us in Davenport. We made an offer and closed on April 30. With a new job and house and a baby just a month away, Krista and I were excited to start the next phase of our lives.

A week before Krista's due date, a gregarious attorney at work stopped by my office to chat and asked whether we knew the baby's gender. I informed him we were having a girl. He asked whether I had a preference. "To be honest," I said, "I don't care one way or the other as long as it's healthy."

Krista went into labor in the early morning of June 2, 2013, one day after her due date. We remained at home until she had a full hour of contractions. Throughout the day, the contractions would cease after fifty minutes before resuming twenty minutes later. Sitting or lying down made them more painful, so she endured wave after wave of contractions while standing. Finally, at 5:30 p.m., Krista hit the magical sixty minutes with recurring contractions. I helped her to the car, and we drove fifteen minutes to St. Vincent Women's Hospital.

The hospital is a long, squat, three-story building tucked behind the main St. Vincent Hospital facility in northern Indianapolis. Delivery and operating rooms are on the second floor along with a small Neonatal Intensive Care Unit (NICU). The main NICU and recovery rooms are on the top floor.

The hospitalist admitted and transferred Krista to a delivery room on the second floor at 6:30 p.m. Krista progressed slowly. Exhausted and in great discomfort after more than twelve hours of labor, Krista asked for an epidural at 8:30 p.m. The drug allowed Krista to finally rest.

Huge aficionados of sixties music, Krista and I entered the gloaming listening to the sounds of The Beatles and Beach Boys. It pained me to watch Krista struggle, and I tried to console her.

> "Babe," I said. "I hate watching you in pain. If we could trade places right now, I wouldn't. But I still hate watching you endure this."

That earned a laugh, which was about as much as I could do. As midnight approached, it became increasingly obvious that our daughter would not be born on June 2. I joked that, for Krista's sake, I hoped the baby would arrive on the third.

My mother arrived from Connellsville at 1:15 a.m. to find Krista comfortable with no indication of distress. Dilation was slow in coming, so we settled in for a long night. At 2:20 a.m., the delivery nurse informed us that the cafeteria closed at the bottom of the hour. Expecting hours of additional waiting, I asked Krista if she minded me picking up a snack. She encouraged both of us to go. With less than ten minutes before closing, we took the elevator to the cafeteria one floor below.

We quickly grabbed a few items in the cafeteria. I offered the cashier a few bills, but she held her hand out like a traffic cop: "We only take credit at night." Seeing the big hand a few minutes shy of the "6" on the analog clock behind her, I left mom at the counter and raced back to my wallet in the delivery room. I barreled through Krista's door and stopped dead in my tracks.

Stark fluorescent light supplanted the dark, restful environment I had left just minutes earlier. Concern bordering on fear filled the eyes of the half dozen staff members clad in scrubs tending to Krista. They had positioned Krista on her side. Blood covered the backs of her legs. I locked eyes with one of the staff members. Her eyes blazing with intensity, she did not beckon me into the room. I nodded my head, hoping to communicate that I knew something was wrong and was stepping out so as not to interfere. She broke our brief connection to focus on Krista. I backed out of the room and, with adrenaline flooding my system, ran down the stairs to inform mom. When I returned, I found an empty room. Towels and bandages littered the bloodstained floor. I headed to the nurses' station when an unfamiliar nurse stopped me in the hall.

> "The baby's heartbeat dropped dramatically, so we took Krista down to the OR for a C-Section. The heart rate went back up, and it looks like both mom and baby are fine. We are going to keep Krista in the OR for a little while so that we can monitor both of them. Krista is doing fine. We'll let you know if anything changes."

I quickly studied her expressions and demeanor. She was sufficiently concerned to assure me that she knew the situation, but not so concerned as to put me on edge. After exhaling with relief, I looked at her nametag: "Stephanie." I retreated to the delivery room and updated mom.

I spent a few minutes pacing, fretting that I had been with Krista for more than sixteen hours of labor yet was absent when she needed me. A now frantic Stephanie bolted in the room, interrupting my self-flagellation.

> "They're going now! Follow me!" She was already in a full sprint when she exclaimed, "Hurry!"
> "What happened?" I asked while chasing her down the hall. She did not pause to answer.

Stephanie stopped outside a set of double doors that led to the OR. She quickly dressed me in a gown, booties, mask, gloves, and cap. Before I could ask her again, "What happened?" she took me firmly by the shoulders, turned me around, put her hand flat against the middle of my back, and pushed me through the doors.

I made my entrance just seconds after Katherine. The scene was much worse than anything I had anticipated. I got a fleeting glance at the baby's head as

I took a seat by Krista. With arms splayed out, Krista was deathly pale, shaking, and complaining that her dry mouth made breathing difficult. Below the curtain, I could see her midsection as they fought to extract the baby. A dozen rolled green towels caked in dark red blood sat stacked like cordwood on a table at Krista's feet. Masks did not hide the furtive expressions on the physicians' faces.

Serendipitously, Krista and the anesthesiologist working the floor that night, Dr. Wright, served on a hospital committee together. Keeping an eye on Krista throughout his shift, he not only ensured her comfort, but also arguably saved her and our daughter's life. Troubled by monitor readings in the delivery room, Dr. Wright insisted that Krista be moved to an operating room. Krista's condition or that of the baby sufficiently concerned him that he remained by her side to monitor the situation. The obstetrician was not present when their condition rapidly deteriorated. The initially indecisive residents delivered the baby in response to Dr. Wright's stern prodding.

Katherine disappeared in a flurry of arms and gloved hands upon entering the world. One anonymous staff member erupted, "Congratulations! It's a healthy boy!" Krista, even in her current state, and I exclaimed in perfect unison, "What?" The nurse practitioner (NP), Shea, corrected him. He repositioned the baby and said anticlimactically with more than a bit of embarrassment, "Oh, yeah ... a girl." Krista then collapsed back on the bed. She repeatedly asked, "Did the baby cry? I didn't hear her cry? Did she cry?" I reassured her that Katherine had a good cry.

Having recovered from his gender miscall, the man cut Katherine's umbilical cord and gave her to Shea. The NP placed Katherine in a bassinet ten feet from Krista's bed and invited me to visit a few minutes later. As I watched Katherine Elizabeth squirm under an oxygen mask, Shea informed me that the umbilical cord had wrapped around Katherine's neck and preceded her in the birth canal. The cord constricted with each contraction, necessitating a C-section. Shea's immediate concern was Katherine struggling to breathe, thus explaining the oxygen mask. Katherine's ribcage and belly expanded and contracted forcefully with each breath; however, having never seen a newborn, I did not recognize that as problematic.

I returned to Krista's side after she called for me. She wanted water desperately, but, consumed with closing the incision, the staff ignored my appeals just as they had hers. Dr. Wright finally directed an anonymous woman to bring water. Once delivered, he helped Krista wet her mouth, and she relaxed. As if on cue, Shea again beckoned me to Katherine.

While I looked for water, Shea had moved Katherine to a larger bassinet in a room directly behind the OR. The new, deluxe model had a variety of accoutrements to heat, provide oxygen for, and God knows what else to keep babies alive. The significance of upgrading bassinets was lost on me.

Shea wanted to take Katherine to an examination room in the NICU one floor above for additional testing. Explaining that "[her] job was to ensure Katherine breathed sufficiently," she suspected Katherine had pneumonia. Shea promised to deliver Katherine to Krista's room after the examination in roughly forty-five minutes. She was concerned, but not terribly so.

The transport team tried to wheel Katherine through the OR so Krista could see her daughter, but the heater on the hulking bassinet slammed hard against the wall above the door. With all of its bells and whistles, the bassinet did not fit through the OR entrance. Shea and a few nurses instead wheeled Katherine out another exit without first visiting her mother.

With my angst over Katherine subdued, my thoughts returned to Krista. The doctors were still closing her incision. A look of profound disappointment fell on Krista's face when I told her the staff had taken the baby upstairs. Since she could not see Katherine in person, I arranged the next best thing. I found Krista's nurse at the nurses' station and asked her to take some photos of Katherine with my phone. Although a little taken aback at the request, she agreed. I returned to Krista, and the tension of a calamitous delivery subsided with every minute. We had weathered the storm and reached calm seas, or so I thought.

CHAPTER 2

Shock and Awe

A NORMAL HUMAN HEART CONSISTS of four chambers, two small filling chambers (atria) atop two large pumping chambers (ventricles). The heart muscles comprising the chamber walls are incredibly strong and resilient, beating more than a billion times in an average person's lifetime. Powerful enough to pump blood through the entire body, the heart muscle is all brawn and no brain. The muscle contracts without regard to where the blood goes, relying on a series of four valves to direct blood in the proper direction. Each ventricle has a valve at its entrance and exit. The atria and ventricles alternately contract in concert with the valves opening and closing to propel blood forward through the circulatory system.

Deoxygenated blood returns to the heart's right atrium primarily through two large veins, the superior vena cava (SVC) and inferior vena cava (IVC). The tricuspid valve blocks blood in the atrium from prematurely entering the right ventricle. Following the ventricle's contraction, the tricuspid valve opens to allow blood in the atrium to pass through the aperture into the expanding ventricle. The pulmonary valve blocks further progress. The tricuspid valve closes and the pulmonary valve opens as the ventricle contracts again, directing blood to the lungs via the pulmonary artery. This process repeats on the left side of the heart, pumping oxygen-rich blood to the body.

The tricuspid valve is itself a complicated little machine. True to its name, the valve is comprised of three flaps (or leaflets) of muscle lying naturally across the opening between the right atrium and ventricle. Rope-like tendons tether the flaps to the inner wall of the ventricle. The force of the ventricle contracting pushes the flaps over the hole, and the tendons restrain the flaps from prolapsing into the atrium. When the ventricle expands, the current of blood from the atrium pushes the flaps down into the ventricle.

Ebstein's Anomaly is a rare congenital heart defect involving the tricuspid valve that affects one in every 200,000 births and comprises less than 1 percent of all congenital heart defects.[2] Malformed valve leaflets and/or leaflets anchored too low in the right ventricle characterize the condition. The malformation allows blood to leak from the right ventricle back to the right atrium. The Anomaly is present very early in the pregnancy, as the heart develops sufficiently to start beating in the first three to four weeks. No known cause exists.

The severity of Ebstein's Anomaly defects varies widely. Some people live long lives without any symptoms; others do not survive gestation. A patient with a mild form of Ebstein's may require only careful monitoring. Moving along the severity spectrum, treatment may include medications, surgical correction, and valve replacement. These methods preserve the functional four-chamber heart, which is impossible in the most severe cases. When tricuspid valve functionality cannot be restored, the only two means of survival are a right atrium and ventricle bypass or a heart transplant.

Tapping a pen against the rough sketch of Katherine's heart, Dr. Abarbanell informed us that the nurse practitioner had x-rayed Katie's chest to confirm pneumonia after the delivery. The x-rays and subsequent imaging revealed something far more insidious. Katherine had an extremely severe case of Ebstein's, the most severe case she had seen in her career as a cardiologist.

Dr. Abarbanell explained Katherine's defect using non-technical language. The flaps comprising Katie's valve were significantly malformed and misplaced, sitting close to the bottom of the ventricle. The muscular support structure anchoring the flaps was likewise deformed. Therefore, the valve

2 Attenhofer Jost, CH, Connolly, HM, *Congenital Heart Disease for the Adult Cardiologist: Ebstein's Anomaly.* American Heart Association Journal. 2007; 115: 277-285.

could not prevent blood from flowing backward into the atrium, depriving the lungs of blood and creating backpressure in both the atrium and organs closest to the heart in the circulatory system. Katherine's heart had grown in size and strength to offset pumping inefficiency. At the ultrasound five months earlier, a doctor failed to notice any abnormality. Another doctor later told us that he mistook a shadow for the valve. Katie's heart at birth, three times the size of a healthy infant's heart, occupied most of her chest cavity. No one could mistake it for a shadow now. Katie struggled even with the aid of a ventilator.

Aggressive surgical intervention presented Katherine's only chance to survive. Even if the operations were resoundingly successful, Katherine would never heal. She would never be normal. She could not be fixed. Calm but firm, Dr. Abarbanell said she could keep Katherine comfortable and recommended letting Katherine go.

Shocked, I slumped back in my chair. Because of my brief time with Katherine and, perhaps, the chaos in the operating room, I did not yet feel a connection. I therefore thought not of my daughter, but of my wife.

Krista began questioning Dr. Abarbanell about the surgical course. The steadiness in her voice left no doubt that she contemplated pursuing treatment. My mom, the only one of us thinking clearly, also asked questions. The doctor's responses mattered little to me since my mind failed to process her words. I could not move past the fact that, after a routine pregnancy, we just now discovered our daughter had a lethal heart defect.

When the questions stopped, Dr. Abarbanell again gave Krista her sympathies and said the surgeon would visit us later. With that, she departed with retinue in tow. Alone in the dark with our thoughts, no one spoke. The doctor clearly believed that we should forgo treatment. Concluding from Krista's questions that she rejected that opinion, I wrestled with how to convince my wife to let our baby die.

I do not know whether it reflects the fattening of America, but hospital beds are enormous. Krista's bed could have easily fit two more Kristas with room to spare. I liken turning the thing to maneuvering a World War II battleship. Krista had asked her nurse, Amanda, if she could see the baby. Amanda drafted two more nurses, and we slowly pushed Krista on her bed to the NICU. Under any other circumstances, the scene would have been comical. As it was, I felt like a guard escorting a prisoner to the gallows. The staff either averted their eyes or stared at us sadly. I pretended not to notice and hoped that Krista did not have to pretend.

The main NICU entrance is a set of double doors at the end of a nondescript hallway. The doors opened as we approached and entered what felt like another world. Dozens of pods comprised of two walls intersecting at their midlines created semi-private spaces for bassinets that filled the giant open bay. Plastic molded branches and leaves topped each pod to give the appearance of a tree. I could imagine the forest depicted in the architect's drawings; however, the presence of staff and medical equipment destroyed the aesthetic.

We snaked our way through the field of pods to Katherine at the far end of the bay, no easy task given the size of Krista's bed. Our slow pace gave me the opportunity to take in my surroundings. I had never seen so many babies in one place. Some were tiny, barely a couple pounds. The extensive machinery they required to live buried them under a cobweb of tubes and wires. Others had no overtly visible problems. Afraid of what I would see at our destination, a feeling of dread increased as we approached Pod 32. My fears were for naught.

After parking Krista's bed alongside the bassinet, I took a position at the baby's feet. Katherine reached my sternum in the elevated bassinet. With her head slightly elevated, she looked like a museum display. I studied my beautiful Katherine, with giant, coal black eyes and hair to match, searching for imperfections. She was breathing hard despite the ventilator assistance. Her belly forcefully expanded and contracted in rapid motion. To my inexperienced eye, she otherwise looked robust and ... perfect.

The heart defect necessitated equipment not required for a normal baby. Tape across Katherine's cheeks held a breathing tube in her mouth. Tiny wires connected a monitor to three EKG leads affixed to her chest. IV lines delivered medicine through her umbilical cord. She had no perceivable imperfections aside from her heart condition. I did not question the diagnosis, but I recognized the incongruity of the baby's appearance and her prognosis.

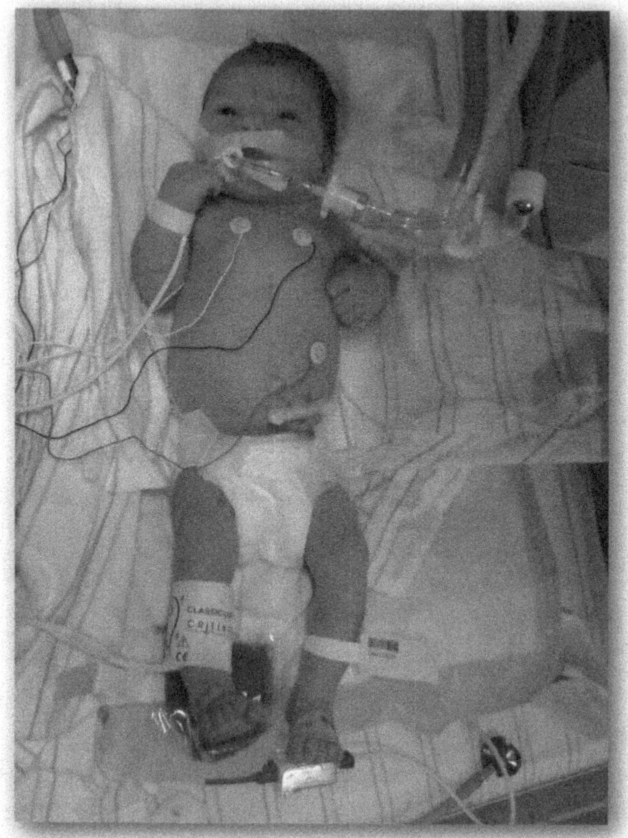

Katherine in the NICU on the day of her birth.

A young nurse explained the monitor and pharmaceutical regimen. A monitor showed the heart and respiration rate and the oxygen saturation level within the blood. The ventilator largely controlled the latter two numbers. The staff used nature's delivery system to give Katherine food and medicine. The umbilical cord does not immediately lose its function after birth. For a couple of weeks, the internal passageways remain. Thus, instead of an IV in her arm or leg, the staff ran lines directly through the umbilical cord. Katherine required intravenous nutrition, milrinone and dopamine to improve cardiac function, and a sedative. Intubation requires sedation as a fully conscious person instinctively struggles against a ventilator.

Dr. Abarbanell checked on Katherine during our visit. After her examination, I took the doctor by the arm and walked with her beyond earshot of those surrounding Katherine.

"If we don't treat, how long are we talking? Years? Months?"

"A few days. Maybe a few days. At best, a week."

"What would that look like? I mean, how does that work?"

"We have a pediatric program at our hospice facility."

"I know. My wife is the pharmacist over there."

"Then she'll know how it works. Katherine will be comfortable."

The hospital started a pediatric hospice service the previous year. Krista mentioned it occasionally, but I knew little about the program other than its existence. I never dreamed we would need its services.

I turned back to my family. Krista, my mom, and a nurse crowded around the bassinet. From her hospital bed, Krista managed to bridge the expanse between her and Katherine to caress the baby's left arm and leg.

The strange procession retreated to the delivery room after twenty minutes. We barely settled in before the doctor ordered Krista's transfer to the obstetrics ward on the third floor. Krista's nurse helped me load our gear on Krista's bed. Using Krista as a cart struck me as somewhat undignified, but I was in no condition to protest.

Krista finally fell asleep after settling into the new room. I left my mom with Krista as I sought out a private place to use my phone. Finding the room next to Krista's empty, I took up residence on a couch by the window and stared at the wall clock that read a few minutes before 8 a.m. At the top of the hour, I called my civilian and Air National Guard supervisors. Knowing that

Krista had gone into labor, both answered the phone with enthusiastic congratulations. The tone of my voice probably conveyed the calamity more than my brief description of events. I told them I did not know when I would return to work and promised to keep them apprised of the situation. Unbeknownst to us at the time, I would remain on leave for more than three months.

I spent the next few hours with Katherine while my mom watched over Krista. The nurse provided some much-needed company as Katherine slept. As we conversed, I placed my pinky finger in Katherine's open left palm. I stopped speaking when I felt four tiny fingers and a thumb wrap around my pinky soon thereafter. With her eyes closed, Katherine held my finger with a vice-like grip. She squeezed as though her life depended on it, which, in a way, it did. After hearing that Katherine was on death's door all morning, her strength surprised me. I started to think I underestimated the fight in this little one.

A nurse informed us in the early afternoon that the surgeon would meet us in the NICU. Krista felt well enough to use a wheelchair, so I pushed her to the unit. We encountered a throng of people signing in at the NICU front desk and waited for our turn. A man wearing a long white coat walked through the crowd and entered the NICU without breaking stride. Noting his unmistakable air of confidence, I told my mom offhandedly as I signed the log, "That guy must be a mover and a shaker around here." I was right. He was waiting for us when we arrived at Katherine's bassinet.

Dr. Simon Abraham was the sole pediatric cardiovascular surgeon at Peyton Manning Children's Hospital. Slight and soft-spoken, he managed to be simultaneously direct and empathetic. He reiterated Dr. Abarbanell's diagnosis and described the defect with greater granularity. The right side of Katherine's heart could not be repaired, but Dr. Abraham believed the other side "looked good." Two working heart chambers out of four is rather dismal, but, given the day we were having, that constituted good news. He was optimistic those chambers afforded us a surgical treatment option.

Katherine required three surgeries in her first two years of life to have any chance of reaching adulthood. The first procedure would create a temporary cardiopulmonary circulation to help compensate for the heart defect, thereby giving Katherine time to grow large enough for additional surgeries. The second and third procedures result in the permanent bypass of the right atrium and ventricle, leaving Katherine solely dependent upon the left side of her heart, or a "single ventricle." These surgeries are performed separately to allow the body time to heal and adjust to the new physiology. Dr. Abraham described the individual procedures:

- A Blalock-Taussig Shunt ("The Shunt"): The right side of the human heart receives blood returning from the body and pumps this deoxygenated blood to the lungs. When Katherine's right ventricle contracted, some of the blood intended for the lungs escaped back into the right atrium through the faulty tricuspid valve. Dr. Abraham would place a 2 mm shunt between the aorta and pulmonary artery. Left ventricle contractions would then push blood out to the body as in a normal heart *and* the lungs. Katherine required this surgery within days.
- The Hemi-Fontan or Bidirectional Glenn ("The Glenn"): The Glenn is the first of two surgeries to divert blood away from the right side of Katherine's heart. Dr. Abraham would disconnect the SVC from the right atrium and attach it to the pulmonary artery. Blood returning from the head, arms, and upper torso would flow to the lungs via the SVC and pulmonary artery, bypassing the right side of the heart entirely. Dr. Abraham would also remove the Blalock-Taussig Shunt since the SVC could provide sufficient blood flow to the lungs. Katherine would not be eligible for this surgery until she weighed 5 kg, or approximately six months of age.
- The Fontan Procedure ("The Fontan"): In the third surgery, Dr. Abraham would repeat the Glenn process for the IVC. Blood returning from the legs and lower torso would bypass the right atrium and ventricle. Katherine would no longer use the right side

> of her heart for pumping purposes. This surgery typically occurs at least eighteen months after the Glenn.

Dr. Abraham expressed confidence that Katherine had a better than even chance of surviving into adulthood provided she survived the three major open-heart surgeries. She would need a transplant as an adult, but, as Dr. Abraham postulated, "Who knows what technology we'll have by then; we might be able to grow a heart for her."

In addition to the tricuspid deformation, Dr. Abraham informed us of another abnormality in Katherine's heart. Normal babies are born with a hole between their left and right atrium through which blood bypasses the lungs while in utero. Blood begins flowing through the lungs immediately after birth. No longer needed, the hole closes within days or weeks. For a small minority of people, the hole fails to close. Dr. Abraham concluded Katherine was one of those people from the heart imagery. This condition, known as an "atrial septal defect," often requires surgical correction. This abnormality fortuitously improved heart function in Katherine's unique case; therefore, Dr. Abraham did not intend to sew it closed.

Having covered the heart issues, the doctor transitioned to quality of life concerns. Katherine's heart defect and the surgical course Dr. Abraham proposed have little if any effect on intelligence. She would have physical limitations. Katherine probably could not tolerate pregnancy. Aerobic activity would be difficult, severely limiting her athletic options. The doctor broke the news that Katherine would "never be a high school track star." I assured Dr. Abraham that genetics determined that when Katherine picked her parents, heart condition or no heart condition.

Dr. Abraham stressed that we had little time to decide whether to proceed with surgery. Katherine needed the shunt as soon as possible, no later than Friday. Before departing, he instructed us to inform the nurse of our decision.

Awake for more than thirty hours and emotionally exhausted, Dr. Abraham's measured optimism only slightly buoyed my flagging spirit. He had not given us a "take two pills and everything will be fine" option. The surgical plan gave Katherine only a chance of living at a certain cost of tremendous pain, thereby tempering my relief that we had an alternative to hospice care. The latter course would at least be painless for Katherine. This marked the first of countless occasions when circumstances forced Krista and me to choose from a slate of unpalatable alternatives. Deciding whether to pursue further treatment weighed heavily on me, and I did not have the luxury of time to ponder the alternatives.

Knowing that Krista intended to proceed with the surgical course, I assessed Katherine. Her eyes darted about as though still searching for something. She appeared so normal. The thought of her squeezing my finger inspired, for the first time since our ordeal began, hope. Maybe it was just delusion or the father in me, but I sensed a strong personality in our Katherine. If she were willing to fight, I would not deny her that chance.

I turned to Krista. "Okay, let's do this."

Once we decided to press with the surgery, Dr. Abarbanell became the driving force in moving the process forward. The pressing question now turned to whether we would stay at St. Vincent. Krista and I wanted the hospital and surgeon with the most experience treating Ebstein's. Katherine could not get a mulligan; she had one chance. Indianapolis had one other capable facility, Riley Children's Hospital. Outside of Indianapolis, the closest hospitals were in Cincinnati and Chicago. We wrestled with the thought of transporting a critically ill, ventilated baby more than two hours away. Katherine's rib cage quivered during respirations even on the ventilator, and I questioned her ability to survive transport.

One of my best friends started researching hospitals after I notified her of our plight Monday morning. Johanna's mother-in-law and a former medical school roommate of her husband were pediatric cardiologists. The cardiologists recommended five premier hospitals, namely Cincinnati Children's Hospital Medical Center, Boston Children's Hospital, University of Michigan C.S. Mott Children's Hospital, Children's Hospital of Philadelphia, and Johns Hopkins Children's Center. As luck would have it, Dr. Abraham had either trained or practiced at the latter three. Meanwhile, my father's wife, who worked for St. Vincent Hospital in Jacksonville, Florida, found that those in her facility who knew Dr. Abraham gave him glowing endorsements. As a St. Vincent employee, Krista was already familiar with his reputation. With Katherine struggling in the NICU, we selected Dr. Abraham as our surgeon. We would fight this war at Peyton Manning Children's Hospital at St. Vincent.

Krista's mother (Mary) and sister (Amy) arrived from Denver late in the evening of Katherine's birth and joined us at her bedside. Katherine slept amidst the sounds emanating from the machines surrounding her. Even with the assistance of a ventilator, the force with which her belly and ribs expanded and contracted had increased. Krista eventually capitulated to exhaustion and suggested that we say a prayer before departing. We said an "Our Father" and "Hail Mary."

Once the prayers ended, Amy began to pull the wheelchair away from the bassinet. Krista stopped her. "Wait, I haven't sung yet," she said. Leaning against the bassinet, Krista then sang the first verse of "Goodnight, Sweetheart, Goodnight."

Goodnight, Sweetheart, well, it's time to go.
Goodnight, Sweetheart, well, it's time to go.
I hate to leave you but I really must say,
"Goodnight, Sweetheart, Goodnight."

I recognized the Spaniel's 1957 hit and listened in puzzlement. I never heard her mention or sing a note of the song in more than a decade together. I asked Krista about it in the slow procession back to her room.

"What was that about?"
"What?"
"The song. Where did that come from?"

"I've been singing it to Katherine at bedtime."

"How often?"

"Every night."

"Since when?"

"I don't know. Since when I thought [that] she could hear me. Months ago."

Her answers did not surprise me. Krista is not one for overt sentimentality. Though one of the kindest and most sensitive people I have known, she does not wear emotions on her sleeve. Krista's practice of privately singing to her unborn baby is indicative of both her caring and emotionally guarded nature.

The impromptu prayers and song became a routine that continued for the remainder of Katherine's life. Not a single night passed without someone reciting those prayers and singing that song. Family, friends, and even staff members often joined us. The routine brought a measure of normalcy to the surreal existence that is life in a pediatric hospital. More importantly, the prayers reminded us that we had so much for which to be thankful. Bitterness and frustration collect on one's spirit in a hospital like barnacles on a ship, a natural reaction to watching a critically ill child. The nightly prayers helped us rejuvenate spiritually.

Amy spent the night with Krista while Katherine's grandmothers and I retired to the house. After forty hours without sleep, I collapsed on a small area of the couch not occupied by our dog, Sam. We rescued the rotund eleven-year-old canine two years earlier. The Humane Society knocked ten pounds off his husky frame over his three months in its facility. He slimmed down another twenty pounds in our charge, but had another twenty to go. Sleep came quickly, and I spent the first night of Katherine's life alongside an obese foxhound.

I thought a lot about prayer that day. Lacking the spiritual life I witnessed in others, I felt like a hypocrite asking God for anything. That did not stop me. Emerson said, "The wise man in the storm prays God not for safety from danger, but for deliverance from fear." In the next ten months, I never asked for a miracle, a desired test result, or a successful procedure. I do not think that is how God operates. I asked God to give us the strength to endure this trial, our own road to Calvary. God did not disappoint.

Since first hearing Katherine's diagnosis, I often found myself coping with sadness and depression. I am fortunate, however, that I never felt anger. Maybe that was denial. Whatever the reason, I accepted the fact birth defects are inevitable given the complexity of life. Until someone can give me a compelling reason why someone else deserved this more than we did, I have no basis for complaint.

CHAPTER 3

Peyton Manning

KRISTA LOOKED EVEN MORE EXHAUSTED Tuesday morning than the night before. Periodic breast pumping prevented a long period of needed sleep. Between pumping sessions, she visited Katherine in the NICU with her sister's help pushing the wheelchair.

Meanwhile, my mom discovered the hospital gift shop and bought an orange PMCH shirt for me. In a brief moment of inspiration, I said, "I'll wear this tomorrow for Katherine's surgery." I thought for a moment before adding, "I'll wear one of these shirts every day Katherine is in the hospital." That Katherine would spend 238 days hospitalized was beyond my wildest imagination, but I kept my promise. Doctors wore lab coats. Nurses wore scrubs. I wore PMCH shirts. To me, these shirts represented my role as Katherine's father in her care team. To others, the shirts evidenced my complete lack of fashion sense, which, unfortunately, was accurate. Dr. Abraham once commented on my wardrobe, "I think you have more Peyton Manning [Children's Hospital] clothes than I do." He was probably right.

Katherine's new day nurse was another "Katherine," although she went by "Kat." By her looks, she should have been racing to third period in senior high school, a testament to either her youthful appearance or the fact I am getting old. Regardless, she was delightful and very attentive to Katherine. Kat had fallen in love with my daughter upon seeing her the day before and asked to be Katherine's nurse. Kat was Katherine's fourth and final nurse in her initial NICU stay. We were fortunate to have such skilled and caring women watching over Katherine.

An unknown neonatologist briefly examined Katherine late that morning. While leaning over the bassinet, he looked up at me and asked whether we planned to baptize our daughter. I nodded my head in affirmation. His eyes returned to Katherine before responding flatly, "If you are going to do it, better sooner than later." Numbed by the proceeding thirty hours, this comment did not faze me. Such news was already our new normal.

An emergency baptism never crossed my mind. Krista and I had big plans for Katherine's baptism in the church where we were married back in Pennsylvania. Both prospective godparents and most of the family were there. Without the luxury of waiting, we improvised.

Not planning to stay in Indianapolis once my sister returned to Pennsylvania, Krista and I never joined a church. The only priest with whom I had some familiarity was Father (Fr.) Jim Farrell, who taught a few classes during our weekend diocesan wedding preparation course. Blending into the crowd with fifty other couples, I do not think we ever spoke with him. Confident he did not remember us three years later, I got his number from the church office and called nonetheless. When his phone went to voicemail, I asked Kat to contact the hospital priest.

The hospital transportation team arrived at 12:30 to take Katherine to PMCH. Although St. Vincent Women's Hospital and PMCH are located on the same campus, they are roughly a quarter of a mile apart. Even for such a short trip by ambulance, the transport procedure was labor intensive and technically complicated. Dressed in flight suits, the crew was anxious to leave. The need of the spirit took precedence over that of the body, however, so they had to hold fast.

Fr. John arrived ten minutes after the transport team to perform the baptism. In the bustling NICU, Krista, Katherine's grandmothers, Amy, Kat, and I stood in silence as Fr. John read the Rite of Baptism. The priest had asked Kat for a white cloth prior to the ceremony. She returned with an old, white, and somewhat raggedy washcloth. I thought nothing of it at the time. Halfway through the ceremony, the priest placed the washcloth on Katherine's legs. The realization struck me that the washcloth served as Katherine's baptismal garment. With all of the new baby clothes at home, the priest baptized Katherine with a rag.

Fr. Jim arrived minutes after the baptism. As the pastor of a parish with more than 1,600 families, he was a very busy man with many demands for his time. After hearing my message, he cleared his schedule to visit a sick lamb not yet in his flock. I met him at the NICU doors and escorted him to Katherine's bassinet. After I introduced the priest to the family, he gave a beautiful blessing. The priest and his parish, St. Pius X, thereafter supported Katherine and our family through the many ordeals ahead.

The transportation team prepared Katherine for her journey, which was no small feat. They disconnected innumerable wires from the monitors and vent and reconnected them to corresponding machinery on the cart. I liken it to hooking up a dozen DVRs to the same TV. The crew then gently moved Katherine from the bassinet to a compartment on the cart resembling a pizza deliveryman's warmer. After watching the team wheel Katherine out of the NICU, Fr. Jim and the grandmothers escorted Krista back to her room while my sister-in-law and I followed Katherine to Peyton Manning Children's Hospital.

Peyton Manning Children's Hospital is an appendage affixed to the back of St. Vincent Hospital. The dark windows and white frames canvassing the walls resemble black kitchen floor tiles. This elegant yet plain aesthetic serves as the counterpoint to the whimsical fixtures distinguishing the building as one intended for children. White pipes ripped from The Beatles' *Yellow Submarine* cartoon spout large multicolored circles up the building's south wall. Eight yellow flags on poles line the roof's periphery. An outdoor playground on the third floor looks down on the parking lot to the south and parking garage to the east. The visual focal point is a large green gear running the entire height of the building and arcing over the roof. The building could be a children's museum.

Amy and I entered the lobby through Door 4, the non-emergency entrance on the east side. The room stretches the building's entire four-story height. Large sculptures of the five symbols on the PMCH crest adorn the inner wall. These symbols represent the hospital's core values: a football (heroism), gear (teamwork), star (inspiration), hand (helpfulness), and swirl (creativity). Lights set in a dozen white spheres a foot in diameter hung from the ceiling by steel cables of varying length. A battalion of wagons carrying the names and/or pictures of former patients lined the outside wall. A welcome desk sits immediately to the left, opposite a wall that illuminates in rhythmic patterns when people pass by and an autographed painting of the facility's namesake. We walked through the concourse to elevator doors directly across from the main entrance.

The elevators opened in the small second floor lobby, directly opposite of the Family Room entrance. A television and recliners occupied the sitting area on the south side of the Family Room. The opposite side of the room consisted of a small kitchenette with a full size refrigerator and table for six. Large windows provided a full view of Entrance 4 and the lobby below. Randomly placed windows in odd geometric shapes in the wall separating the Family Room from the lobby added some whimsy to an otherwise cold environment.

A young woman named "Molly" met Amy and me as we exited the elevators. As a "child life specialist," she helped pediatric patients and their families cope with the challenges of hospitalization. Her duties included explaining procedures to kids in terms they understood, preparing them for said procedures, and, most importantly, providing the comfort of companionship. That morning, Molly helped the father of the PICU's newest patient acclimate to the unit.

The three of us walked around an abandoned reception desk and then southward through a nondescript central hallway toward a set of wooden doors. The closed doors for a patient consultation room and parent sleep rooms on the left and the lactation room on the right made the scene eerily quiet. The white walls and ceiling radiated coldness. Molly pointed out a security panel on the wall just before the doors and told us that family and visitors must buzz the main desk and state the patient's code for admission. Molly spared us this formality. The door locks released after she swiped her badge, and I got my first look into the PICU. My stomach tightened as the door opened. It was, to say the least, anticlimactic. The hallway continued until reaching a dead-end at the top of a "T." Two halls bisected the main corridor, ending on both sides with a set of closed double doors. We turned left at the end of the hallway and passed through yet another set of double doors that opened into the heart of the PICU.

Molly led us around the bustling nurses' station to Katherine in Room 8. Katherine slept while doctors, nurses, transporters, and respiratory therapists buzzed around her. Reticent to interrupt, Amy and I stood back and watched the commotion. Lost in concentration, the staff initially ignored us. Once Molly introduced me to someone as "Katherine's father," the floodgates opened. Half of the hospital personnel introduced themselves and described their roles in the next hour. I tried to remember names, but both the situation and sheer magnitude of information overwhelmed me. A petite, middle-aged woman with chestnut hair in a white lab coat eventually pulled me aside.

Sarah was the cardiology group's nurse practitioner and liaison between Dr. Abraham and his patients. She informed me that Katherine's surgery would be the second for Dr. Abraham the following day. Dr. Abraham would leave Katherine's incision open for a few days should he have to adjust the shunt. The thought of seeing Katherine in such condition unnerved me, but Sarah assured me the wound would be covered.

Having addressed the surgical details, Sarah transitioned to a less medical yet no less important concern: Krista had never held Katherine. Doing so with such a fragile, intubated baby presented great risk. The tiny ventilator tube could dislodge, depriving Katherine of oxygen or tearing her airway. Some risks, however, are worth taking. Sarah promised that, if we could get Krista to PMCH by 8 a.m. the next morning, the staff could position Katherine in Krista's arms until she departed for surgery at 9 a.m. I promised Sarah that I would get my wife to that room.

"One more thing," I said as Sarah turned to leave.

"What's that?" she said.

"I really appreciate you coming here and talking to me. But I need you to call my wife and tell her directly. I won't remember what you said, and I guarantee that she'll have questions I can't answer."

Sarah smiled with a hint of reluctance and agreed. I sensed this was not the first time she received such a request. Then it was Sarah's turn to interrupt her departure.

> "You know, with these heart kiddos, it's a roller coaster. You'll have a great day and then a terrible day. Over and over. You have to remember this is a roller coaster. Ups and downs. Don't get discouraged. That's how it is with these heart kiddos - a roller coaster."
>
> I nodded my head, "Got it."

I did not get it, nor did I appreciate Sarah's prescience. Sarah would be with us through the best and worst of times over the next ten months. Before parting, I would often say, sometimes as a joke, sometimes in exasperation, "A roller coaster, right?" Her response was always the same, a slight smile and nod of her head, "A roller coaster."

With her medical background and, frankly, intelligence, Krista would eventually replace me as the de facto lead in Katherine's care. Less than forty-eight hours since the emergency C-section, however, she was neither physically nor emotionally capable. Amy looked after Krista in the days following the birth, and Krista's mom would nurse her back to health over the next few weeks. This support for Krista freed me to concentrate on Katherine.

Katherine continued gripping my finger late into Tuesday evening. The night nurse arrived for the 7 p.m. shift change carrying a stack of books a foot high. I asked what she was reading. The nurse fanned the stack, revealing titles varying on the theme of congenital heart defects, and said she wanted to "brush up" on Ebstein's Anomaly. I glanced at Amy and could see in her eyes that we were on the same page: We scored yet another great nurse.

I still did not feel comfortable leaving Katherine alone in the PICU. In the NICU, Katherine was in an open bay surrounded by scores of staff members. She was now isolated in a room, albeit with glass doors across from the nurses' station. The ventilator made crying impossible, greatly impairing her ability to communicate. I shared my concerns with Amy, who volunteered to spend the night with Katherine. Anticipating a rough day ahead, I accepted the offer.

Krista made me promise that I would say prayers and sing to Katherine before I left the PICU. I am not one to pray openly. I grew up in a blue-collar coal-mining town where men buried feelings under an exterior hardened by years of hard manual labor. Although the mines closed long before I arrived, the culture, which I absorbed through every pore in my youth, remained. Thus, I waited for a window when neither Amy nor the staff were present. Leaning close to my daughter, I whispered that she had a big day tomorrow and we would be here for her, no matter what. I then made the sign of the cross on Katherine's forehead and recited the "Our Father" and "Hail Mary." After checking the hall to ensure that no one would observe my performance, I sang Katherine's goodnight song and kissed her forehead. Her eyes opened at the sensation, peering at first straight ahead and then turning directly to me. Just inches away, our eyes locked for a few long seconds. Tiny, heavy eyelids fell as Katherine resumed her slumber. I kissed her once again before retreating into the hallway.

I next checked on Krista at Women's Hospital. She was exhausted, but awake to pump. Assured that Krista was safe with Mary, I joined Mom back at the house. Spending the night in our bed with Krista recuperating in the hospital felt wrong. Perhaps I just did not want to be alone with my thoughts, afraid of what would come to my mind. I grabbed a pillow and again joined Sam on the couch.

CHAPTER 4

Good Vibrations

WEARING MY ORANGE PMCH SHIRT, I stopped by a small chapel at St. Vincent Women's Hospital in the early morning of June 5. The room was empty given the hour. I said a quick prayer before going to Krista's room.

On the third floor, the sight of Krista shocked me. Surgery, lack of sleep, and emotional turmoil left her ghostly pale. She had little time to hold Katherine, so rest was not an option. Krista's nurse helped her transition from the bed to a wheelchair and pushed my tired wife to the main lobby. We loaded the new mother in the car, and Krista and I left for PMCH.

Krista, our mothers, and I found Katherine sleeping when we arrived in her room a little after 8:00 a.m. Amy reported an uneventful night. Molly had made paper letters spelling Katherine's name and taped them to the wall, which added some cheer to an otherwise austere room. Unlike the staff that swarmed me the day before, personnel were much more reserved in their contact with the fragile Krista. Sarah informed us that Krista only had until 9 a.m. to hold Katherine, so we did not delay. Katherine's grandmothers helped Krista into the sole chair in the room, a sturdy, wooden model built for function, not comfort, while the nurses went to work.

Moving Katherine required significant effort. The breathing tube enters the mouth, passes down the throat, and terminates just above where the airway splits to enter the lungs. In a normal intubation, a balloon inflated in the throat after tube placement secures the apparatus. Katherine's throat was too small for a balloon, so the tape on her face held the tube in place. Repositioning her tube risked dislocation or a torn windpipe. Two nurses, a respiratory therapist, and my mom lifted Katherine and her sundry tubes and wires from her bassinet and slowly transported her five feet to her mother. Tears of elation and soul wrenching sorrow filled Krista's eyes.

The first surgery ran late, pushing Katherine's procedure back to early afternoon. Despite her discomfort, Krista did not relinquish Katherine. She asked me if I wanted to hold our daughter. I demurred, cobbling together a sentence or two about the difficulty and risks in moving Katherine. In truth, I could not deprive Krista of one second with her Katherine.

Dr. Abraham stopped in the room briefly to obtain our written consent for the procedure. I read the form thoroughly before signing. I found the experience cathartic, as though I finally had some control over an otherwise uncontrollable situation. Dr. Abraham left once I returned the clipboard, and we resumed waiting.

Tremendous musical talent flows through my mom's family, skipping every other generation. I am unfortunately in the "skip" generation, but love music nonetheless. As the transport team collected outside the room, it occurred to me that, should she not survive, Katherine would never have heard music. The thought revolted me. Watching the growing assembly of people in scrubs outside the glass door, I correctly concluded Katherine had time to hear just one song.

I imagine many people have considered the question, "If I could only listen to one more song, which would I choose?" The question was not hypothetical that morning. Only one number came to mind. I sat next to my wife and daughter and played the song on my laptop. Over the hum of the ventilator and the random beeps of monitors, Carl Wilson's voice soared above a Hammond organ and electric bass:

I, I love the colorful clothes she wears
and the way the sunlight plays upon her hair.

Drums, a tambourine, and a flute joined in as Wilson started the second line of "Good Vibrations."

I hear the sound of a gentle word
On the wind that lifts her perfume through the air.

The instruments then dropped away, replaced by pounding cello triplets beneath a soaring theremin:

I'm pickin' up good vibrations; She's giving me excitations.

As The Beach Boys stacked layers of vocals in the chorus, I wondered how those lush harmonies sounded to Katherine and hoped they were glorious.

Good, good, good, good vibrations....

While the exquisite falsettos climbed step by step in the coda, the surgical transport team entered the room and waited patiently. After the cello and theremin faded, a woman in scrubs declared, "It's time." She and a few other nurses took Katherine from Krista's arms and returned her to the bassinet. We took turns saying good-bye and wishing the sleeping Katherine well before the staff wheeled her out of the room. The room turned quiet once Katherine and her coterie departed, but I could still hear those lyrics in my mind:

"Gotta keep those lovin' good vibrations a-happenin' with her...."

Mom drove back to Connellsville after Katherine's departure. She was the primary caregiver for my ailing grandmother, whom we called "Gram," and could not leave her for long periods. More importantly, she appreciated the long road ahead for Katherine. Krista and I would need a tremendous amount of support; therefore, we had to be strategic in terms of visitors to maximize resources. She would return when we no longer had other visitors. I realized the wisdom in my mother's approach in the months to come.

Sarah escorted Krista, Mary, Amy, and me to the surgical waiting room in the first floor of the main hospital. I checked in at the main desk where a stoic receptionist gave me a beeper similar to that used by restaurants. After seeing the age of our patient, she warmly wished us luck.

We settled in a cluster of open chairs in the large, open waiting room. Serving all surgical units, the room buzzed with activity. Both Krista and I craved isolation but found none. A crowd of anxious people conversed loudly and paced endlessly. Krista tried napping with little success. I escaped into the story of a terrible science fiction novel that I bought the previous day at a discount bookstore for a dollar. I rarely read fiction, but I wanted something mindless. As a book, it was overpriced. As a distraction, it was priceless.

A large television screen displayed the patient's surgical progress. The receptionist assigned each patient a code, which was a combination of initials, a truncated last name, and the patient number. Katherine's code appeared at 12:45, indicating the procedure had started. Dr. Abraham opened her chest fifty minutes later. My concern for Krista somewhat overshadowed that for Katherine as the afternoon progressed. I had never seen anyone so pale. So much fluid collected in her lower extremities that I could not feel her ankle-bones through the swelling. Krista could not return to her room at Women's Hospital and again leave to see Katherine as the insurance company allowed only one pass during a hospitalization. A nurse drove over from Women's to deliver Krista's pain medicine.

Our tension eased at 3:40 p.m. when the screen indicated Katherine was no longer on the bypass machine. By this time, only a handful of people remained in the waiting area. An hour later, Sarah arrived to tell us the procedure was over and escorted us to the PICU Family Room. We relished the quiet of the empty room while awaiting the surgeon.

Dr. Abraham, wearing scrubs and his white lab coat, arrived within minutes. He had a measured affect, but I discerned that he was genuinely pleased with the procedure. He spoke briefly, directing his comments to my exhausted wife.

Katherine tolerated the procedure and, thus far, the shunt well. Although hearts are very similar from one person to the next, each has its own idiosyncrasies. Therefore, Dr. Abraham had to make an educated guess as to the appropriate size of the shunt. He left her chest open in case he needed to crimp the device to reduce blood flow. Before departing, he said we could see the baby once the staff finished their post-op tasks. Sarah notified us thirty minutes later that we could go back to Katherine's room.

As we entered the PICU, Sarah and I fell a few paces behind the family. As they continued to walk, I put my hand on Sarah's arm and stopped her. Stammering, I tried to find the words to express my concern. I did not want to admit that the thought of seeing my baby with her chest open horrified me.

> "Ummm … You know, with her chest open, what, uh … what is that going to look like?"
> "Oh, no, you don't have to see anything at all. The nurse has a bandage over the incision. They generally don't use a bandage to allow the wound to breathe, but it's perfectly fine to ask the nurse to put a bandage on if you are in the room."

Relieved, I thanked her and proceeded to Room 8.

Katherine was radiant, resting on a pure white sheet with a white rectangular bandage covering her chest from the lowest ribs to the base of her neck. White tape held her breathing tube in place. A cloth hat of muted pastels covered her black hair. Katherine's eyes were puffy, but her color was normal. The I.V. inserted by the surgical team in her inner left thigh impeded the blood flow in that extremity, causing her left foot and ankle to swell to twice their normal size. The clear, pencil-sized drainage tube protruding from her chest an inch below her right nipple revealed a slow trickle of blood-tinged fluid. Blue and red wires snaked across her torso to their respective leads. Her chest and belly expanded and contracted gently with each breath. Despite the bandages, wires, and tubes, she was beautiful.

Having seen her daughter, Krista finally returned to Women's Hospital with her mother and sister. I remained at Katherine's bedside throughout the evening. The nurse had turned down the lights and closed the clear glass doors before her shift ended at 7 p.m. The medical equipment left very little of Katherine available to touch. I leaned into her bassinet and rested my forehead on hers. Taking Katherine's little hand in mine, I told her she made us all proud. She did not stir. A few moments later, I felt little fingers slowly, slowly encircling my index finger. Once her fingers were in position, Katherine squeezed.

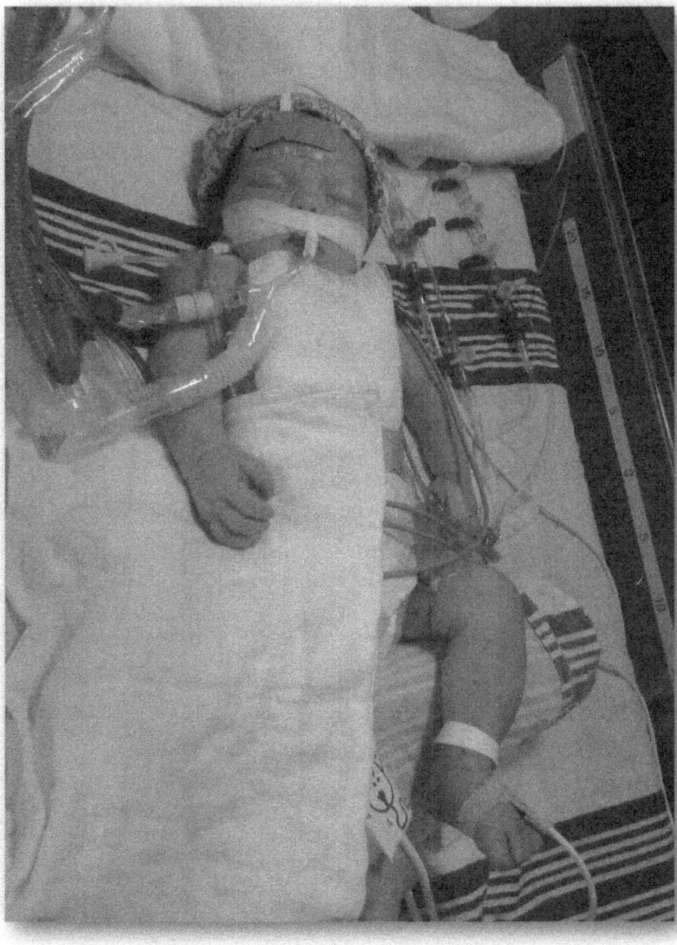

Katherine recovering on the day of her first open heart surgery when two days old.

The overnight intensivist, also known as a critical care physician, interrupted our solitude. He assessed Katherine and reported that she looked "fantastic." I was elated, feeling the weight of the past three days fall off my shoulders. I fulfilled my duty of the bedtime routine, kissed Katherine on her forehead, and departed for Women's Hospital to check on Krista. I relayed the doctor's assessment to my wife, who managed to find enough energy to smile.

Since notifying my supervisors and a few friends following the diagnosis on Monday morning, I had not communicated with anyone else. I knew from text messages and e-mails that the word was out. People were starving for information, and I wanted to share Katherine's story and the news of her recovery. With absolutely no interest in social media, I resorted to e-mail. Once again sharing the couch with Sam late Wednesday night, I started typing. Fifteen hundred words poured out that detailed the events of the past three days.

I abhor mass e-mails, but Katherine's situation warranted an exception. My e-mail program crashed, choking on my large distribution list. Complicating matters, it would not reopen. I played with the settings. Nothing. I restarted the machine. Nothing. As the one o'clock hour passed, the adrenaline that had propelled me through the last twenty hours evaporated, and fatigue seized me. An old, secondary e-mail account still worked, but I was too tired to copy and paste all my addresses. I had not updated its contact list in almost a decade, but I used it anyway after adding a postscript:

> PS: I do not have all of my e-mail contacts. Please do not hesitate to forward to those you may feel interested.

Saying my e-mail went viral would be an exaggeration, but it certainly took on a life of its own. A deluge of responses from friends and strangers over the next few days filled my inbox. Katherine's distribution list, consisting only of those who contacted me, soon numbered in the hundreds. Long after Katherine was gone, I met strangers at work, church, and even a coffee shop who followed Katherine's story via my e-mails that their friends forwarded.

With my mission accomplished, I went to bed looking forward to seeing Katherine's progress the next day. I could not get the post-op image of Katherine out of my mind.

CHAPTER 5

Hope Interrupted

THE PROFOUND SENSE OF RELIEF remained when I awoke the day after Katherine's operation, and I looked forward to her continued improvement and Krista coming home. After updating the family while walking Sam, I met Krista at St. Vincent Women's Hospital. She was packed and eager to return to PMCH. After a couple of signatures and Krista's final wheelchair ride, we left Women's Hospital for what I thought was the last time.

I strode through the halls of PMCH with no small degree of pride that may have crossed the line into arrogance. The physicians gave us a grim diagnosis, yet Katherine had sailed through the surgery. In the early days, I thought of Katherine's accomplishments as "ours," much like a football fan says, "We won the Super Bowl." The fan did not win; the players won. Similarly, Katherine overcame obstacles with her own strength and determination. Hubris initially prevented such realization. Thus, I entered Katherine's room with the aplomb of a conquering general entering ancient Rome. Even Caesar had his Brutus. On that day, my Brutus came in the form of a tall, lanky intensivist.

We found Katherine sleeping unattended. Dr. Williams joined us moments later, taking a position between Krista and me. I did not wait for him to initiate conversation, craving another dose of superlatives describing Katherine's progress.

"Well, doctor, how is she doing today?"

"Not good. Not good at all." His morose expression gave his words force that made me pause.

Dr. Williams proceeded to disabuse me of any notion that Katherine sailed through the surgery. He recited a litany of numbers and readings that meant nothing to me, but, from his tone, I knew they were not good. Confused by the medical jargon, I asked him to speak in layman's terms. Dr. Williams distilled the test results and his observations to one salient point: Katherine's heart was struggling to deliver sufficiently oxygenated blood to her body. I could see on one of the many monitors that her oxygen saturation hovered in the low sixties. Normal saturations range in the high nineties to a perfect one hundred. With her unique plumbing, Katherine's ideal saturation range was 75 – 85. Now looking at Katherine with more discernment, my untrained eyes noted her mottled skin, a patchwork of red and pink hues.

The intensivist explained that one expects a patient's condition to deteriorate somewhat in the days following heart surgery. He compared the experience to getting punched in the eye. In the hours after the strike, the area around the eye may be tender and a little red. The shiner does not appear until the next morning. Likewise, the heart muscle traumatized during surgery swells and bruises over time. Katherine's deterioration exceeded his expectation. He concluded his report expressing his dismay that Katherine's lactate was nine, explaining that increased lactate levels indicate inadequate tissue oxygenation. Again, that meant nothing to me, so I asked him for context. "Normal is less than one, maybe, *maybe* two. Anything over five is critical. Over 10 is very critical, life-threatening. Fifteen is 'you're dead.'" And our Katherine was a "nine."

Krista and I stared at each other, too overwhelmed to speak. All the excitement, all the joy, and all the relief from the night before had vanished. Dr. Williams broke the silence.

"Oh, and she had a stroke."

"What?" I exclaimed. "That's a little more than an 'Oh, by the way,' isn't it?"

"If the heart doesn't work, the brain doesn't matter," he said diplomatically.

"Yes, yes it does," I said. I appreciated that Katherine's heart defect presented the existential threat; however, my concern was not merely

> keeping Katherine alive. "We're not putting her through all of this if there isn't a chance for some meaningful life." As the words exited my mouth, I fought to maintain a measured tone. I fell silent, and Krista resumed information gathering.
>
> "When? How bad was it?"
>
> "We can't be sure of either. It could have happened during the delivery or surgery. It might have happened before she was born. There's no way to know. And we don't know how it will impact her."
>
> "So what are you doing for Katherine now?"

Dr. Williams responded that he added nitric oxide to the standard post-op pharmaceutical regimen for a cardiac baby. Inhaling nitric oxide relaxes blood vessels in the lungs, thereby increasing blood flow and lowering pulmonary hypertension. Dr. Williams did not gild the news, leaving his devastating words hang in the air. Krista and I were too stunned to think of more questions, so he left us with our very sick little girl.

Patience is not one of my strongest virtues. After a few hours sitting in Katherine's room, I explored the PICU. The unit occupied most of the second floor. Fifteen patient rooms arranged in a "U" shape occupying three exterior walls surround a cell of offices, break rooms, a master nurses' station, supply rooms, and medication dispensary.

The patient rooms are numbered counter-clockwise from 1 to 15. Wide glass double doors fronted each room. A counter with sinks and overhead and floor cabinets lined the remainder of the interior wall. The sidewall closest to the counter was plain white. An off-white square column a foot wide with scores of brown and dark orange outlet faceplates stretched from floor to ceiling a few feet from the white wall. Muted pastel paints covered the opposite wall behind a television, computer station for the staff, and built-in cabinets for the patient's use. The exterior walls consisted of windows looking down on another wing of the hospital, a parking garage, or small wooded park, depending on the room location. Furnishings were limited to a wooden chair, a couch that unfolded into a bed, and a rolling chair for the staff. A short, shiny metal tower covered in outlets hung from the ceiling like a stalactite. The ceiling and floor tiles were white and navy blue, respectively. Nothing indicated these rooms housed children.

The key differentiator between rooms is their position relative to the nurses' station. As they say in real estate, "location, location, location." I analogized the PICU to "Monopoly." Room 8, situated directly across from the nurses' station at the bottom of the "U," is "Boardwalk." When the physicians and nurses congregate, they do so just a few feet from the room. Thus, someone is usually nearby. Moreover, the chair the physicians use while charting provides a direct line of sight to the room's monitors. This is the best PMCH has to offer. Rooms 9 and 10, the PICU's "Park Place" and "Pennsylvania Avenue," are also adjacent to the nurses' station; however, the additional twenty feet from the hub of activity reduces their value relative to that of Room 8.

Counterintuitively, some of the sickest kids are not necessarily in the aforementioned primo rooms. Rooms 1 and 2 are the farthest from the nurses' station, but the closest to the main hospital, which may account for their location. The planners fitted these rooms, slightly bigger than the other thirteen, to support a machine that can act as an external lung and/or heart. Referred to as "ECMO," the device temporarily alleviates the stress of circulation in critically ill patients.[3] A complicated process with significant risk, ECMO requires a highly trained staff. The thought of a kid on such a device gave me the shivers, and I avoided that wing of the PICU even when unoccupied.

A massive cookie bouquet with a kind note of support from a law school friend greeted me at the nurses' station when I returned. The bouquet marked the first of numerous gifts of food I used to foster relationships with the staff.

3 "ECMO" - extracorporeal membrane oxygenation

I removed the cellophane and invited the staff to help themselves. Wanting to send a picture along with a note of thanks, I retreated to the room to get my phone. By the time I returned, I found the bouquet stripped almost bare and the nurses' station deserted. A school of piranha could not bone a small cow that fast.

Katherine improved slowly throughout the day. Her lactate dropped to from 9.0 to 5.2 by late evening. Her left leg and foot remained terribly swollen, but her color was better. Her pulse-oxygen hovered in the low seventies.

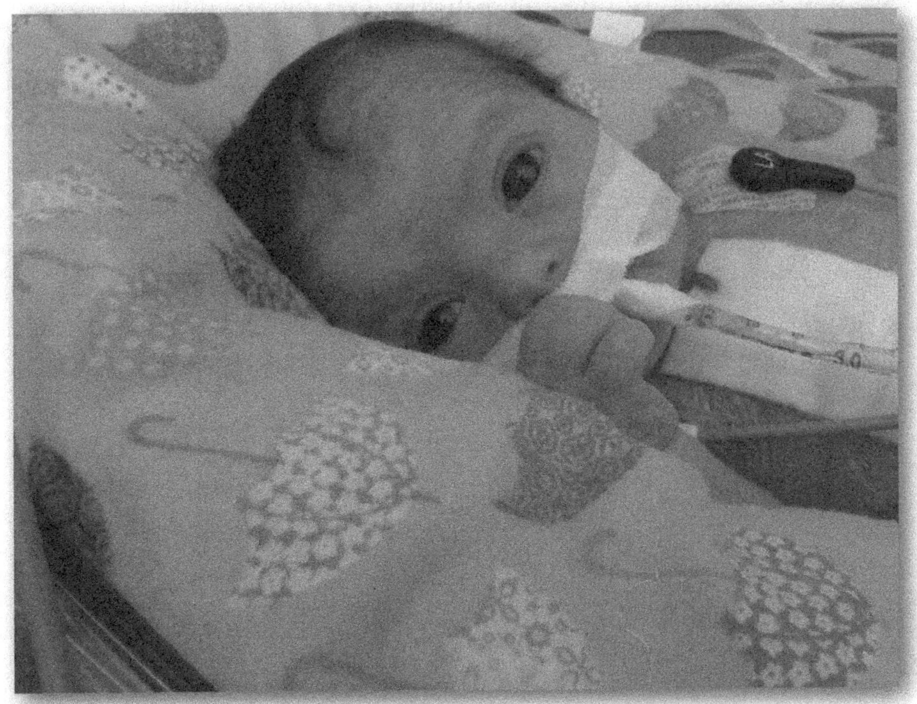

Katherine fully alert one day post-op.

I had the fortune of being alone with Katherine when she awoke late that evening. Her glassy eyes revealed her exhaustion. I took her hand in mine and, as I talked her through the events of the last few days, felt her fingers squeeze my pinky finger. She succumbed to sleep before long, but her grip remained. Hoping she could hear my voice through the fog of drugs and fatigue, I decided to read to her. Not wanting to break free of her grasp, I grabbed the only book within arm's length, a Bible. Starting literally "in the beginning," I opened to the Book of Genesis and, amid the din of monitors and pumps, read to my little girl.

New faces greeted us at the PICU on Friday. Strangers replaced many of the key staff members that cared for Katherine over the last three days. I realized that I needed to know the players in order to participate effectively in Katherine's treatment. I taped a piece of paper beside the staff computer in Katherine's room and asked her nurse to instruct everyone who entered to write down his or her name and specialty. I continued this invaluable practice throughout Katherine's life, referencing the list often while discussing Katherine's care.

Working a fixed Monday through Friday schedule, the PICU's nurse practitioner, Anthony, was the one constant amongst the staff directly involved with Katherine's care. As Krista and I became more acclimated and engaged in the PICU, we relied less upon child specialist Molly and more upon Anthony. I found the doctors intimidating during Katherine's first hospitalization, making me overly deferential. Relying on Anthony as both my intermediary and sounding board, I went straight to him when I needed explanations or translations of "doctor-speak."

Katherine's lactate escalated to 6.0 early Friday morning from 5.2 the prior evening, but started to slowly decline again by sunrise. Radiology performed an ultrasound of Katherine's head, and cardiology ran an echocardiogram to inspect her heart. Both reported normal results. Her urine and bowel movements were normal. The intensivist removed the femoral catheter in the afternoon, which decreased the swelling in her left calf and foot dramatically.

More importantly, Katherine was not only awake, but actively looking around and squeezing anything her little hands could find.

She cried at times, which I found heartbreaking to watch. The ventilator left her mute. Katherine's mouth contorted to scream without making a sound, visibly frustrating her. We tried to comfort Katherine by caressing and holding her hands. As much as I hated watching Katherine cry, her alertness was encouraging. We were also relieved to hear Katherine's progress pleased Dr. Abraham.

The family celebrated the week's ups and downs over ribs and pulled pork before Amy flew back to Denver. Meanwhile, I took a break from the drama at the hospital to address some administrative chores. I had enrolled in a family insurance policy when I began my employment less than three months earlier. I called my carrier to add Katherine to my plan. The customer service agent could not have been more pleasant. After asking a series of questions, he ended our conversation with an earnest and hearty, "Thank you, sir. We truly appreciate your business." As I contemplated the cost of the open-heart surgery and those yet to come, I said, "No, no, you don't." I was an actuary's nightmare. "Believe me, no you don't."

Krista's phone rang at 1:30 a.m. on Saturday morning and interrupted her third night of post-op sleep at home. I listened to Krista's side of the conversation, a staccato refrain of monosyllabic words. She tapped the front of the phone to end the call and turned to me. "Katherine had a seizure."

Hospitals are eerie places at night. Hallways, cramped with staff, patients, and families during the day, feel cavernous and cold. Administrative offices are dark and welcome desks deserted. Children's hospitals are more disconcerting. Light attractions that entertain patients during the day cast unnatural hues. Subdued lighting and chimerical architectural flourishes such as crooked windows and miniature doors intended to distract kids from impending shots and exams create an atmosphere akin to that of a monster movie from the silent screen era. PMCH is no different.

Unable to sleep after the seizure news, I threw on a PMCH shirt and drove to the hospital. The main door to PMCH is locked at 10 p.m., so I entered through the Emergency Department on the other side of the building. I passed a dozen people while crossing through the waiting area and entered PMCH through an exit in the back of the room. The empty hallway zigged and zagged as it snaked through the building, ending in the foyer by Door 4. I took a solitary elevator ride to the second floor and proceeded to the buzzer at the PICU entrance. A minute passed before someone responded, and I detected surprise in her voice. The PICU does not get many visitors at 3:00 a.m.

I found the nurses' station deserted. Whomever buzzed the door open had disappeared. I startled the nurse when I entered Katherine's room.

"Hi. Sorry to bother you. I couldn't sleep, so I thought I'd come in."

I could see from her expression that she knew the seizure deeply unsettled me. Her expression changed almost imperceptibly from that of stoic nurse working through routine exams to that of counselor.

The nurse tried to allay my fears, explaining that she briefly observed tremors in Katherine's hands and feet. However, she could not say definitively that Katherine had a seizure. The staff would continue to monitor for any abnormal neurological activity. Conversation drifted away from the clinical to the personal, such as kids, spouses, and hometowns. This distraction helped me process the new development, which I think the nurse thought I needed. She eventually gave Katherine and a less agitated me some time alone. I held Katherine's hand until daybreak.

I often visited Katherine over the next ten months when sleep eluded me. Nurses responded in one of three ways: First, she may ignore me and go about her duties as though I was not there. This neither surprised nor offended me. Some people prefer the night shift because they do not particularly care for parent interaction. Second, she may or may not offer an update before giving Katherine and me some privacy. I relished this private time with Katherine when I could talk to her without feeling self-conscious. Third, she may act as a counselor to her patient's dad, trying to assuage the ever-present fear, helplessness, and frustration. The response I wanted varied, and the nurses were always accommodating.

Subsequent testing over the following week found no evidence of a seizure, but could not rule out the possibility. A myriad of other issues demanded our attention, and the seizure soon fell off the radar. That early Saturday morning marked our only seizure scare. I did not know that at the time, nor did I have any idea that I was about to meet the real Katherine.

CHAPTER 6

The Great Awakening

PMCH HAS ITS OWN CIRCADIAN rhythm that breaks the monotony of an existence confined within the hospital walls. The atmosphere changes significantly after the sun falls on Friday, an aura of relative calm enveloping the facility. Elective and scheduled procedures and tests occur almost exclusively during the week, leaving most of the departments abandoned over the weekend. Administration and physician offices are closed. Only a handful of cars occupy the parking lots. Treatment is limited to emergency cases and patients on the floors. I would come to relish the weekends with their welcome relief from the frenetic weekday pace of a large hospital.

The slower pace was not the only cause for celebration that first weekend. Katherine's lactate dropped from 6.0 on Friday morning to 2.0 on Saturday and, for the first time, dipped below two the following day. Dr. Abraham, satisfied that the shunt was functioning properly, closed the incision Sunday morning while Krista and I attended mass. A crisscross of black stitches ran along Katherine's sternum as she rested comfortably.

Fr. Jim informed the St. Pius X parishioners of Katherine's birth and subsequent struggles during the service. I found hearing Katherine's name outside of the hospital for the first time exhilarating, a feeling I cannot fully explain. Francis Bacon said, "A healthy body is a guest chamber for the soul; a sick body is a prison." Perhaps the priest's comments represented a symbolic escape from the shackles of Katherine's heart defect. We updated Fr. Jim on Katherine's condition after mass before returning to the hospital.

Katherine now faced two major obstacles before she could leave the PICU. First, Dr. Abraham had to remove Katherine's chest tube. Two membranes encase the heart and lungs, much like "double bagging" at a grocery store. A healthy person has some fluid in the "pleural space," a thin gap between the two bags, which serves as a lubricant to facilitate movement. In the body's response to heart surgery, blood and other fluid often collect in the pleural space. An accumulation of fluid can fatally compress the heart and lungs. Katherine's chest tube entered between ribs on her right side and terminated within the pleural space, thereby allowing excess fluid to drain. Once the volume of fluid exiting the tube diminished to Dr. Abraham's satisfaction, he would remove the tube. Second, after chest tube removal, Katherine needed to breathe without ventilator assistance. For now, all we could do was wait.

Signs prohibiting smoking are ubiquitous throughout the hospital, demonstrating how much the administrators care about the health of patients, staff, and visitors. This concern stops abruptly at the cafeteria entrance, a 38th parallel-like imaginary line across which the hospital serves a vast array of food about which your own doctor warns. Located in the basement of the main hospital, the facility is the primary respite for families of patients enduring extended hospitalizations. Your loved one is having a test? Go to the cafeteria. Your loved one needs rest following the test? Wait at the cafeteria. You received the test results? Discuss them over a snack in the cafeteria. Visiting the cafeteria between endless hours of staring at monitors gave us something to do.

I would be remiss not to acknowledge that the hospital does serve some healthy fare. A salad bar awaits those health conscious souls who can break through the Maginot Line of fried food, ice cream, pop, and pastries. When it comes to food, self-control is not my strong suit. Any chocolate item my wife brings into our house has the same odds of seeing another sunrise as a three-legged zebra in the Serengeti. Adding the stress of a critically ill child removed what little resistance I had. Moreover, empty calories seemed so low a priority as not to merit any concern. Ten months of terrible eating habits took a toll on my health as I blew up like a pufferfish. Advice to take care of myself fell on deaf ears.

Fittingly, Krista, Mary, and I celebrated Katherine's one-week birthday on Monday over an unhealthy, yet tasty, dinner in the cafeteria. Afterwards, Mary and Krista went home to check on the dog. Expecting another quiet evening as Katherine had slept all day, I returned to the PICU.

Katherine awoke while her nurse examined her. Despite the sedatives, she was alert and responsive. Noticing Katherine's dry skin, the nurse lathered her with lotion. The hospital had none in supply, so she used her own personal lotion from Victoria's Secret. Katherine loved it.

After the spa session, I took a position across the bassinet from the nurse. We held out our fingers for Katherine to hold and caressed her legs, amazed to see Katherine's reaction to the stimulus. Her eyes jumped back and forth between us. She occasionally craned her neck to look at the colorful monitors slightly behind her. Noticing Katherine squirming against padding limiting her movement, the nurse slid her hand along Katherine's spine and cradled her head, lifting her a foot above the bassinet.

Katherine looked around in complete amazement, her large, black eyes glimmering with wonder. Although frequently awake, the staff kept her immobilized to ensure lines, tubes, and leads remained in place. Now balancing on a nurse's forearm, her appendages were free to move. The tape across her mouth could not hide her jubilant expression as she flexed her arms and kicked her legs.

I grabbed my phone to get a picture only to discover a dead battery. When the nurse offered her phone, I quickly accepted and took four pictures. Months later, a friend rebuked me for using one of these photos as my phone wallpaper. I could understand her perspective. Tape holding Katherine's intubation tube in place obscured her face. Bright red blood filled her chest tube, which contrasted sharply against the white bandage covering her chest and the opaque ventilator tubes. Monitor leads and wires and IVs clung unnaturally to

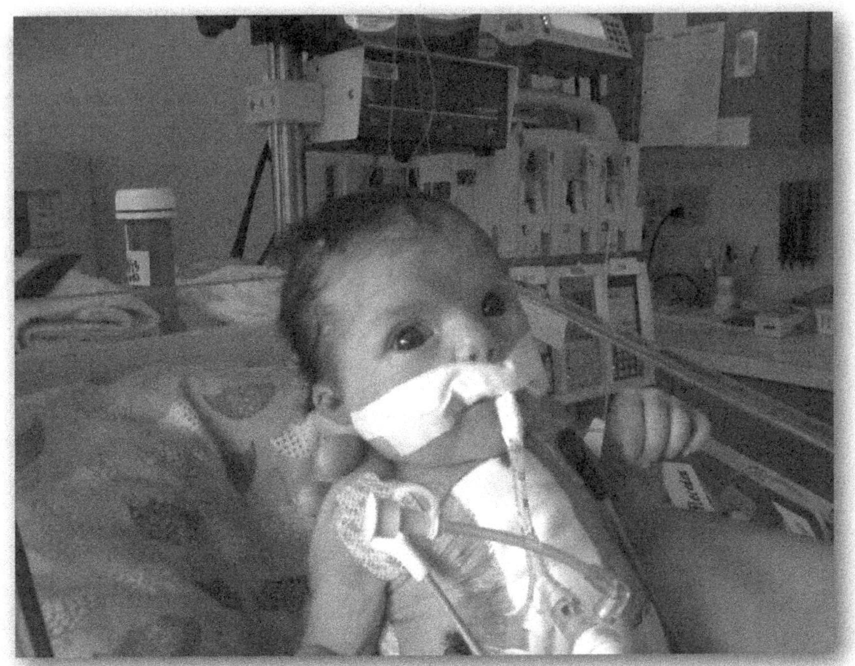

Katherine lifted from her bassinet by her favorite nurse.

her body. My friend saw these things. I saw a beautiful little girl elated by the sheer joy of living. They remain amongst my favorite pictures of Katherine.

During the week, the intensivist conducts rounds as close to 9 a.m. as the demands of the unit allow. The doctor, followed by a team of specialists whose composition depended on the patients' maladies, visits each patient's room after discussing treatment. A nurse practitioner or resident generally initiates discussions by reciting a brief summary of the patient's medical history, status, and care plan. The intensivist may or may not ask questions of the doctors, nurses, and pharmacist before examining the patient. The team then moves to the next room with a new patient and the process repeats. On weekends, the intensivist conducts informal rounds in the nurses' station.

Rounds gave Krista and me an opportunity to not only listen to the staff's thoughts regarding Katherine's care, but also identify communication failures, provide our perceptions, and develop a deeper understanding of the staff dynamic. No one ever directly informed us that we could attend, let alone participate in, rounds. Being in the medical profession, Krista easily assimilated into the group. As for me, I joined the crowd of people gathering outside Katherine's door out of curiosity. Diffident, I remained silent and tried to decipher the medical verbiage. Over time, I became increasingly familiar with the terminology and would occasionally offer information or ask questions. While Krista's expertise made her much more valuable to the discussion, the mere fact of our presence popped the insulated bubble within which the medical staff operated. Everyone acts differently, perhaps almost imperceptibly so, while being watched. A white lab coat does not change human nature.

I learned three valuable lessons attending rounds. First, despite outward appearances, physicians sometimes know much less about a patient than they lead others to believe. As they say in Texas, all hat, no cattle. Interaction between the doctors revealed some physicians were less informed about Katherine's care than they implied when alone with the family. I managed Katherine's care much more effectively upon accepting I was in the presence of mortals, albeit very well-educated mortals. Second, one can discern the strong and weak members of the team by watching the staff interact. For example, an intensivist once asked a nurse, "Did [Katherine] run a temperature during the night?" The nurse responded, "I don't know. I didn't ask." The doctor paused slightly before moving on, but not slightly enough. He obviously expected the nurse to know that fact. Over time, we learned which nurses were top performers and used this knowledge to influence whom the charge nurse assigned to Katherine. Third, communication between disciplines was sometimes lacking. Attending rounds enabled us to bridge the gaps.

Dr. Abraham removed nine-day-old Katherine's chest tube without incident on Wednesday, June 12. The intensivist on duty, Dr. Halczenko cut our celebration short by informing us that a technician discovered a possible second cerebral bleed during a routine ultrasound. He ordered an MRI for that afternoon. We asked for the results when Katherine returned to her room, but the nurse explained we had to wait for a radiologist to write a report. Given the late hour, she did not expect it until the following morning. Her words proved prophetic, and concern kept sleep at bay that night.

Anxious to learn the results of the MRI, we arrived at the hospital when the sun rose on Thursday. The nurse informed us that Radiology had yet to post a report, so we waited. We were still waiting four hours later when Krista left the PICU to pump. Mary passed the time reading a book while I chatted with Katherine's nurse as she performed routine tests.

> "Hmmm … That can't be right," she said to herself.
>
> "What's that?" I asked.
>
> "[Katherine's] lactate is 14. This is the second time I've run it, thinking it was wrong the first time. But again I got 14."
>
> "14?" Remembering Dr. Williams saying, "15 is 'dead,'" I looked at my sleeping daughter and saw no sign of distress.
>
> "No, that can't be right. I'm going to try again." A long minute passed before she received the results and headed to the door. "14 again. I'm going to show [intensivist] Dr. Bob."

I again looked at Katherine and thought her skin might, *might* be a bit darker and mottled than normal. Unconcerned, I slumped back in my chair and closed my eyes.

The stomping of Dr. Bob's heavy footsteps as he stormed into the room snapped me to attention. The nurse followed closely behind. Dr. Bob, the only physician we called by his first name, stood out as particularly personable amongst a very friendly staff. This morning, however, he was all business. Dr. Bob stopped five feet from the bassinet and studied Katherine and the monitors. His eyes darted from screen to screen, his lips moving as he silently worked through his assessment. He then rattled off an array of dictums in what my basic training instructor would describe as "command voice." The intensity of his focus and speech indicated something seriously wrong. Not waiting for direction, I told Mary that she and I had to leave. In the hall, we passed two nurses rushing to assist Dr. Bob. Mary joined Krista in the Lactation Room while I sat alone in the Family Room.

Dr. Abraham came to see me ten minutes later. The surgeon happened to be in the PICU with another patient when Dr. Bob called for assistance. He gave me the working diagnosis: necrotic bowel. He was unsure of the genesis of the problem, but, at Katherine's age and condition, nothing could be done. She had minutes, maybe a couple hours to live. He was sympathetic, but direct. I nodded my head in understanding. He then returned to Katherine's room. Sarah followed Dr. Abraham minutes later, and we repeated the conversation. I was incredulous that Katherine survived an open-heart surgery only to succumb to an abdominal issue.

I handled a malpractice case involving necrotic bowel in my first year out of law school, so I knew something of the issue. The primary source of oxygenated blood to the intestines is the mesenteric artery. The secondary arteries cannot supply the intestines with sufficient blood by themselves. When the mesenteric artery is blocked, the intestines begin to die for lack of oxygen. Without immediate intervention, death is imminent. The doctors believed that Katherine developed a clot, perhaps due to dehydration or her compromised circulatory system. The telltale symptom of a mesenteric bowel obstruction is intense abdominal pain. My physician client described the sensation as "a thousand red-hot pokers stabbing you in the stomach." Katherine showed no signs of discomfort let alone searing pain. The patient in my medical malpractice case likewise felt nothing, and the surgeon found the blockage too late to save her.

Krista and Mary had joined me in the Family Room before Dr. Bob arrived thirty minutes after Sarah. His relaxed demeanor contrasted sharply with the intensity he exhibited in Katherine's room. He explained that Katherine did not have necrotic bowel. The scab on the outer lining of the pleural membrane had opened, which allowed blood and fluid to drain from the pleural space into Katherine's abdominal cavity. When Dr. Abraham positioned Katherine on her side, the liquids gushed from the chest tube incision. Katherine remained in critical condition, but she had dodged a bullet.

Once again, our euphoria was short-lived. The radiology report arrived while the doctors addressed the abdominal issue. In the commotion, I had forgotten about the cerebral bleed Dr. Halczenko suspected the day before. Dr. Bob asked if we wanted to see the pictures and discuss the findings. Bracing for another hit, Krista and I followed him to the physician's office adjacent to the nurses' station.

A life-sized image of Katherine's head appeared on an oversize monitor. Various shades of rippling grey illustrated the brain's anatomy in cross section. A dark black spot immediately drew my eyes to the right frontal lobe. The bleed, the size of a dime, was much larger than I expected. Dr. Bob pointed out a cluster of much smaller bleeds that resembled tiny puffs of smoke, so tiny that I would not have thought anything of them otherwise. He then explained that we would never know when or why the strokes occurred and Katherine may or may not have learning disabilities. Moreover, he could not say how or if the strokes would affect her. She had a sixty percent chance of some degree of cerebral palsy (CP). Confused, I asked him if he saw any signs of coordination issues, which I had not. He replied that CP symptoms manifest by the individual's third birthday. Thus, Katherine's age made a definitive assessment impossible. Dr. Bob ended our conversation on a high note: "Babies are resilient. She is so young, the brain may rewire itself. There may be no long-term ramifications at all."

I left Dr. Bob's office elated. Just an hour earlier, funeral plans filled my mind. Now, I had another evening to share with Katherine. Only one who has been in the valley can truly appreciate the view from the mountaintop. I processed Dr. Bob's words through the prism of my experience with Katherine on Monday. I thought of her gazing at her nurse and the room around her with curiosity and wonder. Stroke or no stroke, my little Katherine was fully engaged in this world.

CHAPTER 7

Katherine of Indianapolis

As we entered the second week in the PICU, the décor in Room 8 slowly began to reflect its inhabitant. Initially, only Molly's letters personalized Katherine's room. Gifts gradually appeared, and we amassed a small collection of religious figurines and stuffed animals. The former kept vigil on a small platform attached to the head of Katherine's bassinet alongside holy water left over from the baptism. Stuffed animals rotated from bassinet to couch to windowsill. Krista covered the back of the couch with a knit blanket from her hospice coworkers. I added The Beach Boys' "Smile" album. The cover artwork featured a whimsical storefront with vibrantly colored cartoon animals. The letters of the title danced across the top: *Smile* - such a simple message. In the trials to come, the album often reminded me to remain positive.

One item gracing Katherine's room came from a graduate school friend. Even as Tracy worked in China, we kept in contact in the decade since our last class together. Katherine received a package from Tracy soon after the first surgery. I opened the envelope and discovered a jewelry case containing a spiral rosary of plastic beads that wrap around a wrist like a bracelet. Tracy explained in an accompanying note that she had been gravely ill at birth; doctors did not expect her to survive. Her grandmother bought these rosaries and placed them on the struggling infant. Tracy proved the doctors wrong. She gave this precious heirloom to our daughter, saying that she "had it long enough, now let it help Katherine."

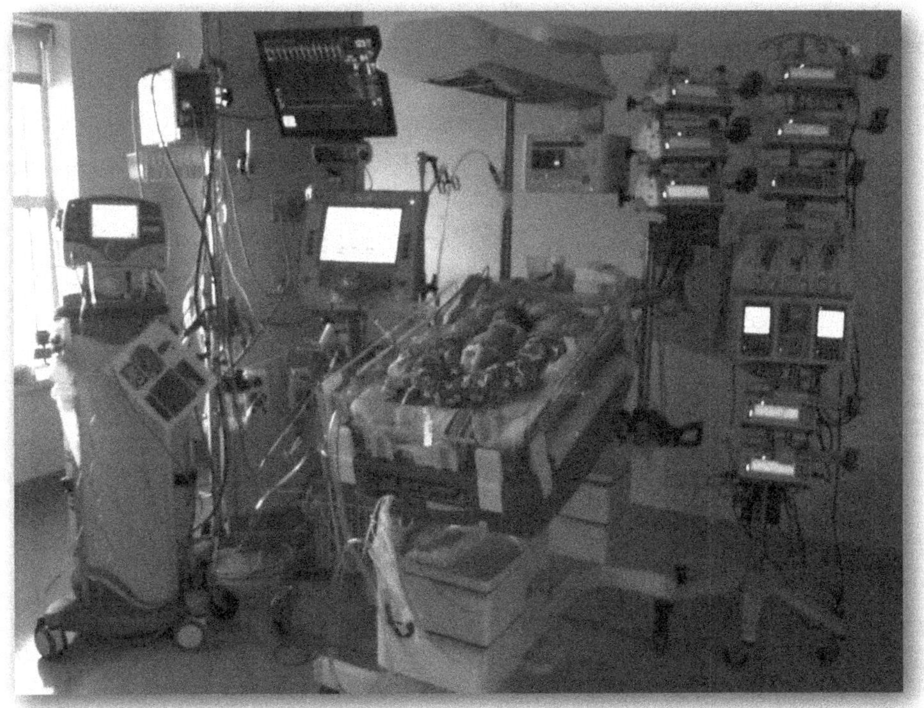

Katherine surrounded by medical equipment in her PICU room.

Katherine needed all the help she could get for the next step in her treatment. The extubation process consisted of four stages: (1) breathing trials, (2) medication reduction, (3) extubation, and (4) independent breathing. During breathing trials, the staff reduces ventilator support to force the lungs to bear some burden of respiration. In addition to strengthening the diaphragm, the trials indicate whether the patient is able to breathe independently.

The second stage of the extubation process, often performed in conjunction with breathing trials, is reducing pain and paralytic medications. Intubation requires heavy sedation to quell the natural reflex to fight an obstructed airway. These medications can suppress the instinct to breathe after tube removal. Thus, physicians need to maintain sufficient medication so that the patient can tolerate the ET tube, but not so much that the patient will not breathe after extubation.

The extubation itself is the simplest yet most dangerous stage of the extubation process. The doctor or respiratory therapist removes tape and deflates the balloon securing the tube in place before quickly pulling the tube from the airway. A patient who fails to breathe must immediately be intubated again. Acute respiratory failure can result in severe hypoxemia, significant blood pressure decline, aspiration, and cardiac arrhythmia and/or arrest. Swollen airways may complicate and delay the intubation process, risking irreparable brain damage or death within minutes.

The final stage of the extubation process, independent breathing, is not just inhaling and exhaling. If the patient continues in struggling to breathe, he will eventually fail from exhaustion. Such failure is fatal without emergency medical intervention. Successful extubation requires the patient to breathe without undue effort, which the doctors describe using the colloquial term, "flying." Not understanding the complexity of human anatomy or appreciating how the heart defect impacted other organs, I never imagined that Katherine would not "fly." Thus, I naively looked forward to extubation without concern.

Eleven-day-old Katherine recovered from Thursday's chest tube debacle with the help of a good night sleep. She had improved so much that the intensivist ordered breathing trials on Friday, June 14. Katherine sailed through multiple thirty-minute trials. Based on these successes, the intensivist reduced her medications. Katherine went into withdrawal Friday afternoon, tremoring slightly in her extremities. This heartbreaking spectacle was difficult but necessary to get Katherine off the ventilator and, eventually, home.

Dr. Bob extubated Katherine on Saturday afternoon without fanfare. Her respiratory rate remained in the sixties and seventies instead of the optimal thirties. An elevated respiration rate was not atypical given her unique cardiovascular plumbing; however, even by that standard, she breathed quickly. Katherine worked hard to breathe, her ribcage expanding and collapsing with noticeable effort. While not a good sign, this did not portend imminent failure. She would probably grow accustomed to breathing independently over the next day as her body abandoned its dependence on the machine. Krista's concern that Katherine was fighting too hard to breathe failed to pierce my confidence. As daylight ebbed on Saturday, I had no doubt that Katherine would breathe on her own.

My confidence faltered when I visited Katherine before mass on Sunday morning. She continued to struggle, evidenced by her forced, quick respirations. Even I, who had yet to develop an eye for mottled skin, detected discoloration. Light red blotches with hints of purple covered her entire body. Exhausted from the strain of breathing and still suffering from withdrawal, she slept soundly.

Krista arranged a present to celebrate my first Father's Day. In the early afternoon, two nurses entered Katherine's room and offered to let me hold my daughter. Unbeknownst to me, Krista had asked Dr. Bob for approval and the nurses for their assistance that morning. Although no longer connected to the ventilator, Katherine was still attached to a half-dozen IVs and monitor lines that made moving a logistical challenge. I sat in a chair next to the bassinet while Krista and the nurses delicately lifted my sleeping Katherine and placed her in my arms. I held her awkwardly, careful not to dislocate the medical equipment. Knowing the hurdles she had overcome made the moment all the sweeter.

Holding Katherine exacerbated her struggle to breathe. She squirmed slightly, as though resting against my chest put undue pressure on her diaphragm. Her ribs expanded and contracted with noticeably more force. As much as I did not want to let Katherine go, I knew she needed to return to the bassinet. Krista and the nurses repeated the transfer in reverse after just a few minutes. I did not hold Katherine long, but I will treasure those minutes forever.

With Katherine resting comfortably, Krista and I took my dad and his wife, Elaine, who were visiting from Florida, to a restaurant for Father's Day.

Dr. Bob phoned me as we pulled into the parking lot. The others secured a table while I paced the lot and listened to the doctor. Katherine's struggle to breathe had escalated. Dr. Bob conferred with his relief physician, Dr. Halczenko, and they concluded Katherine was at significant risk for failure. Dr. Halczenko intubated Katherine and restarted the sedatives. Katherine was currently safe and had not suffered from a lack of oxygen, but she had not flown.

Dr. Bob informed me that, given her failure to breathe independently, Katherine would most likely need a tracheostomy (trach). Her body expended too much energy breathing, energy she needed to grow and maintain her health. In the world of pediatric medicine, tracheostomies often act as a temporary support that allows kids to resolve other issues. Katherine would require the trach for a year, maybe longer. Before moving forward, Dr. Bob would request a consultation from pulmonology. I could tell by his voice that the turn of events disappointed him.

I recounted my conversation with Dr. Bob when I rejoined the family and spent a somber evening contemplating the future. The thought of Katherine tethered to a ventilator made me physically ill. She had already been through so much, with many more challenges in the future. I wish I could say that my concern rested entirely with Katherine, but I cannot. An ocean of self-pity enveloped me as I imagined the demands of caring for a baby on a vent.

A pulmonologist visited us in Katherine's room the following afternoon. Dr. Williams, not to be mistaken for the intensivist by the same name, was a soft-spoken man a decade my senior. He wore his compassion for patients on his sleeve, which instilled in me a feeling of trust. I set my mind to have a non-emotional discussion about a tracheostomy.

Dr. Williams had performed a bronchoscopy earlier that morning, visually inspecting Katherine's airways by threading a tiny camera through her ET tube. He drew an inverted "T" to represent the main airway and two branches leading to the lungs. He then circled the vertical airway and the branch leading to the left lung. These airways, soft as waterlogged rigatoni in infants, harden in the first two years of life. Katherine's enlarged heart pressed against these passages, literally choking her. Dr. Williams believed the problem would eventually resolve as her heart size decreases relative to the rest of her body, her ribcage enlarges, and the bronchial cartilage hardens.

In response to my question of why we could not just keep Katherine intubated, Dr. Williams explained that intubation carries its own set of risks, including internal hemorrhaging and infection. Intubation risks increase over time, becoming unacceptably high and necessitating a tracheostomy after two months for an infant. Dr. Williams recommended a second bronchoscopy in a week in hopes of seeing dramatic improvement. A week of rest would also allow Katherine to build strength and reduce airway swelling. Without sufficient improvement, we would have no choice but to pursue a trach.

The doctor then addressed other considerations. Respiratory diseases took a hiatus for the summer; they would return in force later in the year. Katherine's compromised airways may not be capable of fighting off a serious infection without ventilator assistance. He concluded on an upbeat note, stressing how Katherine would thrive on a ventilator, and I begrudgingly moved a little closer to accepting the tracheostomy.

In the week waiting for the next bronchoscopy, we celebrated a series of small achievements. Using a nasogastric (NG) tube, Katherine took milk for the first time on June 19, sixteen days after her birth. Breastmilk provided all of her nutrition within a few days, and she quickly regained weight lost after the operation. The doctors eased up on her sedatives, thereby allowing Katherine greater interaction with her surroundings. Katherine's eyes danced across the pages of the many books read to her. Her favorite pastime, though, was holding someone's finger or hand. In an existence mostly devoid of physical human contact, this simple gesture allowed Katherine to connect with those around her.

The IV lines in Katherine's umbilical cord finally failed, forcing the staff to establish a PICC line. A "PICC" is a form of IV used for a prolonged period. Although finding a baby's vein with a needle is difficult in the best situation, finding a vein in a baby with a heart defect is akin to placing a needle in a wet strand of angel hair spaghetti under a sweater. I remembered my mom telling me stories of a nurse at her hospital with a gift for finding a vein. A few nurses tried unsuccessfully with Katherine before Anthony, the PICU's savant, secured a PICC in her left arm. Although visually unpleasant, the PICC eliminated the need for any more needle pricks – a very good thing.

In the process of using an ultrasound to locate a suitable vein, Anthony discovered that Katherine had two superior vena cavas (SVC). Blood returns from the head and arms to the heart via two veins in a young fetus. As a normal fetus develops, a horizontal vessel forms between these two vertical veins, creating a capital "H" sitting atop the heart. Over time, more blood flows through the horizontal vein at the expense of the lower section of the left major vein. This section eventually dissolves after blood flow stops completely, leaving one SVC. This did not happen with Katherine. Both of her major veins remained. Krista later asked Dr. Abraham if he had noticed the double SVC during the surgery. He responded dryly, "I don't go looking around while I'm in there," which I found extremely funny and would throw back at Krista often for a laugh. More importantly, Dr. Abraham assured us this anatomical quirk did not present a problem.

After one day with a particularly interactive Katherine, I checked my voicemail before going to bed. Since Katherine's birth, I limited my phone usage to updating family. I simply did not have the emotional energy to relive the PICU events repeatedly with friends. Thus, a large collection of messages awaited me. All but one were messages of encouragement. The outlier came from my new commander in the Air National Guard, whom I had never met. He called to inform me that I had been promoted. Any other time, achieving such a career milestone would have been cause for great celebration. This promotion now paled in comparison to having read "Aladdin" to an alert Katherine just a few hours earlier.

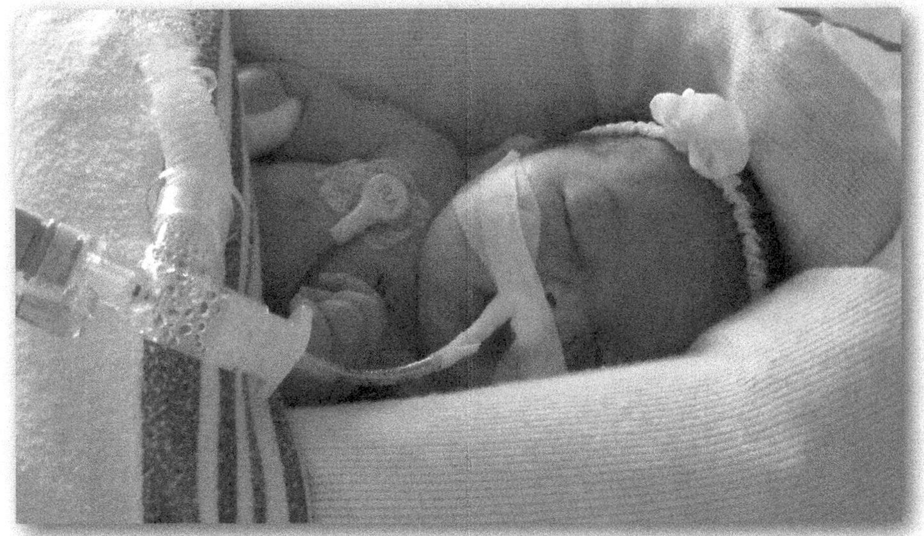

Katherine sleeping in her bassinet – note the ET tube.

Meanwhile, on the other side of the world, one of Krista's fellow pharmacists was cruising the Mediterranean Sea with her family. While exploring Valletta, Malta, she discovered the Church of St. Catherine of Siena. Built in 1576, the baroque structure continues to serve as a parish church for the city's Roman Catholic community. Krista's friend took time from her vacation to pray and light a candle for Katherine. While in the church, she met the pastor and explained her motivation for visiting. The priest, moved by Katherine's story, dedicated the next day's mass to "Katherine of Indianapolis."

Dr. Williams performed a second bronchoscopy on June 25, a week after the first procedure. The degree of improvement surprised the pulmonologist, but was "not clinically significant." In non-medical terms, Katherine did not improve enough to alter Dr. William's opinion that Katherine required a trach. In the week since Dr. Bob first broached the subject, Krista and I had discussed a trach with each intensivist at length. All agreed that Katherine needed a trach to facilitate proper growth and development. Krista and I therefore consented to the procedure. Dr. Williams scheduled Katherine's surgery for 12:30 p.m. on Friday, June 28.

"Did Sarah say anything to you today?" Krista asked as we got ready for bed on Wednesday, June 26.

"No. Why?"

"She stopped by the room and asked if Dr. Abraham had spoken to me yet."

"No, I haven't seen either."

I thought nothing more of it and went to bed.

CHAPTER 8

Breathe, Katie, Breathe

Dr. Abraham appeared in Katherine's room the next morning as Krista and Mary watched the baby. Not one for small talk, he got straight to the point:

> "Do you have any idea how high the mortality rate is for a single ventricle baby on a trach?"

After lengthy discussions with the pulmonologists and intensivists, we thought all parties agreed on the current treatment plan. We were wrong. Dr. Abraham strongly opposed a tracheostomy. His countervailing opinion shattered our illusion of consensus. Krista requested a conference with Dr. Abraham, Dr. Williams (pulmonologist), and the day's intensivist to discuss Dr. Abraham's concerns.

Krista called to inform me of Dr. Abraham's visit and the planned meeting minutes after I notified Katherine's supporters of the impending trach via e-mail. I raced to the PICU without sending a retraction. Sarah had scheduled the conference for 1:00 p.m. in Katherine's room, less than twenty-four hours before the scheduled trach.

Dr. Abraham walked into Room 8 at 12:58 p.m. and sat silently in a rolling chair in the center of the room. Aloof in a white coat, his face betrayed nothing as he casually sipped a cup of coffee. Krista and Mary occupied the couch. I sat beside them in the same PICU chair on which I held Katherine eleven days earlier. The PICU nurse practitioner, Anthony, leaned against the counter next to the bassinet. When the big hand struck twelve, Dr. Abraham started speaking without waiting for the intensivist and Sarah, who were just entering. Dr. Williams could not attend, marking the first of many times we tried unsuccessfully to assemble Katherine's treating physicians.

Tapping his paper coffee cup against a tray table for emphasis, Dr. Abraham asserted that single ventricle patients do not fare well with tracheostomies for two reasons. First, the tracheostomy opening at the base of the throat is a breeding ground for germs. Less than two inches would separate the trach from Katherine's current and future chest incisions, creating a tremendous infection risk. Second, mechanical ventilation disrupts the natural interaction between the heart and lungs, which might stress Katherine's heart to the point of failure.

The intensivist began his defense of the trach on behalf of his fellow intensivists and the pulmonologists by saying, "Some of Dr. Abraham's points are valid, *but....*" This marked the first in a volley of passive aggressive barbs between the two physicians. The intensivist repeated the justifications we had heard from Dr. Williams and the intensivist team for the past week: Katherine expended significant energy simply breathing, energy needed to grow and develop normally. Moreover, her compromised respiratory system left her vulnerable to a myriad of potentially life-threatening illnesses.

The doctors did not speak to each other, instead directing their comments to Krista. Dr. Abraham's gaze oscillated between Katherine and Krista. He never looked at the intensivist. I inferred that the surgeon was annoyed the staff made such an important change in Katherine's treatment plan without consulting him.

The room fell silent once each physician presented his opinion and answered Krista's questions. Four sets of eyes looked at us expectantly. The palpable tension between the physicians indicated that we were not working to find a consensus; Krista and I had to choose a side. I turned to Krista. She remained silent as our eyes met, but I inferred she trusted me to respond. With some feeling for Krista's inclination, I spoke for both of us:

> "We understand that neither course is without risk," I said with more than some temerity. "That said, we don't want to trach Katherine without giving her a chance to breathe on her own. If she fails, we press forward with the trach."

Interpreting Krista's continued silence as agreement, I reiterated the risks the intensivist named to demonstrate we listened to and, more importantly, appreciated his concerns. By adopting this course, we accepted the risk that Katherine might fail to breathe independently and require intubation. Dr. Abraham had no discernable reaction. The intensivist, conversely, was visibly piqued.

The intensivist again reminded us that an emergent intubation presents an even higher probability of brain injury and death. I confirmed that both options were fraught with risk. We chose the better of two bad alternatives. "Okay," he said tersely, "we'll extubate tomorrow."

"No, not tomorrow," I interjected with a firmness that surprised everyone in the room, including me. Dr. Williams said the risk of intubation increased in the second month. Katherine had been intubated eighteen days at that point. We therefore had some time, and I did not want to rush as we had the previous weekend. "You don't buy a car built on a Friday, and you don't extubate on a Friday." The former was some sage advice I recalled from childhood, the premise being that workers are thinking of the weekend, not their jobs. "We only get one chance at this, and I want all hands on deck. This place runs on a skeleton crew on the weekends. No, we do this next week when everyone is here."

Both physicians looked somewhat bemused and surprised at my directness, their only point of agreement that day. The intensivist did not argue. "Okay, we extubate next week." With that, the physicians left. Sarah and Anthony expressed their condolences regarding our unenviable position of weighing conflicting opinions, with Anthony saying he would have made the same choice. Nevertheless, Krista and I had chosen sides, rejecting the advice of the intensivists and pulmonologists. We apostates now had to work with the same treatment team whose opinion we dismissed.

The intensivist ordered breathing trials later that same afternoon. Katherine failed in spectacular fashion, perplexing everyone since she performed so well two weeks earlier when in inferior condition. I blamed the new, larger ET tube. No one else hazarded a guess. The tests did not auger well for a successful extubation.

Krista and I never discussed a nickname for or shortened variation of "Katherine." Not altogether subconsciously, we initially eschewed a different moniker to subdue our emotional connection. Using the formal "Katherine" somehow diminished the heart wrenching tragedy of one so young facing such a serious illness. As the fog of sedatives lifted the week following the surgery, our daughter's personality emerged. She was playful. She was curious. She deserved a suitable name: "Katie."

Even as I began referring to my daughter as "Katie," another nickname slowly grew in prominence. The staff kept Katie immobilized by wrapping a tubular pillow around her. Sleeping in her cocoon, Katie reminded me of a little bunny. I started calling her "Bunny" within a week of arriving at the PICU, a term that soon evolved into "The Hunny Bunny." Krista eventually incorporated the term into her vernacular, and we often referred to Katie simply as "the Bunny" in private conversations. This represented a shift in our relationship with Katie, away from two people scared their baby would not survive the week to parents caring for their child.

After Krista and Mary left at the end of the day, I was alone with Katie for the first time since the big meeting with the surgeon and intensivist. Leaning over my sleeping daughter, I rested my cheek against hers and felt the contrast of her soft skin and the tape holding the ET tube in place. Closing my eyes, I spoke quietly into her ear:

> "Bunny, you've been through so much, and we are all so proud of you. You're doing so well, but I need you to do something for me. I need

you to breathe for me, Bunny. I know it won't be easy, but I need you to breathe. Breathe, Katie, breathe."

Katie disobeyed her dad.

One disastrous breathing test after another did nothing to dissipate the tension between Krista and me and the staff. Katie finally passed a breathing test on Sunday afternoon with significant assistance. The intensivist increased ventilator support, which is akin to a father lifting his kid to the basketball rim instead of making him shoot a foul shot. That Katie required so much support was cause for concern.

Following four days of breathing test disappointments, an intensivist on Sunday again tried to persuade me into the trach. At the time, his dissension from the planned treatment left me seething. We made our decision and expected everyone to pull together; we did not need a fifth column. Looking back, I realize he advocated what he truly believed was best for Katie. God knows how many tragedies he had seen in his career, how many intubations gone wrong. I was upset, not because of the care he provided, but that he questioned our decision. I let my ego distract me from my responsibility, i.e., caring for Katie.

Katie's streak of poor tests continued into Monday with no improvement, prompting another intensivist to cancel the scheduled extubation. During rounds on Tuesday, he announced his intention to extubate Katie that morning, stating, "We're only doing this to humor Dr. Abraham." I do not know if he realized or cared that I stood amongst the staff. Regardless, I took no offense. I knew his position. Our alliance with Dr. Abraham was no secret. As the staff moved on to the next patient, I retreated to Katie's bassinet and repeated the mantra of the last few days, "Breathe, Katie, breathe."

The intensivist extubated Katie just before noon on Tuesday, July 2, while Krista, Mary, and I waited in the Family Room. We did not wait long. Within minutes, Anthony popped his head in the door to announce an uneventful extubation. Success or failure now rested solely with Katie.

Back in Room 8, we found a very upset little girl. The intensivist had ordered 12 liters of moisturized air per minute up her nose. The respiratory therapist used an adult nasal cannula because the pediatric version could not support such a high flow rate. The prongs, too big for Katie's nose, unnaturally distended her nostrils. Katie's eyes opened wide and her face writhed in distress when beads of water accumulating in the opaque tubing broke free and, carried by the pressurized air, shot up her nose. Katie frothed at the mouth as the humidified air entered the back of her throat, frequently choking on a clear combination of saliva and saline. She tried to cry, but the prolonged intubation rendered her inflamed vocal cords inoperative. Her watery, plaintive eyes conveyed her misery. Katie was more than miserable; she was scared.

We asked the intensivist if he could do something, anything, to ameliorate her discomfort. He responded in the negative, stating that Katie needed the air because of her dangerously high carbon dioxide level (CO_2). Katie's CO_2 level measured 61 prior to extubation, considerably higher than the optimal 30-40, indicating respiratory failure or diminished gas exchange in the lungs. Her CO_2 dipped to 58 at noon, and then creeped up to 70 by four p.m. The ordeal was stressing Katie's terribly sick heart.

The family spent the remainder of the day at Katie's bedside to provide what little succor we could. We held her hand, caressed her head, and offered words of encouragement. Most importantly, though, we constantly suctioned Katie's mouth so she would not choke on accumulated fluid. The CO_2 rose throughout the day, reaching 72 by the gloaming. Discomfort prevented sleep. An exhausted Katie struggled hour after hour. The fear of cardiac failure from the strain hung in the air. As we held vigil with the suction, staff visited the room infrequently. Monitors in the nurses' station relayed Katie's vitals, but not her suffering. Katie was fortunate to have family present, which, in fairness, may account for the infrequent staff visits.

Fearing that Katie's chance of "flying" was ebbing away, Krista and I decided to take shifts to ensure someone was constantly suctioning Katie's mouth and comforting her. I called my mom to come out and help; she would arrive early the following morning. Anticipating the next day's possible tracheotomy discussion, I wanted Krista, the most competent member of our team, rested and ready to advocate for Katie. I therefore took the night shift so Krista could at least try to sleep.

I sat with my miserable Katie from midnight until 7:30 a.m. Visits from the nurse were rare and brief. The intensivist may have checked her twice. My hopes that night would bring Katie sleep passed unanswered. Her soundless cries continued. She looked at me with huge watery eyes, pleading for me to ease her discomfort. I held her hand, told her to stay strong, prayed, and suctioned.

I learned a very important lesson that night: One cannot contract out parental responsibilities. Having brought Katie into the world, Krista and I bore the privilege and weight of caring for her. Katie had the right to expect us to exert every effort, explore every possibility, and give our full measure to her well-being. Conversely, Krista and I had no right to expect or demand the same of the staff. They had the expertise, but not the obligation. Despite Katie's struggle, the nurse infrequently checked on Katie. No one else spoke to her that night. No one else held her hand. No one else caressed her tear-moistened cheeks. Although nurses and therapists often provided such comfort, this is a gift beyond the scope of their duties. While such acts of kindness should be greatly appreciated, they should not be expected.

Katie showed no sign of improvement throughout our night together. I was emotionally and physically exhausted when Mary relieved me early Wednesday morning. After a full day without sleep, not even my apprehension could keep me going. Defeated, I collapsed on the couch beside Sam with our mantra still rattling in my head, "Breathe, Katie, breathe."

CHAPTER 9

Independence Day

I WOKE FEELING PHYSICALLY ILL at the thought of seeing Katie continue to struggle. I had developed a tolerance the night before, an intellectual numbness. That numbness dissipated as I slept, leaving me emotionally raw. Knowing that my place was at the hospital, I returned to the PICU at 1 p.m.

The sun, just starting to fall into the western sky, illuminated Katie's room with an ethereal light. I entered with trepidation. No one prepared me for what I would see, not that I would have believed had anyone told me. My mom, who arrived that morning to sit with the suffering Katie, bantered with Krista, Mary, and the nurse. I tacitly acknowledged them and approached Katie. My stomach in knots, I peered down at my little girl.

Katie looked up at me with an expression of serene calm. The tears were gone, her eyes now clear and wide. Lying in her bassinet, she was a picture of contentment. She had turned the corner mid-morning, her body somehow adjusting to the loss of ventilator support. Her CO_2 level dropped from the low seventies throughout the night to 51 by noon. While not ideal for the normal baby, this represented a significant accomplishment for Katie. The intensivist, Dr. Metz, reduced her oxygen to 8 liters per minute, which allowed the respiratory therapist to use a pediatric cannula and eliminated the discomfort of its adult counterpart. Excessive salivating stopped with the decreased airflow, and she took a pacifier for the first time. Katie's alertness and interaction shocked the occupational, physical, and speech therapists who worked with her that afternoon. Before Dr. Metz left for the day, he reported that many of Katie's numbers were better than they were prior to extubation. Pride overwhelmed me, overshadowing feelings of happiness or relief. Katie overcame intense physical discomfort and fear by sheer grit.

Although Katie's progress pleasantly surprised Dr. Metz, he cautioned us that we could not declare success for another few days. Katie could breathe on her own for one day, but we did not know whether she had the endurance to continue indefinitely. His words fell on deaf ears. After watching Katie battle to breathe for hours, we celebrated. Many of the nurses and RTs who had bonded with Katie joined in our jubilation. Come what may tomorrow, trach or no trach, we spent a glorious evening with a very awake and curious Katie.

Before going home for the night, I stopped at a McDonald's to e-mail the latest and happiest update. As I looked at the 10 o'clock crowd going about their daily lives with no idea of the miracle that occurred down the street, I felt privileged to have witnessed Katie's triumph. My distribution list, comprised only of people who reached out to us, had grown close to 200 people over the past month. After hitting "send," I quickly collected my belongings and headed for the exit.

My phone rang as I walked out the door and displayed the name of a law school classmate. Since Katie's birth, I had only taken calls from family and the hospital. Jubilant from the day's events, I dropped my now characteristic reclusiveness and answered the call. My enthusiasm disappeared as I heard Meghann choking back tears. "What's wrong?" I asked with concern. Meghann told me that she had just read my e-mail and, overcome by Katie's success, had to call. She cried tears of joy, not sadness. In the midst of recounting the events of the last few days, I suddenly remembered that it was Meghann's birthday and said, "Think of it as Katie's birthday present to you."

I thanked Meghann for reaching out and invited her to visit before ending the call. I stood in the parking lot and processed the conversation. In her thirty-two days of life, Katie existed within a cocoon on the St. Vincent Hospital campus. I had no understanding of how Katie affected those beyond the PICU. My conversation with Meghann marked the first time I experienced the visceral connection many of Katie's supporters, friends and strangers alike, developed with my little girl.

Katie continued to grow stronger throughout the next day, the Fourth of July. Katie's ever improving respirations prompted Dr. Metz to decrease her oxygen to 4 liters per minute. Her pink skin showed little, if any, sign of mottling. Katie's vocal cords had recovered, and, for the first time since her birth, she could cry. Although an easygoing baby, when Katie wanted her diaper changed, she wanted it changed immediately. She was not shy about conveying her discomfort now that she could scream. Even if Katie ultimately failed extubation, I was thankful just to know her voice. Recovery was not the only item on the schedule that day. Katie had a party to attend.

Krista's coworker and best friend at hospice, Laura, fielded scores of inquiries from their coworkers regarding Katie's condition. Focused on Katie's treatment, neither Krista nor I had invited visitors. Other than Laura and her husband, KC, only family and staff had graced Katie's room. Now that the extubation appeared successful, Laura took the initiative and invited the hospice staff to a party at the PICU on Independence Day morning. Using her employee credentials, she reserved and decorated a conference room off the PICU center hallway. Filling the table with cupcakes adorned with a combination of patriotic red, white, and blue icing, I think she fed every person entering the PICU that morning.

Anticipating visitors, Katie's mom and grandmothers bathed and dressed her for the first time. Although initially unnerved by the bright floral onesie, Katie seemed to enjoy her fashionable attire. As we waited for Krista's hospice colleagues, I asked her how many she anticipated. "A few," she said, reasoning that people were spending the holiday with family or working. That may have been true, but they made time to visit Katie. Upwards of twenty hospice friends came to celebrate Katie's recovery. They were not alone in celebrating with Katie. With a low census and the few patients on the floor stable, the nurses and respiratory therapists spent an inordinate amount of time with the unit's latest miracle baby. I held down the fort in the conference room with the cupcakes as Krista showed off our little girl, who by now had breathed independently for more than two days.

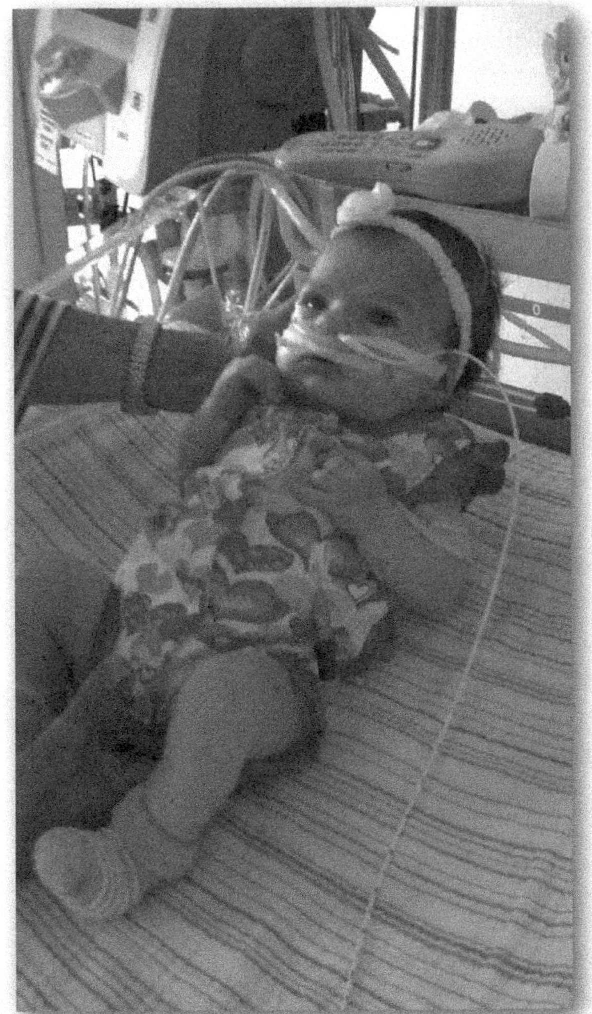

Katie dressed for the first time on Independence Day.

I took a break from the hospital on Friday, July 5. Repeated crises, endless hours of gut-wrenching waiting, plans for the future in doubt, financial strain, and too many sleepless nights on the couch with Sam had finally gotten the better of me. Mentally and physically exhausted, I asked my mom to sit with Katie while Krista and Mary met Krista's brother at the airport. Secure in the knowledge that Katie was in good hands, I settled in at a coffee shop with another book. I barely finished the first chapter when my phone rang.

Before leaving the hospital on Independence Day, both Krista and my mom sensed something amiss. Their intuition proved correct. During rounds, Katie's night nurse reported Katie was uncharacteristically fussy and had developed a fever. Katie's breathing grew increasingly labored throughout the morning. Subsequent tests indicated Katie was septic. Mom called me with the news, explaining that Katie had contracted a blood infection. Lab tests identifying the exact type of infection take two days, so the intensivist started her on a broad-spectrum antibiotic to cover the majority of likely culprits. I relayed the update to Krista, and we convened at the hospital.

The infection threatened to derail Katie's extubation progress. Katie's body diverted energy needed to breathe in order to fight the infection. The sleeping Katie breathed with noticeable difficulty. We feared that the infection might necessitate an emergency intubation or worse. Any stress to Katie's system escalated her already high risk of cardiac failure. Pensiveness replaced the Independence Day joy. Katie slept through the day in stark contrast to the energetic baby just a day earlier. As daylight gave way to darkness, the antibiotics arrested the infection and Katie's breathing improved.

I had not yet recovered from the infection scare when Dr. Bob delivered a bombshell the following day: He would transfer Katie back to the NICU once space became available. The PICU and NICU differ in their focus of care, i.e., acute medical intervention as opposed to stabilizing critically ill infants. The latter includes preparing newborns to go home. Having recovered from surgery and now breathing on her own, Katie no longer required PICU services.

Although Katie required occupational, physical, and speech therapy to reclaim the developmental progress she missed over the past five weeks, ingesting food orally was her major challenge. Katie initially received her nutrition through an IV solution pumped directly into her bloodstream. After a couple of weeks, she progressed to taking breastmilk through an NG tube, which extends from her nose to her stomach. Katie could not go home until she could ingest food without the tube. Teaching babies to eat is a NICU specialty.

For unknown reasons, infants who undergo heart surgery often struggle to take a bottle or breast feed, routinely taking longer to learn this basic skill than recover from the surgery itself. Exacerbating this difficulty, Katie's unique circulation caused her to breathe an average of eighty times per minute, more than twice the normal respiration rate. This fast breathing, known as "tachypnea" (tak-ip-nee-uh), makes eating as difficult as chugging a milkshake during a full sprint.

Krista and I abhorred the thought of leaving the PICU. We had shared, perhaps endured, the greatest trial of our lives with the staff. While they encounter hundreds if not thousands of families in crisis throughout their careers, this was our first, and we hoped only, severe pediatric illness crisis. Our affection for these people accordingly knew no bounds. To carry on with the next phase in Katie's recovery with a team of strangers felt almost disloyal. Despite our reluctance to leave, Dr. Bob convinced us that Katie should transfer to the NICU as soon as possible.

The imminent change in treating staff was not the only personnel shakeup Krista and I experienced that weekend. My mom returned to Pennsylvania to take care of my grandmother while Mary and Krista's brother flew back to Colorado. For the first time in Katie's life, Krista and I did not have local family support. We had leaned heavily on our family since Katie's birth. Anticipating years of medical struggles ahead, though, we had to use their time in Indianapolis and that of other family members conservatively. On the evening of their departure, I remarked, "We're walking [a tightrope] without a net now." Krista nodded her head in agreement.

An intimidating HAZMAT-like sign on the large, closed glass door of Katie's room warned of the biological danger within on the morning of

Sunday, July 7. The intensivist had called earlier that morning to inform us that lab results indicated Katie had contracted a particularly noxious form of E. coli. This strain of bacteria, usually found in the small intestine, is resistant to most antibiotics. He ordered isolation measures to protect other patients and staff from the disease, requiring all who enter Katie's room to wear a mask, gown, and gloves. He also assured us Katie was stable and in no immediate danger.

Krista sped to the hospital after the call while I tended to the dog. She and a nurse were discussing isolation protocols by the bassinet when I arrived. Responding to my knock on the door, Krista gestured to a vestibule adjacent to Katie's room that opened into the hallway.

Fr. John, the hospital chaplain who had become a regular fixture since the baptism, arrived to bless Katie as I entered the small room. He asked me if I had ever taken isolation precautions. I answered in the negative, so he proceeded to show me the process. In one of the premier medical facilities in the State of Indiana, surrounded by an army of doctors and nurses, a Catholic priest instructed me the ins and outs of infectious disease prevention.

Katie responded well to the antibiotics and was already back to her precocious self. The atmosphere was light despite the recent infection. Dr. Bob examined Katie that afternoon. His expression revealed his amazement at Katie's condition. Not only was she breathing on her own, she was thriving. While standing at the foot of the bassinet, he addressed Katie with a slight smile on his face:

"Well, you proved me wrong. You proved us all wrong."

She had indeed exceeded all expectations, with the possible exception of those belonging to Dr. Abraham. The surgeon also checked in on Katie that day, his poker face perhaps betraying a hint of smugness. He had disagreed with the otherwise unanimous treating staff, and Katie proved him correct. As far as I was concerned, he earned the right to be smug.

Dr. Bob did not merely stop by the room to check on Katie. He informed us that a bed had opened in the NICU and this would be our last night in the

PICU until Katie's next heart surgery in roughly five months. While Katie slept that evening, Krista and I packed her belongings.

We found Anthony holding Katie in her room upon our morning arrival in the PICU on Monday, July 8. The sight of tiny Katie in the arms of one who helped save her life gave the scene tremendous poignancy. Moreover, this simple act of kindness symbolized the bond that had developed between Katie and the staff.

Anthony placed Katie back in the bassinet after we interrupted their bonding session. Holding Katie was not his only act of kindness that morning. He also attached a mobile to Katie's bassinet. Its three stuffed animals spinning in the air captivated Katie. I never thought to get Katie such a contraption. That such a simple toy would give her so much pleasure surprised me, and I regret not getting one for her earlier.

The transport team arrived within an hour to take Katie on the quarter mile trip back to Women's Hospital. After transferring her lines from the PICU equipment to that of the transport cart, the nurses and transport staff lifted Katie and slid her into the travel bassinet. Now able to vocalize, she let everyone know of her dislike for the transport cart. Katie wailed all the way to the NICU, her cry fading as the team wheeled her down the hall.

We piled Katie's angel figurines, books, outfits, prayer notes a janitor left for Katie, and the *Smile* album in a red wagon and exited Room 8 for the last time. Before departing, I erased the whiteboard and left the staff a parting note:

Thanks, everyone, I'll be eternally grateful for the care you provided.

Love, Katherine Murtha

CHAPTER 10

Terra Incognita

I DROVE OUR OVERSTUFFED CAR to St. Vincent Women's Hospital after saying our PICU goodbyes. Transferring patients enter the facility through a bay behind the building, but their families use the main entrance. The lobby bustled with mothers-to-be, nerve wracked fathers, and beaming grandparents early on a beautiful July morning.

The elevator doors opened to the third floor waiting room. Krista and I navigated the halls to the NICU's main entrance where a receptionist met us. She presented nametags and explained numerous NICU policies, which differed from those of the PICU regarding visitation. The NICU allowed fewer visitors and suspended visitation for everyone, including parents, for an hour during nurse shift change at seven o'clock in the morning and evening. During our last stay, no one bothered to tell us the rules. Perhaps the staff thought we had too much on our minds, or maybe our brief stay did not warrant the effort. Regardless, we muddled through a short stack of standardized forms before the pleasant woman explained Katie could not return to a pod in the open bay because of the E. coli contamination threat and guided us to a private room.

Katie's new room was much more utilitarian than its five-star PICU counterpart. A bassinet, footstool, and wood chair occupied a majority of the floor space, which was one quarter the area of a standard PICU room. Katie's monitor, a miniature version of that in the PICU, rested on a small ledge high on a wall. A beige curtain hid a large glass door that could open into the adjoining room another baby currently occupied. Scratches and gouges peppered the mustard-colored walls, victims of jostling equipment and furniture in the small space. A white board identical to that of the PICU hung on the outside wall next to a window that looked down on the staff parking lot behind the hospital. The wall opposite the curtain bisected the window, indicating private rooms were not part of the original design. An inch wide gap between the glass and wall edge allowed sound to pass freely between our room and that of our infant neighbor. Unfortunately, the neighbor was learning to "self-sooth," a sophisticated way of saying the staff let him cry. He failed to get the lesson and wailed practically nonstop for an entire week before discharge. The sound did not faze Katie, who slept peacefully in the crib when we arrived.

Krista and I did not have more than a minute alone with Katie before a stream of doctors and nurse practitioners flooded the room. All expressed concern and some surprise at Katie's tachypnea. Expecting her respirations to slow over time as her PICU treatment team predicted, the NICU staff's concerns did not rattle us.

Dr. Wareham, the medical director and neonatologist, outlined the goals Katie needed to meet before she could go home: (1) wean from nasal oxygen, (2) exhibit continued weight gain, and (3) end her dependence on the NG tube for nutrition. The latter presented the greatest challenge. If breast and bottle-feeding did not work, Katie might need a feeding tube until able to feed orally. I dismissed that possibility, thinking the doctor was just being thorough.

The doctor unexpectedly stopped the gown, gloves, and mask requirement before delivering some bad news. Katie's strain of E. coli is often associated with meningitis. He ordered a spinal tap for the following day to confirm the absence of this noxious infection. I protested a little, asking if a less intrusive test existed. Dr. Wareham assured me that babies experience far less pain than adults do during the procedure. I unhappily acquiesced.

Katie's nurse, Cindy, worked around the doctors and nurse practitioners to finish the intake process. NICU nurses typically cared for three or four infants per shift, double that of the PICU nurses, but Katie currently kept Cindy fully occupied. Katie's three nurses during her first NICU stay looked to me like they should be planning for the prom, not caring for a critically ill baby. Closer to me in age, Cindy moved with the aplomb of one with years of experience. After a month interacting with pediatric nurses, I developed a sense for distinguishing the wheat from the chaff. Cindy was amongst the sharpest nurses we encountered at St. Vincent. Knowing that Katie was in her capable hands alleviated much of the anxiety associated with the transfer.

Our confidence in the nursing staff continued into the nightshift. I needed just a few minutes watching Cindy's replacement to conclude Katie was two for two thus far for top-notch NICU nurses. Krista and I remained late into the night to familiarize ourselves with Katie's newest nurse, Karrie. The three of us discussed Katie's history and swapped stories about Sam and Karrie's two dogs. I asked Karrie about her schedule as we were leaving.

> "Oh, I work the next three days. I was supposed to be off today, but someone asked me to fill in for her. I worked last night, too. I work all the time. I love my job. I love my kids."

With that, Karrie left us to check on another patient. When she turned her back, I pointed at her with my right index finger and mouthed to Krista, "Let's ask for her." Krista nodded her head emphatically, "Absolutely."

I never had the opportunity to request Karrie. Smitten with Katie, she asked administration to assign Katie to her permanently. Karrie cared for Katie for almost half her stay in the NICU, which meant many nights of restful sleep for us.

The third and final component of Katie's core nursing team relieved Karrie the following day. Kat, Katie's NICU nurse when she transferred to the PICU, asked for Katie upon learning of her return to the unit. Kat soon became one of Katie's favorite people, responding enthusiastically to the nurse's long curly hair and high-pitched voice. The presence of a familiar face somewhat ameliorated the day's spinal tap ordeal.

The NICU allows nurses to volunteer to be a "primary nurse," meaning the charge nurse assigns the nurse to a specific patient whenever possible. The program is voluntary. Some nurses relish the bonds formed with baby and family during prolonged stays. Others enjoy the challenge and variety of new patients. Most fall on the spectrum in between. Cindy, Kat, and Karrie eschew the practice with few exceptions; however, all three volunteered to be Katie's prime nurses. This scheduling arrangement fostered relationships between the family and these three women unparalleled in Katie's hospitalization, relationships that long outlasted our time in the NICU. Even with Katie's nursing team in place, however, something was missing.

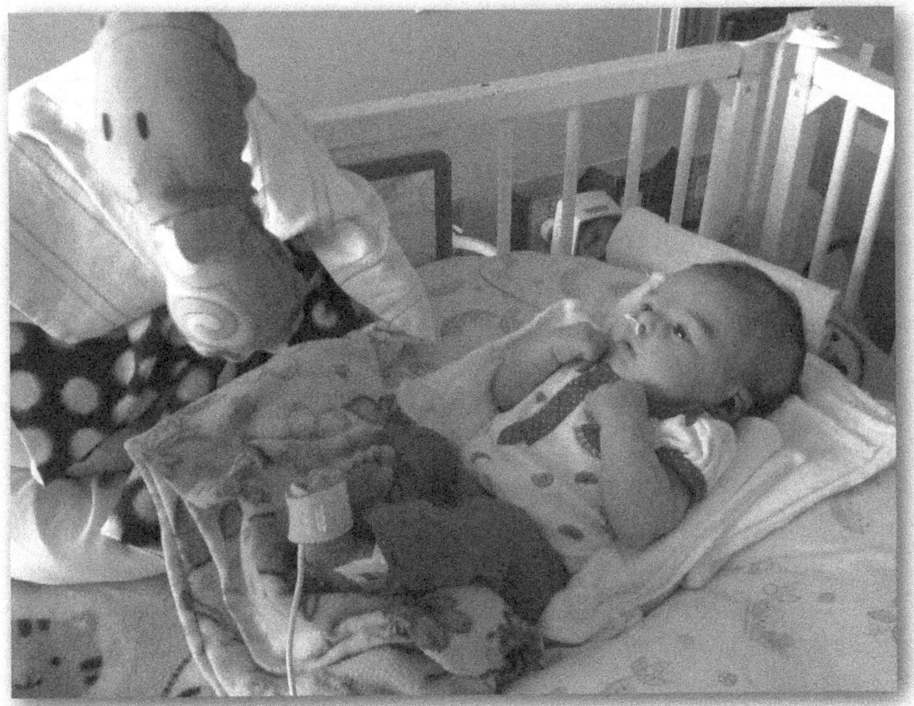

Katie enjoying her mobile in the NICU.

Katie's new bassinet lacked a mobile. The toy Anthony had anchored to Katie's PICU bassinet did not transfer with her. Katie spent her waking hours staring up at white ceiling tiles with an occasional glancing view of the medical equipment surrounding her. These items were hard, cold, and sterile, nothing like what one would expect in a nursery. Perhaps that explains Katie's visceral reaction to watching three colorful animals spin above her.

We requested a mobile, but the unit's only available toy was broken. A mobile that is not mobile is just a few stuffed animals dangling from a hanger. Krista purchased a replacement at a nearby store. Katie's eyes lit up when she saw it and beamed when the animals started rotating. She found the purple octopus particularly fascinating. Surrounded by family and nurses and free of the ventilator and sedatives, Katie found a little bit of paradise while watching her mobile and listening to The Beach Boys.

Katie adjusted to the NICU much better than her parents did. While Katie's nursing care more than pleased us, that care existed within an opaque organizational structure. We had no idea who was in charge. A nebulous group of NPs and occasional neonatologists replaced Dr. Wareham within a few days. None emerged as the de facto care manager. Nursing leadership remained anonymous. Every morning on my way to the NICU, I purchased a drink from a fast-food restaurant that placed the manager's picture and name prominently on a plaque in the lobby. I knew who was responsible for my iced tea, but not my critically ill daughter's care.

On the first morning Katie did not have a prime nurse caring for her, I referenced the whiteboard to check the nurse assignment. No one had updated it. I asked a nurse in the bay for the name of Katie's assigned nurse. She referenced a folded schedule in her pocket. The assignments had changed, so she had to ask someone else. I thanked her and returned to Katie's room, where the assigned nurse met me ten minutes later. This occurred repeatedly. While the search for Katie's nurse was a minor annoyance, the persistent failure to update the whiteboards demonstrated a lack of supervision and attention to detail.

Months later, I debated the significance of the whiteboard at length with undeniably one of the best PICU nurses. Outdated information on the whiteboard was the bane of my existence, and I admittedly became a little obsessive compulsive over it. The nurse maintained the board did not matter, because she knew everything about her patients' care. "I don't doubt *you*," I replied with emphasis on the last word, "but I don't know all the nurses. Plus, if the supervisors don't notice something that obvious, what do they notice … and what else slides by?"

Concerns regarding nursing care and supervision were emblematic of a bigger issue. The NICU had no clearly identifiable process for expressing concerns or asking questions. Katie's nurses were not versed on the specifics of Katie's cardiac issues or long-term care plans, which exceeded the scope of their responsibility. They often mustered an answer, but not a complete answer. Not knowing who knew the answers presented an increasingly vexing problem.

This confusion affected a young married couple struggling with a gravely ill boy just outside Katie's door. Born three months premature, their child faced serious respiratory and gastrointestinal issues. Over lunch in the cafeteria, the young parents relayed some troubling statements one of their boy's nurses allegedly said. Not knowing with whom to speak, they neither reported the nurse nor requested that she no longer be assigned to their son. Instead, the mother said, "We keep our fingers crossed every day that we don't get her again." Watching their boy fight for his life, these twenty-somethings had no recourse. I cannot speak to the veracity of their story or say we encountered any unprofessional nurses, but I shared their confusion as to the nursing hierarchy.

Having initially kept my concerns to myself, the nursing management issue came to a head on July 15. A neonatologist had removed Katie's PICC line the day before. Since Katie completed the course of antibiotics and showed no signs of E. coli, the risk of infection from the PICC outweighed the need for an access port. For the first time since the day of her birth, Katie was free of IV lines.

I joined Krista and my mom for lunch in the cafeteria while an aunt sat with Katie. Visibly upset, my aunt joined us an hour later and reported that the staff spent more than forty minutes trying to draw blood, repeatedly poking Katie's heel with a needle. I was incredulous. Katie's ever-present lines the preceding forty-one days allowed for painless blood draws. On the first day, *the very first day*, Katie did not have an access port, the staff repeatedly stuck her for almost an hour. I rushed upstairs to investigate.

The nurse confirmed my aunt's story and told me what I already knew: "Katie's a tough stick." I asked why the blood was needed, to which she responded that a cardiologist ordered the genetic test. The test had no bearing on Katie's treatment. Moreover, the doctors could have ordered the test at any time since her birth, but no one thought to do it. Seeking affirmation, I synopsized the facts:

> "So the staff spent almost an hour poking Katie, whom everyone knows is a tough stick, the day after her last line was removed for a test she doesn't need because no one thought to order it during the previous 41 days when she had easy access … Does that make sense?"

The nurse reiterated that the doctor wrote the order, an answer that left me wanting. I did not question that she followed the doctor's order; I questioned why she did not push back. After ten, twenty, thirty, or forty minutes passed, why did she not apprise the doctor? My questions did not stop with the nurse. Why was the test not ordered sooner? Why subject Katie to the pain of a blood draw for a test not at all to her clinical benefit? Why not wait until Katie had another access line? Incensed by Katie's purplish blue heel speckled with red dots from numerous needle pokes, I wanted either someone held accountable or an explanation as to why my anger was unwarranted.

Seething from the thought of Katie being stuck repeatedly, I called my dad's wife, Elaine, who worked for the same hospital conglomerate that operated St. Vincent in Indianapolis. After relaying the story, Elaine suggested that I speak with someone in the Risk Management Office. I never thought to ask for NICU management, so I drove to the administrative building adjacent to the main hospital. The receptionist introduced me to a delightful nurse who reminded me of my mom. We discussed Katie's treatment history thus far and the issue that prompted my visit. She seemed to understand both my frustration with the blood draw and the lack of a readily identifiable management structure. Voicing my concerns was cathartic. I left her office without the emotional pique with which I had entered; however, the guilt from failing to protect Katie that afternoon has yet to ebb.

Not more than twenty minutes elapsed after I returned from Risk Management before a senior nurse manager appeared in Katie's room. She was, as we say back home, loaded for bear and castigated me for taking my concerns outside of the NICU. I retorted that I would have been more than happy to discuss my concern with her provided I knew who she was. Her tone softened once I explained I did not intentionally slight her. The initial tension dissipated, and we conversed cordially about Katie's treatment and the blood draw incident. By the time the manager left, we had laid the foundation for a good working relationship. She would routinely stop by the room to check on Katie over the remaining month of her hospitalization.

The next day, headshots of NICU leadership on a new paper sign beside the main door surprised me. I found solace in knowing that Katie's suffering served a purpose: parents now knew whom to approach should they have a concern. Even the whiteboards remained updated for a week before reverting to sporadic use. You cannot win them all.

Administration assigned each NICU patient to one of five teams. Doctors comprised four of the teams. The final team consisted of nurse practitioners (NPs). Although monitored by a physician, the NPs had tremendous autonomy. Katie belonged to the nurse practitioner team, which struck me as odd. Running the numbers in my head, physicians were responsible for eighty percent of patients. Katie was surely one of the unit's more complex cases. That she was not under the direct care of a physician shook my faith in the NICU bureaucracy. I mean no slight to the nurse practitioners or doubt the their capability to treat issues associated with newborns, but Katie's anatomy was exceedingly more complex than that of the average kid.

The unpredictability of the nurse practitioner schedules made the task of monitoring Katie's progress increasingly difficult, particularly without the benefit of rounds. Doctors worked two weeks on, two weeks off. Nurse practitioners worked a fragmented schedule. One NP worked only on Sundays. Other NPs worked as needed. Their schedules had no apparent rhyme or reason. This meant little to those with NICU stays of short duration; however, it deeply affected the continuity of care for those on an extended stay plan. Krista and I sometimes felt as though Katie had a different NP every day. While our perception may not have reflected ground truth, it colored our attitudes nonetheless. We had no issue with the staff members themselves, but with the randomness in which they appeared. Occasionally, a stranger would check on Katie, never to be seen or heard from again. Thinking Katie had overcome the complicated phase of her care, I did not to ask caregivers to write their names on my list as I had in the PICU, a decision I came to rue.

One day, a middle-aged woman in scrubs entered Katie's room as the baby slept and I read a book. Differentiating staff wearing the ever-present yellow gowns was difficult, and I assumed the stranger was a nurse practitioner. "I'm just here to take a few measurements," she said without introducing herself. I greeted her and returned to my book. After a brief pause, she turned to me with a furrowed brow.

"Her head is far too small. Far too small. Has anyone mentioned this?"

Taken aback, I asked, "No. How small?"

Shaking her head, she responded grimly, "Too small, far too small for her age" and left the room in a huff. Concerned, I asked the next doctor I saw about Katie's head. He gave me a quizzical look. "Her head is fine. What are you talking about?" said the doctor dismissively. I told him the story of the mysterious woman. He had no idea of whom I spoke. For a week, I asked doctors, nurse practitioners, nurses, and therapists about Katie's head. They gave me the same reaction the residents of Sleepy Hollow gave Ichabod Crane. At least Crane saw the Headless Horseman every now and then. I never saw the woman again.

Krista reached her breaking point after a few weeks in the NICU. Katie, though cute and adorable, had an extremely rare manifestation of a rare condition. The nurse practitioners struggled to track her ever-changing status. After spending a few days watching Katie struggle to breathe, our concerns regarding pulmonary hypertension resurfaced. Krista asked a nurse practitioner, who had been off for a few days, about the plan should Katie's numbers not improve. The nurse practitioner stared at her, completely unfamiliar with the issue. Krista is quite reserved, but I sensed anger. "She didn't even read the chart," Krista told me that evening in exasperation.

Krista disappeared after we arrived at the NICU the following morning. While I checked on Katie, Krista arranged her transfer to one of the physician teams. The transfer relieved my growing apprehension regarding continuity in Katie's care. I only regretted that we waited so long to make the change. I liken changing care teams to breaking up with a girlfriend and appreciated Krista doing the dirty work. The nurse practitioners continued to follow Katie's progress, initially a little awkward for all involved. As in the PICU, tension dissipated as we watched Katie improve.

Katie thrived in her first few weeks in the NICU. The spinal tap came back negative for bacteria. Kat placed Katie on her stomach to avoid pressure on the puncture wound after the procedure, which marked her first time lying face down. Although a nonevent for most kids, this bit of normalcy constituted yet another milestone. Katie exhibited no sign of infection after completing her course of antibiotics. By the middle of July, Katie weighed more than a pound over her birthweight and outgrew her first onesie. The only setback came two days after the transfer when the infectious disease physician reinstated the isolation protocol. We found humor in Krista trying to breastfeed Katie in a rocking chair while wearing a gown, mask, and gloves.

The staff wasted no time introducing Katie to oral feeding. Krista and I had been equal participants in Katie's care up to that point. The new breastfeeding goal relegated me to a support role. Both Krista and Katie needed all the support they could get. The hospital's lactation consultants, along with many of the nurses, offered suggestions and encouragement to no avail. We doubted she obtained milk on the one occasion Katie latched for thirty seconds. In addition to her rapid breathing, Katie often fussed from discomfort when held. We assumed that she merely felt more secure in her crib. In retrospect, the pressure on her ribcage when held, albeit slight, probably made breathing more difficult.

We gave up on breastfeeding after a week and tried bottle-feeding. The bottle allowed us to ascertain with certainty how much milk, if any, Katie consumed. Katie required 61 mL every three hours for her weight and size. She struggled so much to drink that I felt guilty giving her a bottle. Her face grew dark red, and perspiration covered her brow. I periodically checked the volume, only to be disappointed upon seeing no change. No matter how hard she tried, Katie could not drink.

Katie's struggle to feed independently did not surprise the physicians. Many post-operative infants encounter the same roadblock. In such situations, infants commonly rely on a feeding tube to ensure proper nutrition. Just seven weeks earlier, an abdominal surgery would have horrified me. After open-heart surgery and a potential tracheostomy, I considered a feeding tube rather innocuous.

Immediate medical and quality of life concerns overshadowed my disappointment that Katie would bear another scar. The nurses typically replaced the nasogastric tube every three days. Katie sometimes pulled on the itchy tube, prompting a premature replacement. The nurse would remove the existing tube before inserting a replacement in the other nostril and extending it down to Katie's stomach. I would opt for a feeding tube to escape that process any day.

To prevent Katie from pulling on her NG tube, we put oversize gloves on her hands. Katie did not need long to overcome this obstacle. I put large, powder blue circular gloves on Katie one afternoon. As I hovered over her, poking her belly, she covered her smile with a glove. Her eyes stared directly at me above the blue fabric. She continued to laugh as I tickled her. Sensing something amiss, I moved her glove. She had freed her other hand and, using a glove to hide her devious machinations, pulled the NG tube while staring at me just six inches away. I found the nurse in the bay and informed her that Katie needed a replacement tube. She looked at me quizzically, "Weren't you with her?" I nodded my head sheepishly but did not volunteer an explanation.

Having collected a car full of items during our PICU stay, Katie's smaller room forced us to limit what we brought into the NICU. We culled the decorations to her favorite stuffed animals, a few small religious items and figurines, and Tracy's rosary. I also included my CD player. A mound of boxes in my car buried our CDs; however, I happened to have three on my front seat. I intended but failed to bring additional music over the next seven weeks. A Beatles and swing disc received little playing time. I cannot say the same for The Beach Boys, who fittingly provided the July soundtrack. The CD featured two albums, "Surfer Girl" and "Shut Down Vol. II," that the band recorded exactly fifty years earlier. I did not appreciate the frequency with which the disc played until I heard a nurse sing along to a deep track that the band probably no longer remembers recording. I increased The Beatles' airplay for the nurses' sake.

In addition to patient care, the NICU prepares parents for the responsibility of caring for a baby at home. The nurses, therefore, expected us to care for Katie to the maximum extent of our capabilities. The PICU nurses performed almost all the hands-on care because of Katie's many IVs and lines. I changed one diaper during Katie's five-week stay. I exceeded that number in the NICU before the first sunset.

Learning the art of changing diapers brought with it a healthy dose of humility. Figuring out that the cartoon character goes on the front alone took a few days. I once walked in on a nurse when she discovered I had neglected to replace the dirty diaper I had removed, which earned me a look of bewilderment and castigation. I later found Katie's backside covered in a white pasty substance when I removed her wet diaper. After battling her heart defect for more than a month, she now had some dastardly intestinal issue. I raced out to the main floor in full crisis mode and asked the closest nurse to check Katie. Such was my introduction to diaper rash cream.

CHAPTER 11

Surfer Girl

Our five weeks in the PICU isolated us from anyone other than close family or caregivers. Facing crisis after crisis kept us rather self-involved. Katie's progress now afforded me enough peace of mind to engage with those outside her immediate sphere of care. Most of these relationships took root in the small hospital cafeteria. I once spent an hour exchanging war stories over lunch with the parents of a baby close to Katie's room. Their tiny boy, born at twenty-three weeks and just under two pounds, struggled with a myriad of complications. Listening to his harrowing ordeal, the tremendous will to live within that diminutive body astounded me.

The stories of families who live hundreds of miles away from the hospital made us appreciate our fifteen-minute drive. One woman accompanied her nine-month old daughter on a three-hour emergency ambulance ride to PMCH while her husband remained at home, working and watching their other kids. He joined his wife and daughter on the weekend four days later. The marooned mother arrived at PMCH with only the clothes on her back. We offered her our guest bedroom, but she had already made arrangements.

One mother overheard me telling an aunt how fortunate we were that Katie avoided a tracheostomy. She stopped by our table on her way out and said, "My daughter has a trach. It's not so bad." That afternoon I discovered her daughter, Teagan, had a private room a few rooms away from Katie. Born around the twenty-fifth week, her lungs did not have sufficient time to develop. She needed a trach until her lungs could support independent respirations, which would probably take a few years. The five-month-old looked very small in comparison to the other babies.

Teagan was lucky to have a devoted mom and grandmother. Not all kids were so fortunate. In the two weeks that another baby occupied a room next to Katie, I never saw anyone but staff members enter his room. I asked a nurse how often she sees such circumstances. She said, "It's not common" before pausing and then, slightly quieter, "but it's not uncommon, either."

Not all infants in the NICU are in the extended stay program or face Katie's degree of struggle. I had the fortune of befriending some parents of the "short timers." These ephemeral relationships provided a distraction from the monotony of hospitalization. A portly first-time grandmother of a baby in the pod by the main door planted herself in a rocking chair before the sun came up and held her grandson until midnight. I asked her every time I walked in, "You're still here?" She would laugh with a partially toothless grin and say, "Yep, me and my grandbaby." One father wearing a Notre Dame hat spent seven days with his son in the NICU. Sharing a Notre Dame connection, we spoke a few times. He would follow Katie's progress for the next nine months and send countless messages of support. That is but one example of the bonds forged in the NICU.

Back in the room, I curried favor with the staff by providing an endless supply of donut holes. I cannot say Katie got any extra attention because of my sugary bribes, but earning the moniker of "the donut guy" did not hurt. Katie did not really need my help. As the most popular member of the family, she induced affection amongst a growing cadre of caregivers. The nurses caring for Katie on the days when the primes were off joined the Katie Fan Club. Katie's confinement to the bassinet limited her physical interaction with the PICU nurses; however, their NICU counterparts could hold and rock her, allowing a level of intimacy previously unrealized. Deprived of human contact for so long, Katie reveled in the stimulation.

A team of therapists quickly became a valued part of the treatment team. Spending five weeks practically immobile took its toll on Katie. Babies with cardiac surgery tend to "hang on" tightly with some muscles, elevating their shoulders and tightly flexing their elbows. Five weeks of ventilator tubes pulling Katie's face towards her right shoulder left her neck muscles frozen. As with the nurses, she picked a favorite. Even on the days Katie disliked therapy, Lynne could motivate her little patient to push through the discomfort.

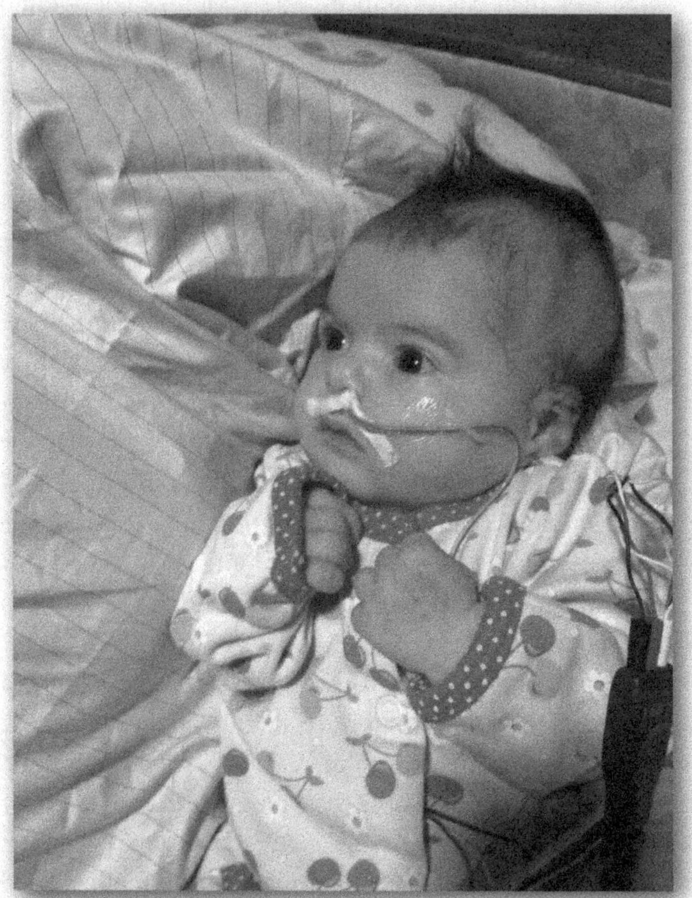

Katie "hanging on" with elevated shoulders and flexed elbows.

The therapists employed a variety of techniques to offset the effects of prolonged immobility. Infant massage improved range of motion, the immune system, and bone strength. Her neck muscles relaxed after a few weeks of therapy. Positive touch helped Katie overcome any aversion to touch after weeks of pokes and prods. Rocking and supporting Katie in an upright position imitated activities that normally occur in typical development at home, thereby improving the vestibular system. Other than impressing people when dropped in casual conversation, the term "vestibular system" describes the body's most influential sensory system. Located in the inner ear, it detects movement and acts like an air traffic controller, directing tactile, auditory, and visual sensory impulses to the appropriate brain location. Katie shared my love of physical exercise, which I charitably categorize as negligible, but she powered through it.

In between therapy sessions, Katie's universe opened up beyond immediate family, caregivers, and hospital employees. Holding a newborn often stirs emotions, but holding a newborn that came so close to tragedy is a spiritual experience for some. Great aunts and uncles drove hundreds of miles to visit the youngest member of the family. Laurie, a friend from a legal assistance organization in Indianapolis, became the first non-relative or caregiver to hold Katie. She would also be the last non-family member to hold Katie.

Watching others interact with Katie always lifted my spirits; but nothing compared to our private time. I often returned to the hospital after Krista and I had gone home for the night. Slipping through the subdued open bay, I entered Katie's dark room and closed the door behind me. After turning on some music, I would gingerly lift Katie from her bassinet and hold her in the rocking chair. Some nights she would sleep, some nights she would stare at me with her coal-black eyes. The music, though, was always the same. Drowning out the monitor alarms, the sound of "Surfer Girl" filled the room:

Little surfer, little one, made my heart come all undone.
Do you love me, do you surfer girl?

For a brief time, thoughts of heart defects disappeared, replaced by music about the sun, crashing waves, and sandy beaches.

As I say from me to you, I will make your dreams come true.
Do you love me, do you surfer girl?

Bathed in darkness and harmony, nothing could harm me and my surfer girl.

From a medical perspective, Katie continued to exceed expectations. The biggest development since leaving the PICU was that Katie transitioned from being a "cardiac baby" to a baby with a cardiac problem. She gained an impressive pound and a half since birth and grew 1.25 inches. Katie exhibited no sign of infection. With lungs void of any fluid, she did not require oxygen through a nasal cannula. No longer subject to mechanical devices, painkillers, paralytics, and needles, her personality fully emerged. Katie used a bouncer for the first time. Her vocal cords recovered from the intubation and were capable of loud wailing. Her respirations remained high, however, doubling or tripling that of a typical baby. Pulmonology believed they would slow over time. Cardiology and neurology considered her condition stable.

Not all developments were positive. Katie began to express increasing discomfort when changing positions. Everyone had an opinion or, more accurately, an educated guess. Some speculated that her muscles were sore from therapy. Others attributed the discomfort to the tachypnea, hypothesizing that shifting positions made ribcage expansion difficult. Unable to isolate the cause, we hoped the issue would resolve. Feeding, however, remained the primary concern.

As hard as she tried, Katie just could not feed from a bottle. Her face would flush dark red as she struggled. Each attempt left her crying, exasperated, and covered with perspiration. Even I as a layman realized the futility in continued attempts.

Krista and I aggressively tried to avoid a tracheotomy, but we resigned ourselves to a feeding tube with little resistance. Katie needed to grow and gain wait before the next heart surgery. One benefit of the feeding tube is the ability to monitor nutritional intake with precision. From a quality of life perspective, the feeding tube alleviates the need for the uncomfortable NG tube insertions. Other than a brief dressing change every few days, Katie had not been free of a tube in either her mouth or nose since birth.

The first order of business was learning the ins and outs of feeding tubes, specifically gastric feeding tubes. Commonly known as a "G-tube," the mechanism allows liquid nutrition to enter one's stomach through a tube in the abdominal cavity. The patient's ability to digest the feeding dictates the rate. Katie's doctor ordered bolus feeds for one of every three hours.

The device implanted in the stomach and abdominal wall, known as a "MIC-KEY" button, consists of a tube and retention balloon. The MIC-KEY, which sounds like the famous mouse, resembles an inverted water tower. The tube through which fluids flow runs lengthwise, capped on the external opening with a port cover. A second port, oriented ninety degrees from the external opening, leads to a balloon an inch in diameter. When deflated, the MIC-KEY takes the shape of a short pencil. After making incisions in the stomach and abdominal wall, the surgeon inserts the deflated MIC-KEY. He then places an air-filled syringe in the second port and inflates the balloon in the stomach, thereby anchoring the MIC-KEY in place.

Feeding tube insertion is about as risk-free as surgery can be, but for Katie, as with everything else in her life, the procedure presented considerable risk. The surgeon scheduled the procedure for July 31, two weeks after the infectious disease physician ordered the PICC removal. Thus, she needed a new PICC or IV line. A notoriously difficult stick, we feared repeated needle jabs while attempting to find a vein. Our fears proved prophetic. Two teams of nurses tried unsuccessfully over the course of a few days, leaving Katie with numerous puncture wounds on her arms, legs, and hands. A team of PICU nurses also met failure. A talented physician working the graveyard shift established an IV just hours before the scheduled surgery.

The anesthesiologist warned us that Katie might not resume independent respiration following the procedure. With her tumultuous extubation fresh in my mind, the thought of Katie once again intubated sickened me. Krista and I waited in the cafeteria until notified the staff had returned Katie to her room. The surgeon greeted us in the NICU and reported no complications from either the surgery or extubation. Katie resumed breathing unassisted before leaving the operating room, once again exceeding expectations.

Katie failed to share my relief and excitement at her success. Her eyes glowered at me below a deeply furrowed brow and above tightly pursed lips. Her nurse, Cindy, hung a stuffed mouse from the warmer above the bassinet. The animal dangling a foot above Katie looked like a skydiver in mid-flight. Katie eyed the mouse suspiciously, not at all amused. I do not blame her. In addition to the feeding tube, she had two other abdominal incisions from the scope. Cindy had also wrapped her left arm in a diaper to prevent Katie from pulling out the IV, rendering the appendage useless. Add an array of medications and you have the recipe for one miserable little girl. No longer needing the NG tube, though, Katie's face was finally free of tubes and tape. Even with a scowl, she was beautiful.

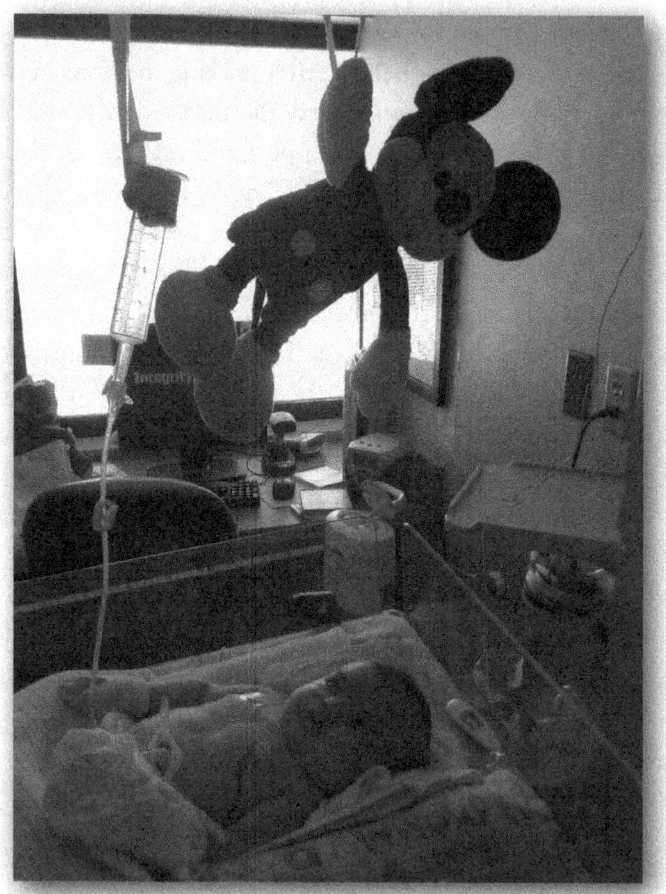

Katie suspiciously eyeing Mickey. Note her arm wrapped to protect the IV.

Katie took the better part of a week to recover. The diaper came off her arm after the physician removed her IV line, leaving her free of any devices aside from a few monitor leads. Despite initial discomfort, she successfully transitioned to G-tube feeding. In just a couple of weeks, her consumption increased from sixty to seventy-five mL of milk and formula every three hours.

"Cardiac babies" are routinely underweight relative to healthy babies. Katie was no exception. Her weight gain slowed while recovering from the second operation, but the ten-week-old plumped up to 8 lbs, 6 oz soon thereafter. With the second surgery behind us, our focus turned to taking Katie home.

Krista and I spent two-plus weeks preparing for life with Katie outside the hospital. The complexity of infant CPR and G-tube training paled in comparison to the insurance paperwork. Our insurance policy provided forty hours of home nursing care a week, a godsend as Krista returned to work the first week of August. Krista arranged for in-home care since Katie's needs far exceeded the limitations of a normal daycare.

With another two months of donated leave remaining, I would become the weekday caregiver after discharge. I had zero experience caring for a baby, let alone one that required twenty-four hour nursing care, monitors, and an army of doctors the first two months of her life. I do not know how I would have met the responsibility of caring for a baby with significant cardiac issues and a G-tube without the nurses. After spending nine months of pregnancy strategizing how to avoid changing diapers, karma had indeed slapped me upside the head.

Although Katie continued to improve as discharge approached, three concerns persisted. First, her shunt might have been directing too much blood into her lungs, causing pulmonary hypertension and making her ineligible for the next stage of the surgical course. Second, Katie continued to breathe very quickly, which might have been related to the first concern. She still breathed two to three times faster than normal with no signs of improvement. Third, Katie spent much of the past two months recovering from surgery, time that she should have been developing physically and mentally. We hoped that various therapy disciplines and our own amateur efforts would accelerate her return to the normal development path.

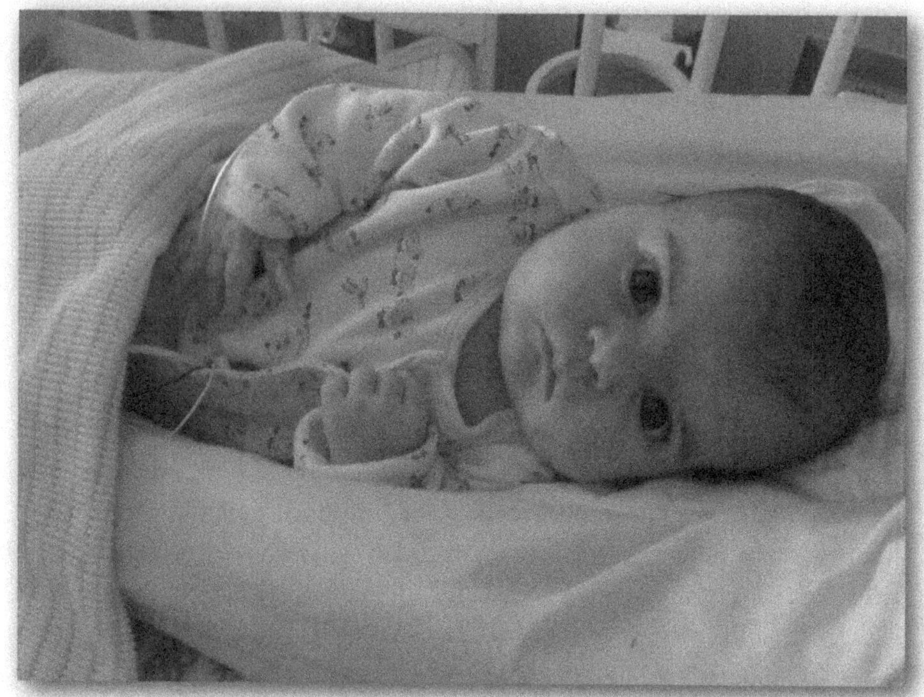

Katie, free of the ET and NG tubes, ready to go home after two months in the hospital.

We spent four great days with Katie and our prime nurses as mid-August neared. All the primes then had an extended period off. As we rotated through new nurses day after day, all of them pleasant, we missed the camaraderie of the familiar staff. We heard rumors of discharge, but nothing definitive. Although Katie remained happy, the hospitalization had grown tedious for Krista and me. Like staying at a party too long, I wanted to go home.

On August 16, one of my favorite neonatologists stopped by Katie's room. He teased me for watching Katie's monitor. "Why are you looking at that? I haven't looked at that for weeks," he said half-jokingly. "I guess it's a habit," I responded. "I just feel more comfortable knowing her numbers." He laughed and slapped me on the back. "You better get over it. She's going home tomorrow."

CHAPTER 12

The Eagle has Landed

AFTER SEVENTY-SIX DAYS OF HOSPITALIZATION, Katie finally came home on August 17. We arrived at the hospital that sunny Saturday morning and discovered bags of gifts for Katie from the staff in her room. A "lovie" from Kat sat atop the books, stuffed animals, and toys. A lovie is a small blanket with a stuffed animal or animal head sewn in the center. Katie loved the bright, plush pink cloth edged in dark pink satin adorned with a small stuffed dove. The staff's affection for Katie made cleaning out the room bittersweet, and I actually started to wish we were staying. That feeling dissipated significantly while waiting six hours for the neonatologist to sign the discharge orders. Once the doctor gave us the green light, Krista strapped Katie in her new car seat. Dressed in a light tan jumper with little raccoons on her feet, Katie looked with wonder as a nurse carried her through the NICU, down the elevator, across the cavernous lobby, and into the world. Confined to two hospital rooms for her entire life, Katie soaked up the new sights like an arid desert absorbs water.

After a fifteen-minute car ride, I carried Katie, still in her car seat, into the house and placed her on the living room floor. Having cried ever since leaving the hospital, Katie finally fell asleep as we unloaded the car. The commotion aroused Sam from his nap, and he lumbered over to Katie for a couple quick sniffs. Any interest in the family addition ceased once he realized she was not a source of food. Sam then thoroughly inspected Krista and me. Satisfied that we did not have food, either, he returned to his nap.

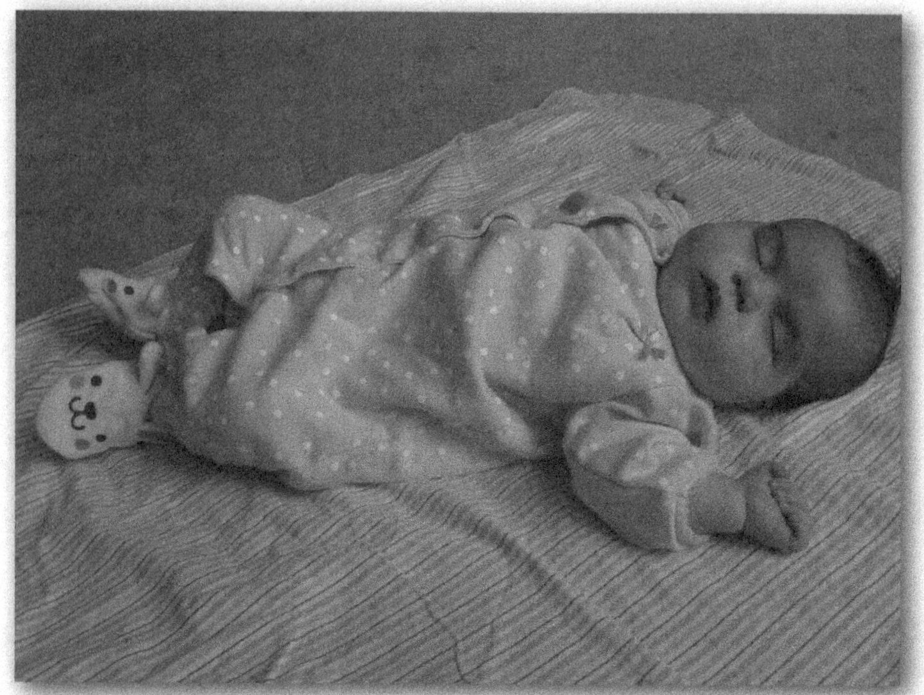

Katie sleeping on the living room floor after finally coming home.

Krista changed Katie and placed her on a blanket in the middle of the living room. Having spent countless hours watching Katie, I never saw her sleep that soundly. Krista and I stood at the living room entrance and looked at the slumbering members of our family. "You know," I said, "we spent seventy-six days at the hospital, waiting for the day we could get her home and have our family together. Now that we do, it's kind of boring." Krista laughed, and life was good.

Krista and I differ significantly in personality as evidenced by our actions that afternoon. Krista focused on Katie's food, medicine, and clothing while I acted like a kid on Christmas morning with a new toy. I carried Katie to the retention pond in the backyard and showed her trees, bushes, grass, and birds before the house tour. After a lifetime in the hospital's palette of white, off-white, and beige, her eyes studied the variety of colors. My collection of framed Beatles and Beach Boys albums fascinated her, but not as much as an old upright piano. I cradled Katie in my left arm and managed to pound out a few songs with my right hand. I could see the wheels in her head turning as she processed the sounds. As in the NICU, Katie started to fuss when held too long. Her protestations limited our time at the piano. For two months, I had promised Katie that I would teach her to play the instrument. We would have time for that later.

Katie looking out the window while holding the lovie Kat, one of her prime NICU nurses, gave her at discharge.

Krista orchestrated a bedtime routine that differed significantly from what I imagined pre-diagnosis. Krista carried Katie to the nursery with me close behind holding the G-tube pole, pump, and tubing in one hand and formula and syringes in the other. Krista changed Katie's diaper while I administered the medication and prepared the G-tube feeding. We continued the hospital practice of ending each day with an "Our Father" and "Hail Mary" followed by Krista singing "Goodnight Sweetheart" on top of my pitchy bass. Katie slept soundly as we kissed her goodnight. I suspect that she appreciated the relative quiet and calm of the house as opposed to the incessant cries, alarms, and conversation in the NICU. Not having to wake for feedings, Katie slept through the night. I cannot say the same for Krista and me.

I found Krista staring at the ceiling after I administered the midnight feeding and meds even though she had retired a couple hours earlier. Neither of us could sleep. Since Katie's birth, medical professionals and the latest technology surrounded Katie. Now, we had nothing. Failing to detect movement, the baby monitor shrieked every few minutes. Theorizing that Katie, accustomed to confinement, did not stir while sleeping, we had no choice but to turn the monitor off. Krista experimented with the device days later and discovered we had a defective unit, but her discovery did nothing for us that fretful first night.

The significant burden of managing Katie's medications fell squarely on Krista's shoulders. The cardiologists prescribed an ACE inhibitor to keep blood vessels from tensing and reduce blood pressure, aspirin to prevent the shunt from clotting, a diuretic to maintain proper fluid levels, lansoprazole to reduce reflux, and a multivitamin. On the day of Katie's discharge, Krista visited multiple pharmacies to procure Katie's prescriptions, some of which required compounding, and created an idiot-proof schedule for me. Initially, I did not intend to administer medications. After all, we had a pharmacist in the house. That plan fell apart within hours as Katie screamed, Sam barked to go out, and general chaos ensued. Krista gave me a quick tutorial, showing me where she stored the medications and syringes. She also instructed me in the science of preparing Katie's food concoction. I calculated the amount of formula based on the available breastmilk and combined and blended the ingredients like a pediatric bartender.

I gave myself forty minutes to prepare the syringes the first time Krista asked me to administer meds. The schedule called for five medications. I could not find the first drug listed, emptying the cabinet and refrigerator in vain. When I asked for help, Krista told me she used the brand name on the schedule, not the generic name on the bottle. After finally identifying the medication, I double-checked the dosage and filled the syringe. After a minute adding and removing the syrupy liquid, I achieved the perfect the dosage and took the syringe and bottle to Krista to verify my work. After her confirmation, I returned to the kitchen, placed the syringe on a glass plate, and began the process again for the second medication. I barely finished before the deadline. By the end of the week, I could prepare meds while making dinner and feeding Sam faster than a NASCAR pit crew changes tires.

My mom joined us for Katie's first week home to help with the transition to the next phase of care. She organized our kitchen, which now looked like an amalgamation of the Iron Chef set and a MASH unit. G-tube supplies and syringes covered the half of the dining room table stacks of medical bills did not occupy. More importantly, she helped us vet home nursing candidates.

Our house opened up to a parade of nurses immediately after Katie came home. We introduced Katie to each new nurse and explained the idiosyncrasies of her condition and care. Their level of skill varied greatly. We liked them all but felt more comfortable with some. We solidified our lineup within a few weeks after choosing four nurses, with one nurse working both Tuesday and Thursday. We would have preferred a single dedicated nurse, but each nurse had commitments with other patients. I realized the benefit for the nurses in this arrangement when Katie unexpectedly returned to the hospital. A nurse can fill a one-day hole in her weekly schedule much easier than finding forty hours of work.

Krista, mom, a home nurse, and I took Katie to her first pediatrician visit on the Monday after discharge. A perk of having a seriously ill child is bypassing the waiting area and going directly to an examination room, thereby avoiding other kids' germs. One has to see the bright side of any bad situation.

We chose Dr. Stoesz, pronounced "Stays," on the recommendation of Krista's coworkers. He visited Katie periodically in the hospital, but this was our first in-depth meeting. He examined Katie and then listened for the better part of an hour as Krista and mom walked him through her history. The doctor, nurse, and pharmacist conversed as three colleagues, each with his or her own area of expertise as the home nurse and I listened. The home nurse met Katie just two hours earlier, so she joined me as a bystander. All of us left Dr. Stoesz's office impressed with our first meeting. Once we were out of earshot, my mom, who worked with more than a few doctors in her forty years of nursing, said, "Oh, that's a good one. Yes he is. He's a good one."

Katie put on a show for Dr. Stoesz and his staff on her second visit a week later. Katie became upset during the thirty-minute ride to the pediatrician's office. She had yet to calm when the receptionist ushered us to a frigid examination room. A nurse arrived to take Katie's vitals and asked us to strip her down to her diaper. The combination of air conditioning, lack of clothing, and perspiration from the crying spell proved too much for Katie. She threw a tantrum to end all tantrums, the results of which matched the severity of Bill Bixby's transformation in the opening credits of "The Incredible Hulk." Her skin turned a deeply mottled hue with the exception of her hands and feet, which grew dark red. Her lips and fingertips took on an ominous blue tint.

Katie's appearance stunned the nurse. I would not say she panicked, but she came very close. She immediately took Katie into her arms to console her, and Katie let out a blood-curdling wail. Krista and I exclaimed, almost in unison, "No!" Krista finished the thought, "She doesn't like that. Put her on the table." The nurse complied and Katie calmed slightly. The nurse turned off the air conditioning as Dr. Stoesz entered. Concerned by Katie's discoloration, he asked the nurse for a pulse oximeter, a handheld device that measures oxygen saturation. The brick-sized device connects to a clothespin-like clip by a wire. The nurse closed the clip on Katie's finger and "63" appeared on the screen after a few seconds. A troubling number for a healthy person, this was only slightly below Katie's optimal range. Although the number did not please the doctor, it did not signify an acute emergency.

Krista and my mom covered Katie in warm washcloths that Krista had requested from the nurse. Wrapped like a mummy, Katie calmed as her temperature increased. Her color returned to a normal pink, and she reverted to her pleasant self after ten minutes. Crisis averted, Dr. Stoesz resumed his routine examination. An outing with Katie was anything but boring.

The doctor's request for a pulse oximeter bemused Krista and me. A pulse oximeter was the only piece of equipment we requested before discharge. The neonatologists and cardiologists dismissed our request out of hand, saying, "Oh, you don't need that," yet the first doctor who saw Katie in distress immediately called for the device. The other doctors never saw Katie's transformation when greatly upset. They never saw her skin turn dark red and lips turn blue. A doctor finally capitulated to Krista's repeated requests during Katie's final hospitalization. The device sat on Katie's dresser, awaiting the homecoming of its intended patient. We returned it unused.

Katie's pediatrician played a critical role in her treatment team, but I did not realize until our second visit that he would not lead the team. His expertise, although vital to infant care, did not include severe congenital heart defects. This is not a critique; few neonatologists and nurses we encountered had an understanding of Ebstein's Anomaly. The same held true for other specialists, and they were legion.

The team consisted in part of cardiologists, pulmonologists, neurologists, gastroenterologists, and occupational, physical, and speech therapists. Name an Indianapolis medical professional in 2013 with a title ending in "ist," and he probably examined Katie. Communication amongst the experts was, to say the least, minimal. The cardiologists did not monitor the gastroenterologists who did not track the pulmonologists who did not consult with the neurologists. None received any feedback from the home nurses or could have told you the in-home nursing provider. Meanwhile, the therapists had their own treatment plans. Krista and I were the only constants amongst all these people; therefore, we had no choice but to coordinate Katie's care ourselves. With her medical expertise, I deferred to Krista. No one, least of all me, doubted who was in charge.

Life consisted of more than juggling doctor appointments, medications, and feeding tube equipment. Our home life was surprisingly normal. With Krista working and me using the hundreds of hours of vacation time my coworkers donated, I spent the weekdays with Katie and her nurses. Thankful for their assistance, the awkwardness of giving strangers full range to our house quickly dissipated.

The nurses interacted with Katie to varying degrees. Some played and cuddled with her in addition to performing their nursing duties. Others were more passive, limiting their interaction to Katie's medical needs. I augmented the former and compensated for the latter, carrying Katie throughout the house and neighborhood, stretching her limbs and neck, teaching her to play the piano, engaging in long one-sided conversations, and generally stimulating her as much as possible.

I often placed Katie's hands on Sam, stroking the dog's thick hair. She did not know what to make of the furry beast, and Sam could not have cared less when she touched him. The two only interacted when we laid a blanket flat on the living room floor for Katie. Sam could not resist a blanket. He would approach the blanket slowly and look at us sheepishly, like a child testing his boundaries. Sam would lie down beside her, often placing only a single paw on the material. There they would remain, sharing a mutual love of blankets.

My favorite time with Katie was the gap between the nurse leaving and Krista coming home. Finally alone in the house, I would sit at the piano and play my repertoire of early rock standards. I am mediocre under the best conditions. Whatever ability I possessed diminished significantly with Katie nestled in the crook of my left arm. Not that it mattered; she made a forgiving audience. In my mind, I could hear the parts she would someday sing against the chords I played. The concerts ended when I heard the garage door open, and I returned to making dinner before Krista entered the house.

Katie and Sam sharing a blanket.

A highlight of Katie's stay at home occurred the weekend after her discharge. My friend Tracy, who had sent Katie her rosary, followed our daughter's story from her birth and desperately wanted to meet her. Tracy's career took a much more exciting path than mine since we first met a decade earlier. She worked for a large multinational corporation in Hong Kong. The company had its own jet that routinely flew to the States and back on which employees could hitch a ride. Tracy seized the opportunity and traveled from

Hong Kong to Indianapolis to spend a weekend with us. Our house was the only destination on her itinerary. Katie inspired such affection.

Krista, Tracy, and I took Katie to St. Pius X for the first time on a Sunday morning. Tracy found a seat in the sanctuary while Krista and I tried to calm Katie, unhappy from the drive, in a classroom adjacent to the main entrance. Flustered, I forgot to unclamp the feeding tube when I connected a syringe full of medicine to the auxiliary port. I felt the plunger resist my push and, without thinking, squeezed harder. The clamp held, but the food intake port did not. The medicine shot back over my left shoulder and splattered on the wall behind me. I jerked instinctively, knocking another syringe clamped to my shirt with more than 60 mL of formula all over the floor, Katie, and me. Krista and I burst into laughing at the ridiculousness of the situation. Katie eventually fell asleep on a blanket on the floor. I cleaned myself up and caught the last minutes of mass with Tracy while Krista remained with the baby.

The congregation would come to know and love Katie through Fr. Jim's weekly updates in the months to come, but the people of St. Pius X would never meet her. We left without taking her into the sanctuary. Thereafter, we limited outings in hopes of reducing infection risk. She never saw the inside of the church.

Katie's first restaurant experience did not fare much better. Our waitress, also named "Katherine," tried her best to cajole a smile from the baby. Still fuming over the fiasco at church, Katie responded with a look of annoyance. The atypically loud environment did not help. We ate quickly and returned home. From that day on, the waitress would ask about Katie whenever she saw Krista and me.

Although these excursions did not go as planned, I treasure my memories of them. A baby's first this and first that are often memorable occasions. For Katie, these were both her first and last visits to church and a restaurant. I am thankful that her life included such experiences, experiences that I took for granted until Katie.

Capping off an already busy day, two of Katie's primes joined us for dinner at our house. Kat and Karrie doted over Katie while Krista regaled them with stories from the day's adventures. Meanwhile, Tracy and I prepared burgers, dogs, and kabobs as Sam paced expectantly in a semi-circle around the grill. We ate on the patio under blue skies and wispy, nonthreatening clouds. Katie rested contentedly in her bouncer at the foot of the table. We talked not only of Katie's progress, but also of subjects unrelated to medicine. Katie's sickness initially brought us together, but friendships grew from our mutual love of her. The idyllic scene, remarkable for its normalcy, resembled a Norman Rockwell painting. The night would have been perfect had I not overcooked the chicken.

CHAPTER 13

Managing Expectations

I LEFT THE HOSPITAL NOT truly understanding Katie's condition. I knew the shunt merely bought Katie time to prepare for the Glenn procedure; however, I did not appreciate her fragility. A mere tantrum presented a significant and potentially lethal cardiac threat. Katie's compressed lungs left her susceptible to infection. Even the common cold presented a grave risk. I wanted more than anything to take Katie to Connellsville to meet my bedridden grandmother. Krista and my mom considered such a trip impossible since our initial days in the PICU, but I did not admit the same until after a week at home with Katie.

My misunderstanding that summer was not limited to appreciating Katie's frailty. I severely underestimated the cardiologists' role in Katie's treatment. Although Drs. Kumar, Parek, and Steinberg were often present in the PICU, I considered them ancillary members of Katie's treatment team.[4] The solution to her heart issue was surgical in nature. I reasoned that, since they were not surgeons, Katie did not fall in their area of expertise. The cardiovascular surgeon directed Katie's care before and after the first operation. Moreover, Dr. Abraham voiced the sole protest against the tracheostomy; the cardiologists did not partake in the conversation. They were affable and quick to answer questions, but that description fit everyone we encountered in the PICU.

4 Dr. Abarbanell, the diagnosing cardiologist, left the cardiology group in mid-June.

My "Road to Damascus" moment regarding the cardiologists occurred a few weeks after Katie transferred to the NICU. In the course of examining Katie, a neonatologist told me off-handedly that a test showed "progressive congestive heart failure" and an enlarged liver. I had not heard of either issue before, at least with this terminology. I asked Dr. Kumar about the comments the next day as he visited patients in the NICU. A hint of annoyance in his voice surprised me when he said, "The neonatologist should have consulted with me before speaking to you about test results." He thought Katie's heart looked fine and explained that Katie's heart defect caused an abnormal amount of blood to collect in the liver. From his tone and command of her history, he left no doubt that Katie was *his* patient.

The large number of people caring for Katie and my naïveté obscured the true relationship between Dr. Abraham and the cardiologists. I incorrectly assumed during our month in the PICU that the surgical side of the cardiology practice did not interact with the general cardiology side. In fact, the surgeon relied on the cardiologists to manage his patients throughout the continuum of care, thereby allowing him more time in the OR. Thus, I mistakenly attributed Katie's cardiac management in the PICU to either Dr. Abraham or the intensivists, who made significant contributions, without recognizing the cardiologists' key role.

I made up for lost time with the cardiologists once Katie came home. We noticed Katie retaining fluid a few days after discharge. Krista contacted the on-call cardiologist, who increased her diuretic. Katie returned to normal size within a day or two. A few days later, Katie exhibited signs of dehydration, including low urine output and lethargy. Another call to the cardiologist yielded a decrease in diuretics. Thus began an endless cycle of calling the cardiologists to increase or decrease diuretics as too much or too little fluid put tremendous stress on the heart. This frequent contact resulted in a strong working relationship upon which Krista and I relied for the rest of Katie's life. Maintaining appropriate hydration, however, became an unsolvable problem for us at home and the physicians later in the hospital.

Katie's many medications caused or exacerbated severe diaper rash. Although Katie experienced occasional bouts of diaper rash throughout her hospitalization, the severity, frequency, and duration of the rash increased dramatically after leaving the NICU. We were never able to isolate a specific cause. My mom and Krista tried a variety of different products to arrest the rash. Krista even broke out her pharmacist skills to make some concoctions of her own. The mantle over our fireplace looked like the back of a bar in an old saloon, except with various diaper rash creams and ointments in place of spirits. They worked to varying degrees, and the rashes subsided after a month. The rash unfortunately ranked amongst the least troubling of new issues we encountered.

After almost three weeks of uneventful G-tube feeding, eleven-week-old Katie developed severe acid reflux almost immediately after she came home. Heartburn is common among babies, but the threat it posed to Katie far exceeded anything an otherwise healthy baby faces. The additional strain on her compromised system risked cardiac distress and failure. Katie would cry inconsolably after feedings. Writhing in agony, her skin mottled and grew moist with perspiration while her lips turned an eerie dark blue. We could do nothing but comfort her until the episode passed.

The first major reflux event my mom and a home nurse witnessed deeply concerned both experienced nurses. With more than a combined sixty years of nursing, they had never seen such a dramatic cardiovascular response to an otherwise benign event. The home nurse swaddled Katie as they discussed taking her to the emergency room. With Krista at work, I deferred to the nurses on the emergency room question, but told the nurse to place Katie unrestrained on the floor. Katie spent almost all of her life in the bassinet and recoiled at cuddling. True to form, Katie began to calm immediately. The reflux dissipated over the next few minutes, her normal skin color returned, and the nurses cancelled any ER plans. We enjoyed the brief respite until the process repeated after the next feeding three hours later.

Krista scheduled an appointment with the gastroenterology nurse practitioner to address Katie's reflux. Krista could not get the time off work, so my mom, a new home nurse, and I explained Katie's symptoms to a NP. I appreciated having two nurses present, as I doubt the NP would have believed my description of Katie's reaction. She informed us that the reflux would eventually resolve. Short of surgical intervention, nothing could prevent stomach acid from working its way up the esophagus; however, she could moderate the symptoms. She prescribed medication to reduce the fluid's acidity, which she hoped would lessen the pain and reduce the subsequent reaction. The NP also changed Katie's feeding schedule. Katie had been feeding for one hour and then taking two hours off. Hypothesizing that Katie's stomach may not tolerate so much formula in such a short time, the NP directed continuous feedings. After implementing the NP's guidance, the heartburn appeared to subside somewhat.

Krista addressed the reflux issue with another nurse practitioner at a subsequent pulmonology appointment, broaching the subject as an afterthought while saying our goodbyes. The NP asked us to wait while he spoke to the pulmonologist. I expected Dr. Williams, but a larger, soft-spoken man clad in scrubs joined us a few minutes later. Dr. Sufi and Krista had spoken previously in the PICU, but this was our first meeting.

Dr. Sufi expressed concern over the reflux. Specifically, aspiration posed a significant threat. Katie's enlarged heart prevented the lungs from fully expanding, thereby diminishing the organs' capacity to cope with foreign substances. As Katie's heart shrinks relative to the rest of her body after the next two surgeries, the lungs will have more space in which to operate. However, that was a long time away. Fearing Katie might not survive a serious respiratory infection, Dr. Sufi prescribed respiration therapy to improve lung function. For Katie, "respiration therapy" consisted of breathing vaporized medicine for fifteen minutes, twice daily, to expand her air passages. He also scheduled a visit with a gastroenterologist. The first available appointment was eight weeks later. Frustrated, I asked if we could seek another doctor with a shorter waiting time. Dr. Sufi shook his head emphatically. Surprised we got an appointment that quickly, he doubted whether another practice would be faster. We thanked him profusely as we repeated our earlier goodbyes. I never would have thought to mention acid reflux to a pulmonologist. Katie was fortunate that her mom made the connection.

After taking Sam for a walk in late June, I found the first hospital bill in the mailbox. For a couple weeks, we received a bill every few days. The rate increased to every two days. After a month, bills came fast and furious, at least one a day. Some were negligible, not even twenty dollars. Bills for physicians reached the low thousands.

Frustratingly, the physicians billed individually by the day. For example, intensivists staffed the PICU in roughly twelve-hour shifts. Katie's first stay encompassed sixty-nine shifts. We received scores of bills to cover said shifts for more than a year with no rhyme or reason. If a doctor worked the day shift from Monday through Thursday, the hospital billed us for Tuesday one month. A couple of months later, it billed us for Monday and Thursday. The bill for Wednesday arrived eventually. Someone had to be making a fortune on this bureaucratic disaster as such an impressive level of dysfunction cannot occur naturally.

The first huge bill arrived in September. The hospital charged $763,402.70 for Katie's forty-day NICU stay, not including tests, surgeries, and specialists, a daily burn rate of $19,084.07. If I knew they charged that kind of money, I would not have bought them so many donuts. They should have been giving us donuts.

The hospital staff was not the only beneficiary of my gifts of edible treats. In mid-September, I stopped by a fast food joint to buy Sam a burger, a rare treat that he loved. Failing to hear the clatter of Sam's nails on the hardwood floor when I arrived at home, I walked around the house in search of the dog. When I reached the lower landing of the staircase, I looked up to see Sam standing motionless in the middle of the staircase with his front paws two steps below their rear counterparts. He apparently stopped in the process of coming down the stairs but did not appear distressed. Puzzled, I tried to coax him down, but he remained motionless. I got his attention when I lifted the to-go bag in the air, but he still did not budge. I assumed the combination of dim lighting and cataracts hindered his sight so significantly that he froze. I took Sam's paws in my hand and walked him down the stairs. When he reached the landing, Sam trotted off with his burger without a care in the world.

I found Sam stuck on the stairs two more times over the next week. Concerned that he might fall, I fastened the baby gate to the bottom of the stairs, not to keep Katie out, but to keep Sam from going up. I felt terrible restricting Sam to the first floor. I trained Sam to come up to our bedroom at night immediately after his adoption two years earlier. After turning off the light, I would break five animal crackers in half and throw them on the floor. The sound of "crunch, crunch, crunch" as Sam found his treats resounded in the darkness. After clearing the floor of treats, he slept the remainder of the night on a giant pillow. Now relegated to the first floor, Sam would forevermore pout on a couch in the living room regardless of the number of animal crackers I used to console him. Already emotionally strained from Katie's struggle, I willfully denied age taking a toll on "my puppy."

"Dr. Stoesz's office just called," Krista informed me as I sat at my desk sorting insurance bills on Monday, September 9. "Katie's blood tests came back. Her potassium is 6.5." Earlier that day, the nurse and I had taken the fourteen-week-old to an uneventful checkup with Dr. Stoesz. Katie now weighed 10 lbs, 6 oz, a respectable rate of growth. I had Krista on speakerphone while the doctor examined Katie. She mentioned no one had checked Katie's potassium since the hospitalization. Medications and heart defects can alter the body's potassium level, two factors that Katie obviously satisfied, so Dr. Stoesz sent us to PMCH for a blood draw. The phlebotomist specializing in tough sticks like Katie succeeded on her second attempt. I carried Katie out of PMCH content that the test was a formality. Krista's voice now portrayed concern and disbelief.

"I take it that's bad?" I replied nonchalantly

"Very bad," Krista replied pointedly.

"Why?"

"High potassium can cause a heart attack."

"What's high?"

"Anything over 6.5 is a heart attack risk. Dr. Stoesz wants us to take Katie to Peyton Manning for another blood draw. Now." I looked at Katie watching her mobile. "She looks fine, but okay, I'll take her over." Krista replied, emphasizing the urgency, "Her potassium is *really* high." I hung up the phone and asked the nurse to pack for the hospital.

Excess potassium can affect the heart's electrical conductivity, causing the heart to beat at an abnormal rate. The heart requires more oxygen as it beats faster. At the same time, these "arrhythmias" decrease the heart's efficiency and deprive the heart and other organs of oxygen. The lack of blood flow and oxygen can cause cardiac arrest. A normal potassium range for a healthy person is 3.5-5.2 mmol/L. For someone *without* a heart defect, a potassium level exceeding 6.5 mmol/L is a clinical emergency; exceeding 8.5 mmol/L can be fatal.

The staff was not as successful drawing blood on the second visit. A different phlebotomist could not find a vein after multiple attempts. I suggested someone from the PICU with experience with Katie might have better luck, but the PICU nurses also failed after two attempts. A nurse in the ER finally struck a vein. Exhausted by the ordeal, Katie slept as the home nurse and I waited for the lab results. The new potassium reading indicated a decrease to 5.7 mmol/L. Although not in the preferred range, the number had significantly declined. Krista reported the results to the cardiologist who subsequently adjusted Katie's medications and ordered another blood draw for the following Friday.

No one could say with certainty when or why Katie's potassium escalated. The experts considered one or more of the drugs the most likely cause. Her unique physiology reacted unpredictably to the variety of medicines she imbibed. Why exactly that combination of medicines caused Katie's potassium to rise that particular day remains a mystery. In Katie's complicated condition, one had to accept that some mysteries go unsolved.

I planned to attend Air National Guard training in Springfield, Illinois from Friday through Sunday, my first Guard duty since Katie's birth. My absence placed the burden of the next blood draw on Krista's shoulders. I offered to cancel training, but Krista encouraged me to go, saying, "Don't worry, it's just a blood draw." We should have known the misnomer of "just a blood draw" when speaking of Katie.

Krista took an hour of vacation time on Friday to take Katie to PMCH. The phlebotomist did not even try this visit, instead directing Katie to the ER. The nurses struggled to find a vein, ultimately withdrawing blood from Katie's scalp. The needle mark and bruise remained for days. Krista left Katie with the home nurse and returned to finish her shift at hospice.

The nurse found Katie's MIC-KEY button, the feeding tube port in Katie's abdomen, loose in her diaper three hours later. The balloon had deflated and allowed the device to slide out of the incision. A nurse mentioned that remote possibility during training. I asked for the probability, to which she answered dismissively, "Oh, that never happens. Maybe one in a hundred come out. Maybe." Once again, Katie defied the odds. Krista left work, retrieved Katie at the house, and returned to the ER for the second time that day. A nurse replaced the MIC-KEY button four hours later and sent the exhausted mother and daughter home. The grueling day ended with some good news: Katie's potassium had decreased to 5.5 mmol/L.

Krista had a treat in store for Katie on Saturday: a professional photoshoot. Krista scheduled a photographer to come to the hospital after Katie's birth but cancelled in the wake of the diagnosis. Katie finally got her time in front of the camera three months later. After a difficult week of needle sticks and G-tube issues, the photographer faced a grumpy subject. Katie stared intensely at the camera with dark black eyes. Jan somehow managed to frame Katie's stern expression into something resembling a curious intensity.

Jan asked Krista if she wanted Katie's chest scar covered. Krista replied, "No, that's who she is." Katie earned that scar, a symbol of all that she overcame. She would not be Katie without it.

I returned from Guard duty Sunday night and resumed my role as daytime caregiver. On Monday morning, three days after Katie's MIC-KEY button fell out, the visiting nurse knocked on the bedroom door as I was shaving.

"What is it?" I asked.

"Katie's MIC-KEY button came out," she said with concern.

Incredulous, I threw the door open with my face half covered in shaving cream. She repeated herself. The words did not register. The deflated MIC-KEY button in her hand distracted me. "You gotta be kiddin' me." The trainer placed the odds of a MIC-KEY coming out at one in a hundred. Katie's came out twice in three days.

The three of us immediately went to the Med/Surg office adjacent to the first floor lobby at PMCH.[5] A nurse placed Katie on a table in a small examination room and removed her clothes. Feeling no pain with MIC-KEY insertion or removal, Katie pleasantly observed the nurse examining her. The nurse then removed the catheter, which the home nurse had inserted to keep the incision from closing, and bandage from the pencil-sized opening in Katie's left abdomen.

The nurse hypothesized that Katie received a defective unit and rifled through a drawer until she found a suitable replacement. She then turned to me and stated authoritatively, "Okay, you are going to put it in." I can only imagine the shock on my face.

"Oh, you can do it. I'm good," I said while waving my hands.

"No, you need to learn how to do this." Her stare indicated the discussion was over.

I meekly took the MIC-KEY and approached Katie. "Don't forget to lubricate it," said the nurse as she handed me a lotion packet. I paused after preparing the MIC-KEY, took a deep breath, and looked Katie in the eye.

> "I must really love you, Honey, because I wouldn't do this for anyone else."

I placed my left hand on Katie's lower abdomen, slid the MIC-KEY in the football-shaped incision, attached a syringe, inflated the balloon, and threw

5 The office was closed the previous Friday, forcing Krista to use the ER.

my hands victoriously in the air. Mission accomplished and bragging rights secured, we returned to the house.

Dr. Kumar performed Katie's first echocardiogram since her hospitalization on Tuesday, September 17, the day after my successful MIC-KEY insertion. Also known as an "echo," an echocardiogram is a type of ultrasound that creates moving images of the heart. Pointing to the screen, Dr. Kumar explained various aspects of heart structure and blood flow. Katie's heart function as well as her overall condition pleased the cardiologist. He remarked that the left side of Katie's heart looked particularly strong. He had discussed Katie's case with Dr. Abraham; both of them agreed that a "one and a half ventricle repair" might be an option. This cardiac structure is an intermediate state between a normal two-ventricle heart and the single-ventricle heart originally planned for Katie. Simply speaking, the surgeon routes some blood through the damaged ventricle in order to provide some pumping assistance to the healthy side of the heart. Such talk was premature at this point. Before moving forward with the next surgery, Katie required a cardiac catheterization.

A cardiac catheterization, also referred to as a "heart cath" or "cath," yields an internal image of Katie's heart and the pulmonary artery and can measure pulmonary pressure. Dr. Kumar would insert a catheter into a major vein in Katie's upper leg and thread it through the inferior vena cava and the heart to the pulmonary artery. This procedure is the only method to determine the pressure in the artery carrying blood to the lungs. Potentially a deal-breaker, we could press forward with the Glenn surgery only if Katie had sufficiently low pulmonary pressure. Dr. Kumar scheduled the procedure for October 30. If all went well, Katie would have the second heart surgery soon thereafter.

Katie's fast respirations continued to vex both Dr. Kumar and Dr. Sufi, whom we visited after the echo. Neither the cardiologist nor pulmonologist had a good explanation as to why Katie's breathing never slowed. They hoped the next surgery would resolve the issue.

With Katie stable, I finally returned to work the next day. Some friends and family members questioned this decision, and I understood their position. In a perfect world, we would support Katie without financial concerns. Actually, in a perfect world, congenital heart defects would not exist. However, they do, and we could not ignore the financial aspect of her illness. With no idea what lay ahead for Katie, we needed to plan for an extended course of treatment. When possible, we prepared for the unknown future. As they say back in Connellsville, "Make hay while the sun shines."

Unfortunately, three-hundred miles of farmland separated my house from the office. Katie's diagnosis scratched our plans to relocate, leaving me in the untenable position of living in a different state than my employer. I left Indianapolis before the sun rose on Wednesday and arrived at Rock Island midmorning five hours later.

My supervisor had reassigned almost all of my clients in my absence, so I essentially started over. Many of my coworkers kindly offered their support. No two people deal with such an ordeal in the same way, so no safe, rote words exist. My strategy consisted of keeping and focusing on the positive.

While in Rock Island, my thoughts never left Indianapolis. Not only did I miss Krista and the baby, but I also knew the burden of caring for Katie. The nurses went home around 5 p.m., which made for a long evening. Working full-time and caring for Katie left Krista physically and emotionally exhausted. This arrangement, currently the best of bad options, was unsustainable.

After accepting Krista and I could not care for Katie alone, I felt no inhibition in asking for help. I mentioned our predicament to Laurie, my friend from Legal Aid, in casual conversation. She mentioned it during a church meeting. However the word spread, I received an e-mail from a stranger in early September. Dawn explained that the last of her two children just left for college, and she had time to help. I immediately invited her to our house.

Dawn helped Krista some evenings once I returned to work in Illinois. She played with Katie, prepared her for bed, walked Sam, or just provided conversation, anything to ease Krista's burden. Both Krista and I looked forward to Dawn's visits. Krista appreciated and relied on the emotional support and company. I found great relief in knowing that Krista was not alone.

Like a top that wobbles before tipping over, Katie became cranky on Wednesday, September 25. I was in the middle of my second week back in Rock Island when Krista mentioned off-handedly that Katie seemed "to be crying a lot tonight." I thought little of it until Krista reported Thursday morning that Katie kept her up most of the night. Katie continued to fuss the next night. I arrived home Friday after a full day of work and a five-hour drive to find an exhausted Krista with an equally exhausted Katie. Neither one had a decent night's sleep since Tuesday. I told Krista to go to bed and that I would watch Katie. Having spent more than a month at home with her, I felt confident that I could get Katie to sleep.

I placed Katie in the middle of the living room floor and lay down beside her. A pacifier immediately calmed her … for a minute. She then spit it out and resumed wailing. I dutifully gave Katie the pacifier and again she spit it out. This routine continued hour after hour. I tried the mobile. I tried carrying her around the house. I tried rocking. Nothing worked. The incessant crying so annoyed Sam that he opted for the couch over sharing Katie's blanket.

Krista relieved me in the morning, but she did not have better luck. Krista hypothesized that the G-tube might be in the incorrect position and causing discomfort. I suggested an ER visit, but Krista told me to give Katie a little more time. An hour later, she came around to the idea of an ER visit, but now I demurred. I did not want to take Katie to the ER every time she did not feel well. Early that afternoon, Krista said, "You know, maybe her potassium is up." That was all I needed to hear. With the potassium saga fresh in my mind, we headed to the ER.

After taking Katie's vitals in a small room adjacent to the waiting area, a triage nurse escorted us to a slightly larger examination room in the ER. Krista released Katie from the car seat and placed her on the gurney. As soon as Katie hit the sheet, she cheered up as though she had not a care in the world. Krista and I looked at each other incredulously. "That figures," I said just before the nurse practitioner entered. Krista tried to describe the prolonged tantrum of the past three days while the NP examined the perfectly pleasant Katie. "Really, she was inconsolable and mottled. *Really.*" The NP was very understanding, saying Katie was not his first patient that miraculously improved after passing through the ER doors. He ordered a potassium test, but otherwise said Katie looked fine.

Krista and I whittled away the afternoon playing with Katie or watching her sleep peacefully before new lab results arrived. An elevated potassium level of 6.1 mmol/L prompted a call to the cardiologists and a med change. We thanked the NP and departed. The visit reassured us nothing seriously afflicted Katie, so the endeavor was not a complete loss. We drove home blissfully unaware that a major crisis awaited just hours away.

CHAPTER 14

Back to Where We Once Belonged

KATIE REVERTED FROM HER MIRACULOUS ER recovery to the inconsolable crying late that evening. Krista and I spent another sleepless night trying unsuccessfully to console her. The crying continued into the next day. We discussed another ER visit, but both of us were slow to pull the trigger after the "boy crying wolf" episode of the previous day. Katie stopped crying late Sunday afternoon. I initially thought she had finally overcome whatever bothered her, but then I noticed that she was listless, not just calm. Her eyes tracked in response to stimulus, but she appeared too exhausted to react. Krista noticed the same and took her temperature. Katie had a low-grade fever, so we headed back to the hospital.

The triage nurse gave Katie a cursory exam and escorted us to a large examination room. A gurney occupied the middle of the room, and a bassinet sat flush against the back wall. Medical equipment covered or rested against the walls, yet the room did not feel cluttered or cramped. Two nurses stripped Katie to her diaper and placed leads on her chest. A monitor suddenly came to life with a red line jumping to peaks and valleys representing heart rhythm and numbers showing pulse, respirations, and oxygenation. The oxygenation read in the mid-eighties, which was low for Katie but within the appropriate range given her physiology.

A middle-aged doctor in scrubs appeared a few minutes later. Krista provided a succinct history and answered his few questions. The doctor directed the nurses to establish an IV and start fluids, said he would be back, and left. The nurses suggested we step out of the room. Watching a baby get a shot is unpleasant. Watching a nurse repeatedly poke a baby to find a vein is sickening. We took their advice, visited the cafeteria to get a drink, and returned to the waiting room. One of the nurses greeted us before we settled in and reported, to our surprise and relief, that she and the other nurse encountered no difficulty in establishing an IV. We followed the nurse back to Katie, asleep with an IV in her right wrist. And then the waiting began.

We waited, continued to wait, and then waited some more. Minutes turned to hours. A nurse occasionally checked on Katie, telling us everything looked fine and that the doctor would be in soon. The doctor did appear briefly a couple of times, but I spend more time picking out a piece of fruit at a grocery store than he spent in total examining Katie. To be fair, I am particular about fruit. "Okay," he would say, "let's keep an eye on her" and leave. I inferred from the attitude of the doctor and nurse that they thought we were overreacting parents.

As the hours mounted, the lack of attention became increasingly disconcerting as Katie declined. Her face and torso grew pale and extremities mottled. Her oxygenation ominously dropped out of the eighties, through the seventies, and into the low sixties. An alarm blared when it fell under sixty into the mid-fifties, yet no one responded. Krista asked the nurse the next time she came in if we should do something, at least give Katie oxygen. The nurse dismissed her, saying, "No, we don't give heart babies oxygen" and again disappeared. I am no doctor, but that made no sense to me. Krista, equally perplexed, broke down in tears watching Katie's oxygenation continue to drop.

Katie continued to decline as we hit our fifth hour in the ER. My concern for Katie's well-being turned into cold fear. Not only did Krista feel the same, we both felt hopelessly trapped. We briefly discussed taking Katie to Riley Children's Hospital in downtown Indianapolis, which I estimated at least thirty minutes away without traffic, but neither of us thought she would tolerate the move. Lacking options, neither of us spoke. An alarm shattered the silence, signaling that Katie's oxygenation dropped to forty-eight. It returned to the low sixties after a long minute. The staff did not respond at all. Nothing. They did not come to us, so I went to them.

Two young women in scrubs sat in the nurses' station at the intersection of the unit's two major halls, no more than fifteen feet from Katie's room. I positioned myself so I could see down both halls. A few people milled around at the far end of one hall, but the immediate area was empty save the two nurses and me. I fully understood that staff prioritizes patients due to the level of emergency, and personnel could be working to avert tragedy in another room. That was not, however, my impression. My grandfather taught me to hold a train rail to feel for the vibration of an impending locomotive before crossing the track. I observed the ER and, like a cold rail on the Pennsylvania Line, felt nothing.

I approached the desk and said, "Excuse me. My daughter in Room 2 is de-sating to the low fifties and forties, and no one has come in to see her." Both nurses looked up at me with annoyance.

> "We can monitor her from out here," a brunette whose age I would put around thirty said brusquely.

I glanced at the monitors over her shoulder and saw Katie's oxygenation again fall into the fifties. The number flashed red, but no alarm sounded. I paused a few seconds and watched the number turn to a blue "62."

> "Did you see that? She just did it again." I said matter-of-factly.
> "Sir," the nurse said sternly, "go back to your room, and I'll tell the nurse you are looking for her."

Her tone left no doubt that our conversation had ended. She was as helpful as a rubber crutch in a polio ward. I shook my head in frustration and retreated back to Katie's room.

I took a seat against the wall and watched Krista hold our fading daughter's hand. As we entered our sixth hour in the ER, I realized that we had one card left to play. "I'm calling the PICU," I told Krista. Focused on Katie, she did not respond. The administrative aide answered. I asked which intensivist was on that night. She hesitated before answering slowly, "Dr. Helzcenko."

The staff was generally reluctant to divulge staffing information, so her tone did not surprise me.

"This is Jack Murtha, Katherine Murtha's dad. She was in the PICU a few months ago."

"Oh, yes, I remember you."

"I need a favor. Please tell Dr. Helzenko that Katie is in the ER. She is de-sating in the low fifties to high forties. We've been here for six hours, and no one is doing anything for her."

"Okay. Got it," she said with some urgency in her voice.

"Thanks."

I hung up and slid the phone back in my pocket. Out of options, I leaned back in the chair and watched Krista cry.

While watching Krista, I sensed someone watching me. Instinctively, I glanced around the room. My eyes passed over him, at first not registering the image. The realization set in slowly, like an engine turning over on a winter morning. Dr. Halczenko peered in the room from the dark outside hallway. A combination of relief and adrenaline flooded my system. I greeted him as he entered the room, my right hand outstretched. I tried to say his name or thank him for coming, but the best I could manage was an exuberant "Hey!"

Dr. Halczenko spoke with characteristic formality in a calm voice. He stated that Katie's numbers were off and she was dangerously dehydrated. He would admit Katie to the PICU and intubate her upstairs to ensure sufficient oxygenation. Her body was working too hard to breathe, and he feared Katie could not maintain that effort indefinitely. Dr. Halczenko called in a PICU nurse whose shift had been cancelled due to a low census. As soon as the nurse arrived, she would take Katie upstairs. We thanked him profusely before he left us waiting for the nurse.

The tone of our visit changed radically after Dr. Halczenko's visit. Once shunned and ignored, Katie was now the belle of the ball. The doctor never returned, but a constant stream of nurses paraded through, asking if we needed anything and checking on Katie. They wore big smiles and expressed deep concern. No one alluded to the reason for the sudden change in treatment. Fairly or not, I was bitter that I had to call the PICU and did not appreciate their newfound sense of duty. The only nurse I cared about arrived as we marked our seventh hour in the ER.

Melissa had frequently taken care of Katie during her first PICU stay. We had so many phenomenal nurses that I could not select a favorite. I could, however, recognize the best of them, which certainly included Melissa. Thus, I was ecstatic when she arrived. Apparently sensing our emotional strain, she was very kind. More importantly, she was ferociously protective of her little patient. I do not know what transpired outside Katie's room, but Melissa had little patience for the ER staff. Melissa never criticized anyone in front of us, but her unmistakable passive aggressiveness betrayed her thoughts. She curtly declined the nurses' entreaties to help with the transfer, saying that she could manage it herself. Avoiding the neighboring room that now contained a dysfunctional family arguing loudly, Melissa guided us through an alternative route to the staff elevators. The doors opened up to an inner hall in the PICU one flight above. The three of us wheeled Katie to Room 4.

Katie woke from her stupor en route to the PICU. Agitated, Katie's respirations and CO_2 level increased. Katie's numbers rebounded following intubation, and she returned to a healthy color. As much as I hated to see her intubated again, I was thankful she no longer struggled for breath. She pulled out her IV line during transport, requiring Dr. Halczenko to secure another access line. Struggling to find a vein, he inserted the IV in the right side of Katie's neck. We sat with our very ill, but stable, daughter for another couple of hours. Satisfied with Katie in Dr. Halczenko and Melissa's care, we returned home for a few hours of sleep.

Room 4 buzzed with activity when we arrived the following morning. The oncoming nurse busied herself inspecting Katie as Melissa completed her charting and the RT checked the ventilator. Two unfamiliar middle-aged women in scrubs stood post outside the door. They stopped me as we entered the room and introduced themselves as part of ER management. Distracted, I did not pick up their titles or names. I shook their hands, gave them a cursory "Hi, Jack Murtha. Nice to meet you," and stepped into Katie's room. Laser focused on Katie, these women immediately slipped my mind. They were persistent, however, telling me that they wished to discuss our ER experience from the night before. That got my attention. Still seething, I turned to face them. They started to speak again, but I told them to hold fast until Krista, who Melissa was debriefing, joined us.

I was ready for a throw down over the events of the previous night. Knowing that Katie depended on the ER staff, I bottled my frustration and anger prior to her PICU admission. No longer in the ER, I did not need to restrain myself. Angry and exhausted, I wanted to unload on someone, and these two targets availed themselves to me.

The nurses broke the ice by apologizing for our treatment in the ER. "It shouldn't have happened," one said. "I am really sorry. It shouldn't have happened." Her heartfelt sincerity completely disarmed me. With my anger abated, the four of us conversed congenially. Krista and I described the events of the night before from our perspective and answered their questions. They ended the conversation with another apology and a promise that a future visit would be different. We in turn invited them into Katie's room to see our sleeping daughter. After some pleasant small talk, we exchanged handshakes and they wished Katie well. I never saw those women again.

I have no doubt that the ER staff failed to provide Katie adequate care. Apparently, I was not alone in my conclusion. Management, instead of ignoring the failure or offering a slew of excuses, owned it. The women reached out to us and acknowledged the mistakes. They listened to our version of the story and promised to address the incident with those responsible. By the time they departed, the animosity festering within me was gone. To this day, I can recite the events of that night without hard feelings or emotions, a testament to the management staff.

Back in Room 4, Katie was a very sick little girl. The intensivist described the working diagnosis as respiratory and secondary bacterial infections based on blood and sputum samples. Katie's numbers were terrible, including those measuring liver and kidney function. The intensivist pumped antibiotics through her IV. The combination of infection and sedatives kept Katie unconscious. Meanwhile, Krista considered the long game. "You know," she told the intensivist innocently, "Katie was scheduled for a GI consult next month for reflux. Since she's here...." The intensivist did not wait for the end of the sentence. "I'll order a GI consult." And that is how one gets things done in the PICU. "Good job, babe," I said after the doctor left, "Good job."

Not only did we get a GI consult, but the head of the GI department appeared the next day. Dr. Maisel recommended replacing the G-tube with a gastrostomy-jejunostomy (G-J) tube, which required another surgery. A G-tube delivers food to the stomach where it continues the normal journey through the digestive tract. A G-J tube extends through the stomach and into the small intestine; therefore, food bypasses the stomach altogether. With less content in the stomach, the liquid available to reflux decreases significantly. The G-J requires continual feedings since the small intestines cannot tolerate large amounts of food over a short period. Tethering Katie to a feeding apparatus was a small price to pay for reflux relief.

Before the G-J placement, Dr. Maisel would first perform a colonoscopy and endoscopy to check for other possible GI issues. With Katie already intubated, we consented to the procedures on the spot. "This is routine," she said. "In my thirty-five plus years of experience, I've only failed to place a G-J once." Dr. Maisel set the procedure for that Friday, October 4, more than a month before our scheduled GI appointment. Hospitalization had its privileges.

"You gotta be kidding me," I said when Dr. Maisel entered the Family Room following the surgery. I could see by her expression that she failed to place a G-J for the second time in her career. She explained that the incision placement from the G-tube surgery made the angle to enter the small intestine too difficult to navigate. On the plus side, both scopes revealed nothing abnormal. Concerned that the MIC-KEY balloon may be blocking food from leaving the stomach, Dr. Maisel ordered a barium test for the following Monday to get a better idea of how Katie's stomach functioned.

Notwithstanding her G-J issue, the four-month-old had improved sufficiently by Saturday, October 5 for the intensivist to order breathing trials in preparation for extubation. Shocking everyone, Katie failed miserably. The intensivist attributed the failure to one or more factors, including (1) an accumulation of fluid in her lungs from the respiratory infection, (2) depleted red blood cells from multiple blood draws, and (3) the enlarged heart compressing the lungs. I did not understand the latter since Katie's heart to lung ratio could not have dramatically changed from a week before. The intensivist replied that the abnormal anatomy could not overcome the infection's effect on her body.

The breathing trials made for a rough day. The intensivist reduced Katie's sedatives, thereby allowing the body's natural instinct to breathe to reemerge. Katie writhed in vain to free herself of the extremely uncomfortable intubation tube. The nurses used restraints on Katie's wrists to prevent her from pulling out a line or tube, allowing her only a couple inches of free movement in either arm. I asked if we could release the restraints provided Krista or I remained at the bedside. The nurse relented after we promised not to let Katie interfere with the equipment. While The Beach Boys played in the background, Krista and I did our best to distract Katie until she finally calmed down that evening.

Exhausted from the day's hospital drama, Krista and I pulled into our garage just after 10 p.m. Krista preceded me into the house as I unpacked the car. I jumped when Krista screamed my name from inside the house, dropping our bags and running to the sound of her voice. Quickly walking out of the laundry room connecting the garage and the kitchen, she said someone had broken into the house. I told her to wait on the driveway, grabbed a broom hanging on the wall, and slowly walked into the kitchen.

The house was trashed. Stuffing from the couch and loveseat covered the carpet in the living room. The couch sat crookedly on the wrong side of the room. Katie's crib was on its side behind, not in front of, the couch. The loveseat had been dragged from the living room, through the kitchen, and into the dining room. Pictures on the wall littered the floor. The smashed wooden dining room table and chairs resembled flotsam on the kitchen floor. Meanwhile Sam, guard dog that he was, slept peacefully on the loveseat now beside the refrigerator. I dropped the broom, took a knife from the kitchen island, retreated to the driveway with Krista, and called the police.

I remained on the phone with police dispatch while we waited for the officer. She asked if we had a dog, and I laughed. "My dog needs help getting on the couch, let alone moving one. He can't even manage stairs." Besides, someone had already stolen the American flag from the front of our house in July and rifled through our cars in August. I attributed the disaster in the house to a mini-neighborhood crime spree.

A young officer straight out of central casting arrived and inspected the house with gun drawn. Krista and I stood in the driveway and watched the illumination from the officer's flashlight dance in the windows from one room to the next. After a few minutes, the policeman exited the house through the open garage door. "I think it was your dog," he said.

"Can't be," I said. "That dog gets winded walking up stairs."

"Well, I didn't see anything missing. There were laptops in the living room and cash on the kitchen counter."

I suddenly remembered seeing a few singles when I first entered the house, but, in the excitement, failed to note the significance.

"And there are bite marks in the furniture."

It was that precise moment that I felt like a complete idiot. The three of us reentered the house. One need not be Encyclopedia Brown to crack this caper. The readily apparent telltale bite marks in the upholstery left no doubt as to the culprit. While Krista and the police officer surveyed the damage, I stealthily returned the knife to its block. The policeman left after graciously listening to our profuse apologies. We surmised that thunderstorms rumbling through Indianapolis agitated Sam, who apparently was not as disabled as we previously thought. Throughout the drama, Sam never moved from the loveseat in the kitchen, happily panting and enjoying the company.

Katie sailed through the barium test on Monday, October 7. As far as medical procedures go, a barium test with a G-tube is about as easy as they come. A technician delivered a mixture of barium sulfate and water through the tube just like a normal feeding. A series of x-rays showed how the fluid moved through her system. Confirming Dr. Maisel's suspicions, the MIC-KEY button balloon partially blocked the stomach's exit port when inflated and prevented food from entering the intestine. The blockage contributed to, if not caused, Katie's reflux. Dr. Maisel subsequently referred Katie to interventional radiology. The specialty performs minimally invasive procedures with real-time imagery from x-rays, MRIs, and similar tools. An interventional radiologist successfully inserted a G-J tube the following day. We noticed a significant decrease in reflux thereafter.

I fully expected our second PICU experience to be an extension of the first, but they differed significantly. Room 8, typically reserved for the highest-need patients, is directly across from the nurses' station. To reach Katie's new accommodations from the station, one walked a hundred feet west past Rooms 6 and 7 on the left and the dispensary on the right and then turned right where the hallway hit the top of a "T." Room 4, the PICU's "Marvin Gardens," sat twenty feet down the hall to the left. Traffic outside Room 4 dropped precipitously when the neighboring rooms emptied, leaving us feeling very isolated. Instead of having the nurses' station across the hall, Room 4 had the room in which the staff stored garbage. This was not the prime PICU real estate to which we were accustomed. Our physical location was not the only change.

The composition and therefore chemistry of Katie's nursing team varied significantly from the original lineup. Katie's favorite PICU nurse was out on maternity leave. Some of my favorites either moved into management or nurse practitioner training positions. Nurses trained for critically ill cardiac patients eschewed Katie, now a patient suffering from a respiratory virus who happened to have a heart defect. Their replacements were no better or worse, but they were strangers. We once again had to build relationships from scratch.

We also noticed a change in staff attitude during our second stay. I felt like a one-hit wonder that once played the main stage with a record on top of the charts now opening for a high school band at a county fair. Katie first presented at the PICU with an extremely rare condition requiring immediate surgical intervention to save her life. Administering IVs for an infection paled in comparison. For the PICU staff generally, Katie presented somewhat of a distraction from the more complicated cases. Understanding their reasoning, I held no grudge and adjusted my expectations.

The single biggest change was Anthony's withdrawal from Katie's care team. He remained on the unit, but we saw him far less frequently. I felt a huge sense of loss from his departure. He had been our rock, the one weekday constant in the PICU to whom we turned to answer questions and decipher the doctor-speak. No one replaced him, perhaps because he exceeded the formal scope of his position. His absence left a permanent void but taught me that I no longer needed someone to facilitate dialogue with the physicians. The staff members were not the only ones who had changed since Katie's discharge on July 8.

CHAPTER 15

The Queen of Hearts

WITH THE GLENN SURGERY TENTATIVELY planned for the following month, the cardiologists of The Children's Heart Center became the de facto treatment leads. The Center consisted of two distinct functional areas: Dr. Abraham and Sarah on the surgical side and Drs. Kumar, Stein, and Parikh in the general cardiology practice. During Katie's first hospitalization, we dealt primarily with Dr. Abraham and Sarah, particularly the latter. Contact with both of them decreased sharply once Katie transferred to the NICU, where the cardiologists managed Katie's care. Katie saw Dr. Kumar exclusively at every cardiology appointment after discharge; however, managing Katie's fluid levels necessitated almost daily contact with one of the three cardiologists during her forty-two days at home. These frequent interactions laid the foundation for a solid working relationship between the cardiologists and Katie's family, which proved invaluable as Katie faced a series of cardiac issues in the following months.

Katie's ability to breathe independently once again came into question following five grinding days of calamitous breathing trials. After breathing for months off a ventilator, Katie now inexplicably failed every breathing test. The risk of another infection from the ET tube grew daily. Weighing the risks, an intensivist decided we could not wait for a successful trial, let alone a series of good trials. We once again rolled the dice.

A few hours before the scheduled extubation on Monday, October 7, the breathing tube slipped into Katie's right lung. No longer receiving air from the ventilator, the left lung partially collapsed. Katie recovered from this setback for two days before the next extubation attempt. Krista and I waited in the Family Room during the brief procedure. The nurse walked in the room with a large grin on her face. "She's extubated. Her respirations are high, but she looks good." Katie once again surprised many, but not all. I never doubted she would breathe. She had earned my complete confidence long before.

Katie once again suffered through sedative withdrawal following extubation. Concerned with the pharmaceutical regimen, Krista asked a nurse if she could talk to the intensivist the following Friday evening. A wave of admissions kept the intensivist preoccupied, and he never came. Sensitive to higher priorities, Krista did not press the issue. When we returned to the hospital the next morning, she again asked Katie's nurse to see the intensivist and, again, the intensivist did not respond. Her patience started running thin by 8 p.m., so she went to the nurses' station to ask the charge nurse directly to see the intensivist. The nurse promised Krista that she would deliver the message.

Sure enough, a doctor walked in Katie's room ten minutes later. The doctor was not, however, the intensivist. Clad in a white lab coat, the resident had the swagger of a cowboy in a 1950's western and the cockiness of an Ivy League legacy student. Krista sat on the couch while I stood between the two at the head of Katie's crib.

"You had a question about her meds?" asked the doctor.

"Yes," Krista replied. Before she could utter another word, the resident nonchalantly rattled off a list of drugs and dosages before turning to leave. Krista asked a short question, stopping the resident in his tracks. He paused before turning and sizing up the mother before him in blue jeans and a sweatshirt. The resident gave a brief answer chock-full of confidence. Drugs are not my forte, but I sensed a class-A guess. He again turned to leave when Krista asked curiously, "Why that diuretic?" If diuretics can restore blood to one's face, the resident could have used a dose stat. Calling his bluff, Krista peppered him with a few additional softball questions. The resident, who had probably glanced at Katie's chart, thought he could recite a few scripts, and amaze the ignorant parents with his doctor-speak, stammered. Unfortunately for him, this parent happened to be a pharmacist in his own hospital. Clearly in over his head, he politely excused himself, saying meekly, "I better go get the intensivist." We never saw him again. The intensivist visited us within an hour, seemingly unaware of the earlier exchange.

I initially thought the comeuppance hilarious and got a good laugh out of it. Recalling the scene later that night, I started wondering whether I, too, had spoken to and believed doctors feeding me a line. I thereafter made a concerted effort to ask questions both for a substantive answer and confirmation that the doctor at least knew Katie's pertinent history. I do not know whether it worked, but I made the effort nonetheless. Still, I had to give credit where credit was due. As we walked out of the hospital that night, I put my arm over Krista's shoulders and said, "Kris, you were great tonight. That was classic."

Despite the rounds, meetings, and endless discussions with the treatment team, the monotonous PICU existence was often mind-numbingly boring. Reading proved all but impossible as the constant distraction of monitors and staff made concentration impossible. I managed to maintain correspondence with Katie's supporters, who had grown in number significantly since June. After my first e-mail notifying people of Katie's birth and heart defect, I built a distribution list comprised only of those who reached out to us. People forwarded my messages to such an extent that they took on a life of their own. By the end of Katie's second hospitalization, fully a third of my e-mail recipients consisted of strangers. That number exceeded half by year's end. I greatly appreciated both friends and strangers caring so for my little girl. Moreover, I felt pride that she inspired and touched so many people.

A project I started during Katie's first hospitalization occupied some of my time. I purchased a hardcover notebook from an office supply store the week before Katie's birth. I intended to fill it with notes chronicling Katie's life, such as the story of her first day at school, her first Christmas, and the like. In the chaos marking her first week of life, I struggled to remember the voluminous information the doctors presented. Not trusting myself to remember, I kept fastidious notes on the only paper available: Katie's book.

Hardbound with a dark crimson cover and the word "RECORD" emblazoned in gold across the top, I kept an almost daily log in what became my bible of Katie's treatment. The book took on an entirely different purpose after Dr. Abarbanell's last visit in June.

Dr. Abarbanell stopped by Katie's room to say goodbye before moving to Georgia. Unfortunately, neither Krista nor I were present at the time. Finding the room empty, the cardiologist wrote a message to Katie in the hardcover book she found on the counter:

> Katherine,
>
> You have absolutely amazing parents. The first few weeks of your life have been a crazy rollercoaster for them. I am honored to have met your parents and pray for "smooth sailing" in the future.
>
> Blessings,
> G. Abarbanell
> (Pediatric Cardiologist)

Sitting alone with Katie that night, I imagined Katie stumbling across her diagnosing physician's note years later when a solution to a vexing problem popped into my head.

Katie received e-mails, cards, gifts, and prayers from hundreds of people. I wanted to capture these acts of kindness so Katie would someday know how many people supported her. I initially planned to keep all the correspondence; however, it soon grew too voluminous. Rather than maintaining these items, I resolved to ask those who cared for or supported Katie to write messages in the book similar to that of Dr. Abarbanell. After further consideration, I decided to ask for signatures instead. I reasoned that, like a high school yearbook, everyone would write essentially the same message. After combing through emails, texts, cards, and my records, I assembled a list of names and sought out family, staff, and friends to sign Katie's book.

The number of those involved with Katie's care is staggering. In just her first PICU stay, four cardiologists, two pulmonologists, thirty-six PICU nurses, six intensivists, two chaplains, and one neurologist and infectious disease physician cared for Katie. This is in addition to the surgical team, nurse practitioners, RTs, environmental technicians, pharmacists, therapists, child life specialists, and social workers.

The responses to my request for signatures were almost entirely positive. Some people demurred, particularly those who participated in Katie's first open heart operation. I asked Sarah for the names of the surgical team personnel, but administration rejected my request. The surgical team members I could identify were reticent to sign the book, so I eventually gave in to my better angels and let it go. Happily, most of the other staff members felt flattered to be included in Katie's book.

I bought material for a cover to protect the book in a Davenport, Iowa fabric store. The saleswoman asked me why I needed the vinyl-like material. After I told her the purpose of my purchase, she instructed me to come back the next day. She made a cloth sleeve herself and refused payment.

The book is the lone item touched by Katie and so many of those who cared for and about her. More than 600 signatures represent the individual relationships people shared with Katie. The book also includes, in part, handwritten copies of my update emails, a list of the music played in Katie's room, donors to the hospital in her name, the funeral masses, and the names of elementary children who made cards for Katie. As the anthology of Katie's life, I value no possession more.

The intensivist announced during rounds on the morning of Monday, October 14 that Katie had finished the withdrawal process, the final obstacle before discharge. Katie dashed our hopes of leaving PMCH when she spiked a fever of 102.5 degrees that afternoon and slept for ten straight hours. This became a pattern. The doctors told us of plans to discharge so many times only for another issue to arise that I felt like Charlie Brown trying to kick the football. For every issue we resolved, another jumped up to take its place. Katie battled viruses, respiratory and intestinal infections, dehydration, hyponatremia (low sodium in the blood due to too much fluid), and fluctuating temperatures and blood pressures. Katie finally turned the corner on Thursday, October 17 and became her normal, happy self.

Hospitalization has a connotation of misery, but not so with Katie. When healthy, Katie reveled in the constant stream of attention and stimulus in the PICU. In addition to the companionship of the PICU staff, physical and occupational therapists returned to remedy deconditioning from eleven days of intubation. All three "primes" from the NICU visited Katie throughout the month. Our friend, Laura, and Fr. John visited regularly. Family visitors complemented Katie's large PMCH retinue. Great-aunts and uncles from both sides of the family kept Katie busy in between therapy and examinations. Katie let Krista's Aunt Pat hold her for more than two hours, an achievement not matched since the morning of Katie's first surgery on June 3.

While Katie enjoyed her first great weekend in almost a month, a series of tragedies cast a pall over the PICU. A baby girl born with a heart defect in May suffered cardiac arrest during her second heart surgery on Friday. A nine-year-old girl experienced a severe asthma attack Saturday. Both incurred devastating neurological damage. Physicians removed life support for each on Sunday. I shared an elevator with the older girl's father, who told me her story. At a loss for anything more profound, I simply said, "I'm so sorry." He thanked me as we parted ways at the elevator doors. Despite the grief, he conducted himself with a quiet dignity, and I thought of him often in the months to come. Meanwhile, we celebrated Katie's recovery. As my mom often said, "There but for the grace of God go I." Katie's room became a haven for staff who desired a little break from the pervasive melancholy. We were ready to go home.

Under an impression of imminent discharge on October 22, the nurse manager and I discussed procuring an oxygen tank for home use when Dr. Kumar joined us. He changed the topic to Katie's pulmonary pressure. After five months of growth and relative health, only one obstacle prevented the now eleven-pound Katie from having the second of three surgeries: We did not know Katie's pulmonary pressure. The only means of measuring pressure is a cardiac catheterization (cath), which Dr. Kumar had originally scheduled for October 30. He rescheduled the procedure for the following day when an opening in his schedule coincided with that of Dr. Abraham. The two physicians decided that, should Katie encounter trouble during the cath or fail extubation, they would immediately proceed with the second heart surgery. With stars aligning, Krista and I readily consented.

Acceptable pulmonary pressure is a requirement for the Glenn procedure. Picture a thousand-yard straight track. The track's first 800 yards are red while the remainder is blue. You try to drive a car the length of the track; however, you can only step on the gas twice, once at the start and again when the track changes color. You slam on the pedal, and the car lurches forward. It continues to slow until reaching the blue track where another blast of acceleration propels the car to the finish line. The cardiovascular system essentially works the same way. The pumping left chamber of the heart, the first depression of the gas pedal in this analogy, propels the blood through the body and back to the heart. The right side of the heart pumps the blood through the lungs, symbolized by the blue track. Katie's heart defect robbed her of that second pump. Thus, Katie could only hit the gas once and then coast the entire thousand-yard track, which is difficult but possible. Pulmonary hypertension increases the incline on the blue section of track. Without the second burst of acceleration, that is one hill Katie's car just could not climb.

The October 23 cath constituted Katie's fifth surgical procedure. Memories of the previous week's fatalities put my nerves on edge. I no longer enjoyed the benefit of ignorance. Dr. Kumar told us the procedure would not take long, so Krista and I waited in the Family Room with my Aunt Elaine. I worked on a half-finished puzzle to distract myself. When Dr. Kumar finally arrived, he, Krista, and my aunt joined me at the table. Dr. Kumar assured us Katie did well and successfully extubated. He then transitioned to the less than positive test results: Katie had pulmonary hypertension. Dr. Kumar measured her pressure at 27 mmHg. High but tolerable for an otherwise healthy baby, the pressure was much, much too high for the Glenn surgery. Katie required a pressure at or less than 15 mmHg. The lifesaving surgery we had hoped for since June would kill Katie if we proceeded.

PMCH allows one to name a hospital room in return for a considerable donation. The names of deceased kids accordingly adorn PICU Rooms 7, 8, and 9. The latter had a beautiful scrapbook underneath a plaque chronicling the life of a girl who succumbed to pulmonary hypertension almost a decade earlier. I fully understood the condition could be fatal, but failed to appreciate how a less severe case of pulmonary hypertension could present an existential threat to one with a heart condition. Surely, I thought, a drug could decrease it. I did not fully grasp the threat for another few months.

Drs. Kumar and Williams, cardiologist and pulmonologist, respectively, developed a tripartite approach to reduce the pressure. First, 24-hour oxygen delivered through a nasal cannula would ease the strain on Katie's struggling lungs. It also ignited "The Great Cannula War." The device quickly became the bane of Katie's existence, and she fought the cannula like a mortal enemy. Second, twice-daily nebulizer treatments in which Katie breathed in vaporized medicine would open the bronchi, making breathing easier and decreasing the probability of infection. Third, daily doses of sildenafil would decrease arterial pressure in Katie's lungs. The drug, better known as Viagra, is most commonly used for erectile dysfunction. In both applications, sildenafil dilates arteries to facilitate blood flow. I hoped we would never need such a drug in our house, and certainly did not think my daughter would be the one using it.

All other treatment continued unchanged. The doctors believed the new course would decrease Katie's pressure over the next three months, but the degree of improvement was at best a crapshoot. We would not know of Katie's eligibility for the second surgery until Dr. Kumar performed another cath in late January, 2014.

Doctors from multiple disciplines speculated that Katie's recent respiratory illnesses elevated her pulmonary pressure to some degree, a double-edged sword. Were that true, her pressure should fall to an acceptable level as her body recovered. On the other hand, if a respiratory illness could escalate her pressure that significantly, a similar reaction would be lethal after the Glenn surgery. The shunt only bought us limited time to allow Katie to prepare for the next two surgeries. She could not depend on it indefinitely, so we had no choice but to accept that risk. In the meantime, we had to keep Katie healthy. Needing to avoid communicable diseases as the cold and flu season approached, Katie entered her "Howard Hughes phase" upon discharge. She would remain in the cocoon of the house until the next cath. With more than a little luck, she could avoid another respiratory infection.

If everything went as planned, Katie's pressure would decrease sufficiently to proceed with the next surgery. During the Peloponnesian War, Phillip II wrote a long, threatening letter to Sparta, boasting, "If I invade Laconia, you will be destroyed, never to rise again." The Spartans gave a one word response: "If." That is one big word.

Katie quickly recovered from the catheterization. With no signs of infection, Dr. Helzcenko discharged Katie in the early afternoon of October 28. Krista brought a frilly dress for Katie to wear home, but I had other ideas. Reluctant at first, Krista eventually conceded.

A friend from law school and her husband sent Katie a Supergirl costume in the weeks following her birth. I had been holding on to it for just such an occasion. We slipped the blue onesie over Katie's head, a giant yellow "S" emblazoned across her chest. Red boots and a cape finished the ensemble. Krista strapped our little superhero in the car seat, and I carried her out of PMCH after a twenty-nine day hospitalization.

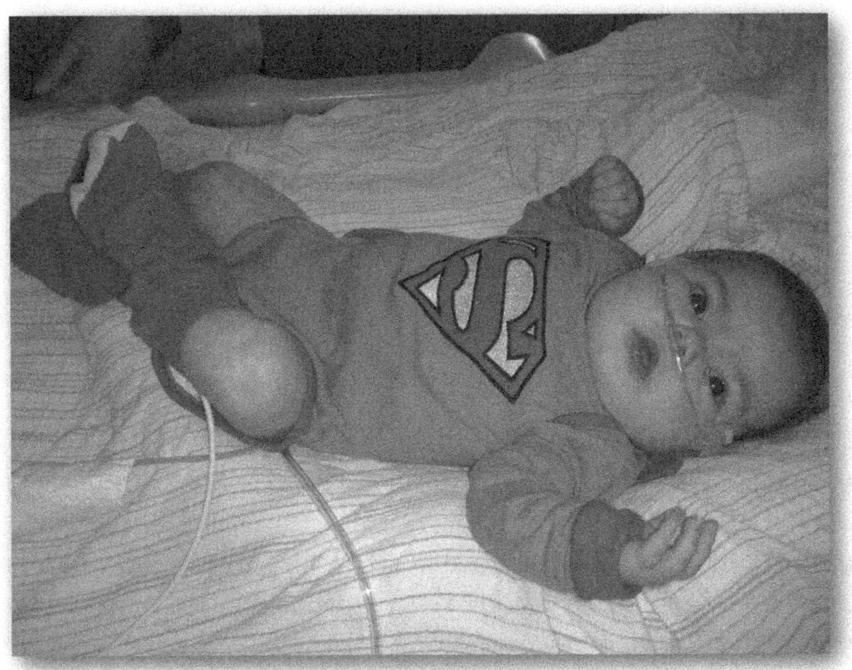

Katie leaving the PICU in her Supergirl outfit.

We first stopped at the nurses' station to thank the staff and show off Katie's attire. Another month together made for an emotional good-bye. When Dr. Helzcenko walked into the nurses' station, I lifted Katie onto the counter and said, "She looks much better than when you first saw her in the ER." He smiled, agreeing wholeheartedly. "That is perfect," he said in reference to the costume. "She earned it."

CHAPTER 16

Be It Ever So Humble

LIFE RESUMED ONCE KATIE CAME home as though the second PICU stay never happened. As the weeks passed in the PICU, I fretted about finding new home nurses. We were fortunate that all four women returned. Physical and occupation therapists continued to work with Katie at the house. Dawn immediately resumed her weekly visits, rounding out the original roster. Krista's Aunt Pat, an empty nester living in Denver, volunteered to stay with us indefinitely to help with Katie. With Pat carrying some of the responsibilities at home, I returned to work.

My employment complicated an already complicated situation. I started working for the Army at the Rock Island Arsenal the previous March. We planned on Krista and Katie joining me in July, going so far as to buy a house in Davenport, Iowa. Unsure of Katie's future needs, Krista and I resolved to work when possible so we would have the resources not to work if needed. Therefore, I started commuting to the Arsenal again in November.

My supervisor authorized a modified schedule to facilitate my travel requirements. I left home at five o'clock on Monday morning and drove through western Indiana and the breadth of Illinois in just over five hours. I had a short day Thursday, which allowed me to arrive home around eleven-thirty that night. I worked longer on the remaining three weekdays to offset lost time on travel days. I worked from home on Fridays, spending only three nights a week in Rock Island.

Maintaining the Davenport and Indianapolis houses bled us financially.[6] Krista and I leased the Davenport house to a military couple with a toddler in October. Seeing a family that so resembled us living in our first house was surreal. The tenants signed a three-year lease, which thrilled me as I fully anticipated Katie would need to remain in Indianapolis for years to come.

For the few nights I stayed at the house in May and September, an air mattress, old television, card table, and folding chair constituted the sum total of my furnishings. I moved my meager possessions into an apartment I shared with a coworker after leasing the house. He and his ill wife lived in Chicago, but he spent the week working in Rock Island. The inexpensive second floor apartment of a friendly retired couple within a mile of the Arsenal served our needs perfectly.

Even with Pat and Dawn's help, I still felt guilty being so far away. The fear of something happening to Katie never subsided. Krista and I were determined to make the unsustainable situation work in the short term, although we had no idea how long or short that "short term" would be.

Ensconced in the comfort of her own house, Katie thrived in the month following discharge. Her respirations slowed to fifty to sixty breaths per minute, down from an average of ninety prior to hospitalization. When Dr. Halczenko admitted Katie to the PICU, she weighed in at the lowest percentile for her age. She doubled her birthweight by mid-November, reaching the tenth percentile of six-month-olds. The neurologist saw nothing of concern in her first consult since August, including no signs of cerebral palsy. In regards to development, Katie rapidly made up for time in the hospital.

6 Neighbors and a coworker voluntarily maintained our Davenport house and lawn for four months. I contacted a small Indianapolis lawn service to cut our grass since I had already moved our lawn equipment to Davenport. I explained my situation, and the owner quoted me a price. Ten minutes later, he called back to say that he and his men would take care of our lawn for the entire summer at no cost.

Not everything on Peregrine Boulevard was sunshine and rainbows. Katie hated the cannula and the tape that held it in place. The prongs often distended her nostrils, leaving her nose red and sore. I trimmed the prongs to give her a little relief with mixed results. Meanwhile, the tape left the skin on her cheeks raw. Krista searched for adhesive products and methods to affix the cannula before finally concocting a workable combination of tape and skin cream. Katie also developed a cough as we entered the third week of November. Given the ordeal of the last respiratory virus, the possibility of yet another infection deeply concerned us. We discussed the cough with Dr. Stoesz, Dr. Williams from pulmonology, and the cardiology staff. They advised us to monitor for changes.

GI-related issues continued to vex us. The G-J diminished Katie's reflux as promised, but did not eradicate the problem. When Katie suffered reflux with the G-tube, the fluid going backwards up the esophagus consisted of gastric juices, breastmilk, and formula. Breastmilk and formula bypassed the stomach with the G-J tube, leaving undiluted stomach acid as the only fluid to reflux. Thus, we reduced the amount, but increased the potency of, the fluid. A surgical fix to prevent reflux constituted too extreme a remedy for a problem of this relatively minor magnitude. The physicians assured us reflux would decrease with age, leaving us to comfort Katie through yet another struggle.

The GI problems were not limited to reflux. The skin around Katie's MIC-KEY button adhered to and grew up the device's stem as Katie's body tried to heal the wound. The inflamed area around the MIC-KEY made movement painful. A home nurse, my mom, and I took Katie to a GI appointment on November 12. The nurse practitioner (NP) spent almost an hour discussing Katie's case with us. Concerned about skin breakdown, she said she needed to apply a "caustic pencil" to the affected area. The word "caustic" gave me pause, but I never imagined the scene about to unfold.

A "caustic pencil" is a long stick with silver nitrate on one end like a match head. The nitrate reacts to moisture on the skin, chemically burning the underlying flesh. The NP asked me to hold Katie's arms and shoulders down as she approached with the pencil. The NP could not apply a topical numbing agent because the nitrate needed to touch the skin directly to trigger the desired chemical reaction. She applied the burning agent to an already tender wound. Katie bucked and screamed so violently that I struggled to keep the twelve-pound baby still. The home nurse grabbed Katie's wildly kicking feet.

To this day, I do not know whether we could have done anything to ameliorate the pain. I felt terribly guilty afterwards for not at least asking. The guilt has not diminished. That I did not know the level of pain involved provides no solace. I do not think Katie experienced that degree of agony before or after. My mom spent more than an hour calming her.

As my grandmother's primary caregiver, my mom left Indianapolis to resume her responsibilities back in Connellsville. Years of advancing Parkinson's disease confined Gram to her room at an assisted living facility. The affliction left her body's life-sustaining systems intact but destroyed those providing quality of life. Numerous mini-strokes over the previous six years took a cognitive toll and, along with the Parkinson's expressive aphasia, made communication difficult. A common manifestation of the disease is the brain replacing one word for another during speech. For example, a person may want to say "car," but instead speaks the word "pie." The combination of strokes and Parkinson's had rendered Gram practically speechless for months. My mom and other visitors carried on one-sided conversations, not knowing what, if anything, Gram comprehended. And so it was when mom returned from her November Indianapolis visit.

As mom took Gram's vitals and tidied her room, she reported the latest on Katie. In a moment of complete lucidity and with a clear voice, Gram spoke, "Is the baby okay?" Initially taken aback by the outburst, my mom realized that Gram had understood at least some of her countless Katie monologues. She sat in a folding chair in front of Gram and said, "No, mother, she isn't okay, but…." She proceeded to give Gram as much detail as possible, taking advantage of this moment of clarity.

Gram did not speak again. That she feared for Katie's health while overcome with her own medical issues is a testament to her loving nature. Despite the adversity she faced, she still thought of others. I have often heard the term, "living one's faith," but I never witnessed anyone display it so fully. While I carry the disappointment that she and Katie never met, I find a measure of solace in Gram knowing of, and I am sure praying for, her youngest great-grandchild.

My expectations on Katie's second homecoming differed significantly from those in August. Just a few months earlier, thoughts of her future decades occupied my mind. Instead of a transplant, could we grow a new heart for Katie? How long would a transplanted heart last? Would she require a transplant before her twentieth birthday? The repeated scares over the previous five months greatly diminished my ambitions. I now hoped that Katie would reach her fifth birthday. Fearing others may think me pessimistic, I kept my new goal close to my vest, sharing it initially with only a small core of confidants. That group grew as winter slowly gave way to spring, and my hope turned from cynical to wildly optimistic.

After putting Katie to bed one November evening, Pat alluded to Katie growing up. I replied, "Five years. I just want five years." Pat rebuked me. "No, no, no. She's going to be just fine." Her response was not atypical, and I let it go. Almost all of Katie's supporters outside the medical universe shared my initial naïveté. The question was always when, not whether, Katie would come home. Many people told me with absolute conviction, "It's terrible that she's still in the hospital, but she'll be okay." Maybe she would, but she might not.

The brain's natural inclination when contemplating a sick child is to assume a happy ending. Children bury parents; it is the natural order. But life is not a movie. I had seen Katie too sick too many times not to appreciate the peril she faced. I witnessed, albeit from afar, death take other children. I saw their inconsolable mothers and grandmothers. I observed grief break hardened men. We had no immunity from catastrophe. Of that, I had no illusion.

I seized the five-year goal, going so far as to work out celebration details in my head. Katie's fifth birthday would fall on a Sunday. We would throw a huge picnic at a local park and invite all the people in Katie's book. She would wear a bright summer dress, her incision visible above the collar. Her long brown curly hair and dark eyes would betray no indication of the struggles that came before. The doctors, nurses, and therapists who had seen her on death's door would stare with astonishment and remark how good she appeared. I so looked forward to that day.

My mom and Pat were not the only visitors in November. Krista's mom and Pat's husband visited us for Thanksgiving. With Katie confined to the house, Krista and I took on cooking responsibilities. I consider the result passable, by no means gourmet, but the adults enjoyed a nice dinner while Katie slept in the living room. Krista and I savored a fleeting moment of normalcy.

Katie with her parents on Thanksgiving.

In the days before the Thanksgiving, Katie started exhibiting the same behaviors that preceded her last hospitalization. She became irritable and seemed pained by the MIC-KEY button. Krista collaborated with Dr. Stoesz and cardiology, which resulted in some medication tweaks. I noticed a large bump on Katie's abdomen and Katie exhibiting discomfort when moved. Krista and I suspected the MIC-KEY balloon slipped out of place. We monitored the bump for a few days, discussing whether we should take Katie back to GI.

On Saturday, November 30, Katie started breathing hard. That, combined with her crankiness, cough, and bump on her abdomen, prompted another ER visit. Once again, Katie reverted to her baseline as soon as we entered the hospital. Unlike our last ER experience, the staff was very attentive. The doctor X-rayed Katie's abdomen to confirm the G-J remained in the correct position, and Krista and I left the hospital with peace of mind. The three of us spent the evening at the house, which would be our last.

The wailing started at one o'clock Sunday morning. Krista and I took turns trying to console Katie for the next eight hours. She took a pacifier for a few seconds, sometimes up to a minute, before spitting it out and resuming her crying. We tried lying beside her on the floor in the nursery, rubbing her back as she squirmed in her crib, carrying her around the house, turning lights on, turning lights off, sitting her up on the couch, playing her mobile, simply holding her, and combinations thereof. Nothing worked. Exhausted by eight hours of continuous struggle, Katie finally fell asleep at 9 a.m.

Krista and I discussed me staying in Indianapolis in case Katie took a turn for the worse, but Katie awoke happy and content around noon. With the weather turning cold, we thought it safer to drive during the day on Sunday rather than the pre-dawn morning Monday. I spent the afternoon playing with Katie and Sam on the living room floor while Krista and Pat decorated for Christmas. At three o'clock, I took a picture of Katie to send to family, kissed her good-bye, hugged Krista by the newly erected Christmas tree, and left for Rock Island.

I arrived at my apartment seven hours later. I typically drove straight through, but the lack of sleep hit me hard in central Illinois and I stopped for dinner. My cell phone rang as soon as I finished unloading the car. Krista informed me that Katie's crankiness returned with a fury around 8 p.m. Despite Krista's attempts to console her, Katie continued to escalate. Her temperature rose to 99.7 degrees. Krista asked me whether she should take Katie to the ER. We agreed that Krista should first call the pediatrician. Another physician in Dr. Stoesz' practice answered. Unfamiliar with Katie's case, the doctor told Krista that she knew Katie better than anyone and advised Krista to "trust her instincts." Krista then called my mom, who echoed the doctor's sentiments. Krista called to tell me they were leaving for the ER.

I asked Krista if I should drive home. She said, "No, that's alright. We'll just keep an eye on her." Feeling too tired to drive safely, I conceded. "Okay, but call me if anything changes." Krista promised she would and hung up. Cautiously optimistic, I collapsed on the mattress. This, too, would probably pass.

CHAPTER 17

Once More Unto the Breach

FEAR DRENCHED KRISTA'S VOICE WHEN she called back an hour later. "They're admitting Katie. Her temperature is 106.8 degrees." The number hung in the air for a second before I responded in shock, "What?" Krista shared my exasperation. Katie's temperature measured 99.7 degrees just before leaving the house. It skyrocketed during the fifteen-minute drive to PMCH. I asked how that was possible. Krista did not have a definitive answer, but the ER doctors and PICU intensivist suspected infection. I asked again, more to myself than to her, "How could her temperature go up so quickly?" Whatever the reason, the doctors stabilized Katie using IV fluids and antibiotics.

Too exhausted to drive safely, I reluctantly followed Krista's direction to get some rest before driving home. Concern prevented me from getting much needed sleep. After a couple hours staring at the ceiling, I donned a PMCH shirt and left for Indianapolis in the pre-dawn darkness. I found Krista in the PICU when I arrived at seven a.m., where she gave me a brief summary of the night's events.

Krista had carried Katie, still in her car seat, through the main ER doors and into the waiting area at 9 p.m. the night before. As soon as the triage nurse set eyes on the six-month-old, she directed them to a large examination room in the ER. This marked the only ER visit wherein the triage nurse did not examine Katie prior to entry. A doctor followed them into the room seconds later and directed Krista to take Katie out of the car seat and place her in the bassinet. The doctor's tone was calm and her actions methodical, but Krista sensed deep concern underneath a placid veneer. The doctor then ordered the nurses to establish an IV line in the unresponsive Katie. They quickly found a vein in Katie's scalp above the hairline on the right side of her forehead. After an expedient examination, the doctor admitted Katie and transferred her to the PICU. The intensivist immediately intubated Katie upon arriving. Without a definitive diagnosis, he ordered a slate of tests and medicines, hoping something would arrest the fever. I imagine a technical medical term exists for this, but, back home, we would call it "shooting in the dark."

Katie battled the fever, which fluctuated between 103 and 106 degrees, throughout the night. Melissa, the nurse who had rescued Katie from the ER in September, never left Katie's side. A head CT scan and chest x-ray were clear; however, her extremely high white blood cell count indicated severe infection. Tests also revealed diminished kidney and liver function. Katie's BNP, however, caused the greatest concern.

Heart ventricles secrete BNP, short for "B-type Natriuretic Peptide," in response to developing and worsening heart failure. Higher numbers correlate to more severe heart failure. BNP levels below 100 pg/mL indicate no heart failure. BNP levels exceeding 900 indicate severe heart failure. Katie's BNP was 1,900.

Under the close watch of the intensivist, nurse Melissa, and the respiratory therapists, Katie's fever finally fell to 100.7 degrees in the six o'clock hour. Remaining in critical condition, she still teetered on the edge of disaster, but now a little further from that edge. Throughout it all, Katie continued to hold Krista's fingers with a vise-like grip.

Krista and I spoke little after Krista recapped the night's events. Intuitively, I knew this marked a dramatic vector change in Katie's treatment. I could see in Krista's demeanor and expression that she agreed. Dejected, we steeled ourselves for another battle in what now seemed an endless war.

The third PICU hospitalization ushered in a new phase in Katie's treatment. The June admission followed a predictable course: Dr. Abraham surgically inserted a shunt and the PICU staff nursed Katie through her post-op recovery. Her treatment generally followed a standard plan for a myriad of congenital heart defects. In the NICU, we had the defined goal of successful feeding. The second PICU stay concerned a known problem, i.e., a respiratory virus. The textbook solution provided for breathing support until the infection passed. We now found ourselves in uncharted waters. The latest fever forced us to reassess our initial plan for three reasons:

- Now six months old, Katie had limited time left with her current cardiovascular configuration. She depended on her shunt to feed oxygen-depleted blood from an artery to the lungs. The amount of blood passing through the shunt relative to her body size decreased as she grew. The quantity would eventually be insufficient to provide adequate oxygen to Katie's organs. No one could say with certainty when the shunt would fail, but Dr. Abraham estimated another three to six months. The risk of shunt failure increased with each passing day.
- Katie's recent respiratory infections may have exacerbated her pulmonary hypertension. Dr. Abraham could not proceed with the second surgery unless the pulmonary pressure fell to acceptable levels. The doctors originally planned three months of medication, oxygen, and breathing treatments to lower Katie's pulmonary hypertension. Short of another cardiac catheterization (cath), we had no way of measuring the treatment's effectiveness. During Katie's last hospitalization, Dr. Kumar scheduled the next cath for late January, 2017, almost two months away. Only five weeks separated the scheduled cath and the lower range of Dr. Abraham's estimate for shunt failure.
- In nine weeks, infections so violently overtook Katie's system that she required ventilator support and prolonged hospitalizations. The doctors and family alike questioned how many more infections Katie could withstand.

Aggressiveness in terms of treatment replaced the standoffishness we observed in October. The cardiologists, intensivists, and pulmonologists engaged in robust discussions as to a course of action. The latest crisis called

Katie's existing treatment plan into question, and everyone had a preferred course of action.

Katie improved over the first few days in the PICU. Her BNP fell to 400, and liver and kidney numbers returned to normal. A culture from a spinal tap in the early morning of her admission came back negative. The only positive test result indicated the Rhinovirus, more popularly known as the common cold. The intensivist started partial feedings on December 3; Katie returned to full feedings two days later. Dr. Parikh performed an echocardiogram on December 5. The overall heart function pleased the cardiologist; however, he could not see the shunt. This did not concern him since the small device is often difficult to identify. Happily, Dr. Parikh could not see "vegetation," either. The term describes the phenomena of an organism, such as bacteria, attaching to the surface of heart valves or a shunt.

Time stood still after Katie's initial progress. Elevated temperatures ranging from 99 to 104 degrees persisted despite negative blood cultures and scuttled hopes of extubation. The intensivists refused to extubate until Katie's temperature returned to normal. Katie woke infrequently. On the rare occasions when she opened her eyes, the drugs and fever left Katie in a haze. We saw no forward movement. I found the monotonous grind difficult to endure, perhaps because it gave me time to contemplate our predicament.

Increasing frustration permeated the PICU. I maintained an upbeat demeanor, faking it when necessary. Krista did the same. We tried to keep Katie's room a positive healing environment, a task that grew more difficult with each passing day. In this morass, an issue long ago decided once again raised its head.

Dr. Williams met with Krista and me on the afternoon of December 10 in Katie's room. The pulmonologist wanted to revisit our decision regarding a tracheostomy. He conceded that Katie could breathe independently; however, recent events troubled him:

> "We now have two data points, *two data points*, within three months where she failed. We didn't have that data back in June when we decided not to pursue a trach. I think we need to reconsider, factoring all the data we now have."

Dr. Williams believed the data points indicated a need for ventilator support. Manipulating the numbers in my head, I calculated the period as five months, not three. I grasped for anything to undermine his position, but eventually accepted the futility of my number games.

I could not disregard Dr. Williams' well-reasoned argument. Katie struggled to fight off otherwise non-threatening diseases. She might not have the strength to survive the present or future infections. Moreover, these infections may increase her pulmonary hypertension and prevent the second lifesaving surgery. Dr. Williams recommended another bronchoscopy to assess Katie's airways before making any decisions. Surrendering on the trach issue after such a long, hard-fought battle turned my stomach, but I opened myself to the possibility.

Turning to the pulmonary hypertension concern, Dr. Williams wanted to add a chemotherapy drug, Bosentan, to the current pharmaceutical regimen. Katie relied on sildenafil to dilate vessels in her lungs since the cardiac cath in October. Bosentan is a much stronger drug. Only recently approved for infants, very little data existed regarding the drug's efficacy or safety for such patients. Signaling his degree of concern, Dr. Williams was willing to try it. Krista's research turned up very little empirical evidence, so we placed our trust in Dr. Williams and gave our consent.

As closely as the pulmonologists followed Katie, they served in an advisory capacity. While she remained hospitalized, the intensivists had sole prescription authority. The arrangement ensured someone maintained a global perspective on the patient's care. Bosentan can cause kidney damage and an irregular heartbeat, so an intensivist initially prescribed a two-week course at half strength once she overcame the respiratory illness. After Katie did not exhibit any side effects, he increased the dosage to full strength.

Dr. Williams performed a bronchoscopy the next day, December 11, threading a tiny camera down the intubation tube to photograph Katie's bronchial tree. The previous test in June showed the enlarged heart significantly compressing the main airway and that leading into the left lung. He now observed significant improvement, far more than expected. The hard and open airways pleasantly surprised him. That we conquered one issue was cause for elation. It also threw gasoline on the tracheostomy conflagration.

After rounds the following morning, Dr. Williams discussed his findings and a possible tracheostomy with Drs. Steinberg and Metz, cardiologist and intensivist, respectively. The three men differed on the best course of action, and the discussion grew heated. Dr. Williams advocated for a trach. His voice remained calm and controlled as he lobbied for his position. The equally adamant Dr. Steinberg, on the other hand, was much more effusive.

The cardiologist argued strongly against the trach. Echoing Dr. Abraham's arguments almost six months earlier, Dr. Steinberg listed three major risks: First, the ventilator tube is prone to viral and bacterial infections. Katie did not have a good record fighting off either. Second, mucus and other secretions can block the ventilator tube. Katie may not be strong enough to clear the blockage. Third, positive pressure destroys the natural interaction between lung and heart function. The heart and lungs work in tandem while reacting to the body's needs. The ventilator eliminates the lungs' ability to fluctuate, thereby stressing the heart. Healthy hearts can handle such stress. Single ventricle hearts may not.

Dr. Metz diplomatically forged a compromise. Dr. Kumar would cath Katie after the current virus ran its course. If Katie were not ready for the Glenn procedure, a surgeon would immediately perform the tracheostomy while Katie was on the table. The three physicians did not ask us to consent immediately. They all agreed we should wait until Katie recovered from the current infection before pressing forward with any surgical procedure. I listened to the doctors intently, but Katie's twelve-day battle to overcome the latest infection monopolized my thoughts. I put the trach out of my mind and focused on getting Katie off the vent.

I remained in Indianapolis the entire month of December. Working from home proved impossible as thoughts of Katie always occupied my mind. Remaining on emergency leave freed me to spend time at the hospital and attend rounds.

The intensivists tried to start rounds at nine on weekday mornings, but patients do not abide by the doctors' schedule. Aside from the patients' needs, doctors from the many disciplines flittered in as their own schedules permitted. When the neurologist arrived, his patients jumped up on the queue. The same held true for other disciplines. Krista tried to attend rounds, but their unpredictability often thwarted her attempts. We developed a strategy wherein I attended rounds, took notes, asked questions Krista gave me beforehand, and called Krista with an update. She frequently had additional questions. I sometimes found the answers myself, but, for extremely complex questions, I asked the intensivists to call Krista directly at work. They always obliged.

Low-grade fevers persisted for days after the tracheostomy discussions. On Friday, December 13, the infectious disease physician discovered bacteria colonizing the IV line. Colonized bacteria are extremely difficult to kill using antibiotics. The preferred method of treatment is removing the infected item. Given the difficulty of starting a new IV, the doctors tried a battery of antibiotics in hopes of salvaging the line.

The new antibiotics were not the only treatment changes. Dr. Metz observed a significant increase in Katie's lung secretions and "wet" lungs on her x-ray. Concerned with accumulating fluid, he delayed starting Bosentan until the lungs cleared. He also increased the enalapril dosage to improve heart function, ordered potassium to return Katie to the normal range, and started limited physical and occupational therapy. Meanwhile, the dietician increased Katie's caloric intake. Katie passed the 15-pound mark; however, fluid retention may have accounted for some of the weight gain.

Each day began with hope and ended with another series of failures. Concerned that prolonged intubation may undermine Katie's ability to breathe without the vent, Dr. Metz directed breathing tests. Katie failed them miserably. Meanwhile, she broke her personal record for the longest continuous intubation. Lobbying in vain for extubation, I argued, "She's done it before [breathed on her own] without passing the breathing tests. She'll do it again." Watching Katie knocked out by sedatives day after day grew increasingly maddening. I wanted my Katie back.

Blood tests the following Monday indicated we were losing our fight against the colonized IV in Katie's scalp. The infection elevated Katie's temperature to 102 degrees. Tylenol, which initially arrested the fever, lost its efficacy. The infectious disease physician declared the fight to save the infected IV over that afternoon. The bacteria had won; the line had to come out. A team from Radiology failed to get a PICC line in two attempts. Anthony, who successfully established a PICC in July, once again succeeded on his first try.

The bacteria proved resilient. The day after the IV replacement, cultures indicated bacteria had colonized the ET tube. Again, doctors hoped antibiotics would keep the infection at bay. After a few days, bacteria once again proved mightier than drugs. The intubation tube had to go. Ready or not, we had to extubate.

The forced extubation presented a quandary. The physicians had planned on extubating in conjunction with another surgical procedure: a tracheostomy, catheterization, or a combined catheterization and Glenn surgery. Every physician believed with absolute certainty that recent respiratory infections exacerbated the pulmonary hypertension; therefore, a catheterization at this point would be meaningless. (Within a week, Dr. Abraham would delay the catheterization until February to ensure Katie sufficient time to recover from the infection.) Thus, our immediate choice was to trach or not to trach.

Intubation is inherently miserable. Katie spent almost a third of her life drugged into semi-unconsciousness instead of learning and developing. A trach obviates the need for intubation. On the other hand, the Glenn procedure may do so also. The former is a sure thing; the latter is uncertain. Most doctors thought the Glenn would greatly improve Katie's respiratory function. Dr. Williams disagreed, holding that Katie remained at great peril without the trach even after the Glenn procedure. The issue was academic at this point.

The Glenn was only possible if Katie did not have pulmonary hypertension. Some questioned whether she ever had it, hypothesizing that the previous respiratory illness artificially elevated the pressure during the October cath. We had to wait another month for the current infection to clear so the lungs could return to normal pressure before attempting another cath. Thus, without knowing the pressure, the Glenn was currently off the table. That left us with two options:

- Katie proceed directly to surgery where a tracheostomy would replace the intubation tube.
- Try extubating Katie and allow her to breathe independently. If she failed, proceed with an emergency intubation or tracheostomy.

Before consigning Katie to a trach, Krista and I first wanted to know whether she could breathe independently. Therefore, we consented to extubation when the intensivists determined appropriate.

The appropriate time turned out to be late Thursday morning on December 19. Krista and I waited anxiously in the Family Room while Dr. Metz and Anthony extubated Katie. We raced back to Katie's room when the nurse gave us the "all clear" after only a few minutes. The sleeping Katie fought hard to breath. Katie's temperature hovered just north of 100 degrees; her oxygenation sunk to the bottom of her acceptable range. Perspiration glistened on her mottled skin. Fighting infection and withdrawal, she faced long odds.

Fr. Jim gave Katie the Sacrament of "Anointing of the Sick" on the day after extubation. The Sacrament consists of a priest anointing the forehead and hands of a Christian experiencing the difficulties of grave illness accompanied by prayer asking for special grace. Meanwhile, two nurses went about their business in the room, seemingly unaware of Fr. Jim reading the rites. As he concluded with the sign of the cross on Katie's forehead, though, the nurses joined us in an "Amen."

Katie slowly improved over the next few days. Her fever fell, breathing became less strained, and color improved. By the morning of Monday, December 23, she was a new Katie, and I mean a *new* Katie. She made great strides in cognitive development since November. Her personality emerged from the haze of sedatives and fever. She was magnificent. Playful, happy, and inquisitive, Katie interacted with her surroundings like never before. She loved the stuffed animals hanging above her from thick gauze crisscrossing the crib's corner posts. A bear, zebra, and turtle dangling above were just part of her menagerie. Now free of the ventilator, she loved the attention she received in the hospital.

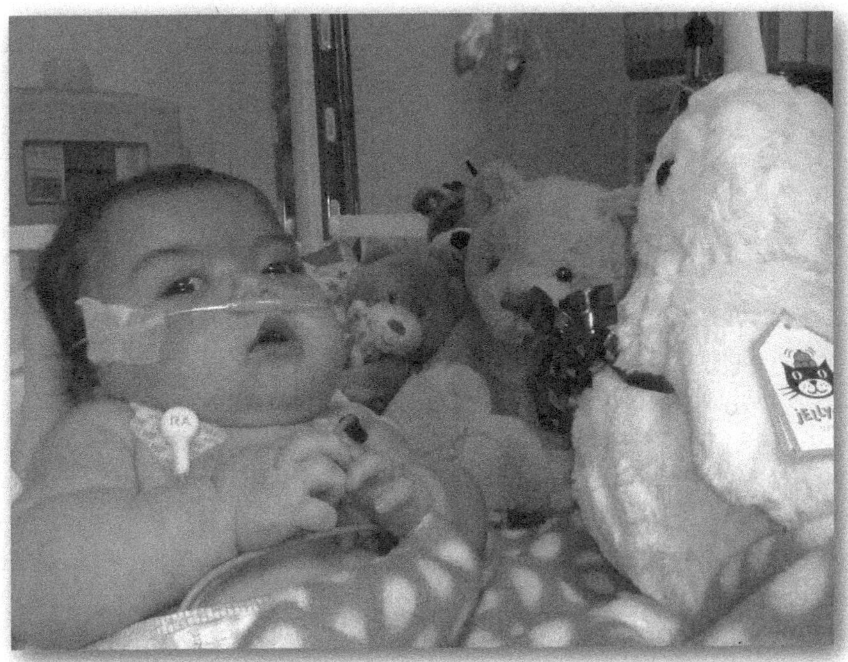

Katie surrounded by her stuffed animal friends.

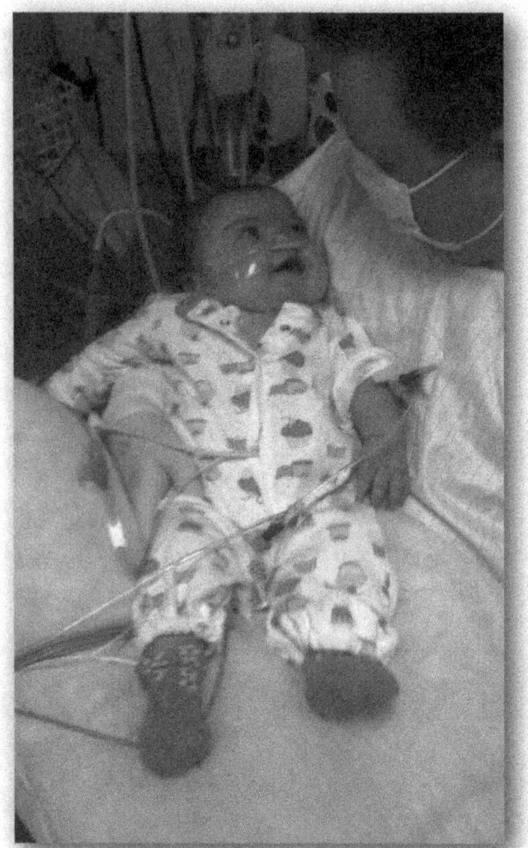

Katie and her dad listening to The Beach Boys.

The PICU emptied out in the days before Christmas as the number of scheduled procedures dropped off and families pushed to get their kids home for the holiday. Our neighbors in Room 3 and 5 went home, leaving us isolated in an otherwise empty hallway. Krista arranged for a transfer to Room 6 so we could be closer to the nurses' station. I was initially indifferent; however, the move yielded an unexpected psychological benefit. Leaving Room 4 ended three weeks of grinding stress, frustration, and fear. The room change heralded a new beginning and a renewed hope.

My research into Ebstein's Anomaly never abated. Many papers and websites explained the deformity, symptoms, and treatments in minute detail. Each piece addressed a range of treatment from regular exercise to surgical tricuspid valve repair for mild to severe cases and then stopped. Deformities of Katie's caliber in which valve repair was impossible merited just one sentence at or near the end: "The severest cases require advanced surgical intervention." And that was it. I did find some great videos of the general three-step single ventricle surgical process on the internet, which doctors use to treat an array of heart defects. One video stood out.

The video told the story of the Wilson family from Akron, Ohio. Doctors diagnosed Mia, the youngest of the couple's four daughters, in utero with severe Ebstein's Anomaly. Seven days after her birth in February, 2011, Mia was airlifted to the University of Michigan's Mott Children's Hospital in Ann Arbor, home of one of the nation's largest pediatric cardiovascular programs. Like Katie, Mia's heart occupied 70 percent of her chest cavity as opposed to the normal thirty percent. She had undergone the same shunt surgery as Katie in addition to the Glenn procedure. Their courses were strikingly similar, including struggles with cerebral bleeds and GI issues. Seeing Mia's story was like watching a favorite movie with a different cast. She and Katie resembled twins. I had to inspect the clothing in a few photos to identify my daughter.

A need for comradery compelled me to reach out to the Wilsons. None of the many parents we met over the prior six months battled Katie's condition, and I felt somewhat alone. I tracked down an e-mail address on their webpage and sent the parents a message along with six pictures of Katie:

> Bobby and Wendy,
>
> I came across Mia's website while researching Ebstein's Anomaly. Our daughter, Katie, was diagnosed in the hours after her birth on June 3, 2013. In her case, the tricuspid valve barely formed at all. She received a shunt on her second day of birth. Katie also had two cerebral bleeds, but we're not sure when exactly they occurred.

I then gave Katie's history in two hundred words and remarked how fortunate we were to live so close to PMCH. In contrast, the Wilsons lived three hours from Ann Arbor, forcing the mom and three girls to stay in a Ronald McDonald House for eleven months during Mia's first hospitalization.

> I so enjoyed finding your site. To date, we know of no one with severe Ebstein's. It's a lonely battle. Mia's story is both familiar and inspiring. Moreover, I am shocked at the physical similarity between the girls. There are a couple of shots on your site that could easily be Katie.
>
> Jack, Krista, and Katie Murtha
> Indianapolis

Mia's mother, Wendy, responded within an hour:

> Jack, Krista and Katie,
>
> Thank you SO much for contacting us. We are honored that our story has been helpful in some small way….
>
> Please feel free to contact my husband or me AT ANY TIME. I really mean that. Even if it's at 2:00 a.m. We have done it to other families, particularly during rough times, and there is something valuable about knowing that someone in your same shoes is on your side. We also would be happy to talk with you anytime about our journey, what the future holds, talking about tough stuff that other people don't really understand. God has just laid it on our hearts to share our story and use our situation to help others in any way we can.
>
> God Bless,
> Wendy and Bobby Wilson

The Wilsons became one of our most valued resources over the next five months.

Katie improved so significantly in the days before Christmas that we invited friends to visit. Laurie, my Legal Aid friend who held Katie in the NICU, stopped by along with her husband, Bill, and nineteen-year old daughter. I helped Laurie and Kaitlyn, who also went by "Katie," don the mandated gown and gloves in the anteroom while Bill, a kidney transplant surgeon at another Indianapolis hospital, geared up and entered the room in seconds flat. Bill asked a general question regarding kidney and liver function. Krista's response must have tipped him off that she had a medical background because their subsequent conversation became very technical. Meanwhile, I gave Laurie and Kaitlyn the layman's version of Katie's condition. The host loved the attention, charming her visitors and showing off her handholding skills.

Once our visitors departed, Krista filled me in on her conversation with Bill and his concern regarding Katie's liver and kidneys. Katie's deformed heart valve allowed some blood to flow in reverse when the right ventricle pumped, causing blood to accumulate in the veins and organs closest to the heart, including the brain and liver. Bill's interest rested with the liver, which interacts closely with his specialty, the kidneys. The engorged liver struggled to remove toxins from the blood, thereby forcing the kidneys to pick up some of the slack. Bill's concerns intrigued Krista, but I thought little of them. I expected a kidney transplant surgeon to fixate on the kidneys. "It's just like a guy with a hammer," I told Krista. "To him, every problem's a nail." Krista grasped the reasons for his concern and referenced their conversation often. Bill's prescience became evident in the months to come.

I received a text from Laurie early the following day while going through hospital bills at the house. She asked if Kaitlyn could visit Katie that morning, which happened to be Christmas Eve. Always enjoying company in the PICU, I typed, "Sure, I'll be there at 8:00. Any time after that." My thumb paused over the "send" button, and I reconsidered.

Katie was blessed with many loving supporters and caregivers, but she lived in a world populated entirely by adults. Although Kaitlyn was a gifted college student following her father into medicine, she had yet to shed the optimism and innocence of adolescence. I wanted Katie to experience that, to relate to someone as a peer.

I deleted my message draft, instead texting Kaitlyn that she could visit at any time and to text me when she left. I refrained from going to the hospital until Kaitlyn departed, giving Katie and Kaitlyn some girl time. After calling the nurse for a status check and informing her of Katie's impending visitor, I smiled at the thought of the girls spending the morning together.

When I recall her life, one of the many things for which I am thankful is that Katie had a friend.

CHAPTER 18

A Merry Little Christmas

My family has celebrated Wigilia (pronounced "va-LEE-a"), the traditional Polish Christmas Eve supper, for as long as anyone can remember. My grandmother grew up with the tradition, so a century would be a conservative estimate. I had never missed Wigilia in almost four decades despite nine years of active duty military service. I once flew into Washington D.C. on the morning of December 24, drove five hours to Connellsville, celebrated with family, and flew back to Cheyenne, Wyoming early Christmas Day. With Katie in the hospital, Connellsville might as well have been a million miles away. More than one chair sat empty that night. Too ill to leave the assisted living facility, my grandmother missed what would have been her ninety-seventh Wigilia.

Krista and I tried our best to recreate the tradition at our house in Indianapolis. Pat returned to Denver that morning to spend the holiday with her husband, but our friends Laura and KC joined us. Fish and pierogi comprise the centerpiece of the meal. I burned the fish, but the pierogi, which we ordered from a specialty store in Pittsburgh, were perfect. Side dishes included sauerkraut, sautéed onions, rice, white rolls, and cabbage. Our efforts proved successful. Admittedly, one needs creativity to ruin an intentionally bland meal. Knowing that we had no choice but to stay in Indianapolis made the separation from family tolerable.

The PICU patients, families, and staff enjoyed an uneventful Christmas. The census was low, and the few patients present were critically, but not acutely, ill.

The skeleton crew running the place certainly had the Christmas spirit. Gifts of food and candy from appreciative families filled the nurses' station. None of us wanted to be there, but we made the best of a bad situation. Besides, I read somewhere that a baby once spent Christmas in a stable. At least the PICU had plumbing. And it smelled better.

Katie enjoyed her first Christmas, particularly a giant balloon in the shape of a Christmas tree that Laura and KC gave her during an early morning visit. Friends left gifts for her at the reception desk, which the nurse arranged on a table at the foot of the crib. Santa even stopped by to say, "Hello." Given everything Katie experienced that year, she made the "nice" list by default. Krista dressed Katie in her own Santa costume. Her potbelly gave old St. Nick a run for his money.

Katie thrilled by decorations on Christmas.

We spent the day listening to Christmas music and watching Katie play with her new stuffed animals. The sporadic fevers took the holiday off. Aside from being in the hospital, the holiday was everything one could hope for a baby's first Christmas. We had enjoyed good days and weathered bad days in the past seven months, and we counted Christmas a merry one.

The pre-Christmas PICU exodus reversed as the last carol faded. Nasty germs waited until the city's kids celebrated the holiday before wreaking havoc. Kids suffering from respiratory illnesses flooded the unit. In a stunning reversal of fortune, Katie ranked as the healthiest patient in the PICU. That is akin to winning "Best Complexion" in a leper colony, but we took the wins when we got them. No longer the problem child, the charge nurse began assigning Katie floating nurses from other floors. Krista and I were not pleased to have unfamiliar personnel, but we accepted without complaint the harsh reality that other kids had greater need for the regular PICU staff. For the first time that anyone could recall, the unit reached its capacity on December 29, so the intensivist transferred Katie to the Pediatric (Peds) floor to make room for another kid. Thus, we planned to start the New Year in a new environment with new caregivers.

Although only one floor higher, the Peds floor differed considerably from the PICU. The Peds physicians did not conduct formal rounds, which bothered Krista and me. Katie's current stability mitigated the harm to some degree, but we still felt out of the loop. Moreover, each nurse cared for four patients, double that of their PICU peers. The Peds nurses, however, have the benefit of technicians (techs), identifiable by their red scrub pants, to share the load. Aside from rounds, the rooms were considerably smaller than those in the PICU and contained much less equipment. The size forced us to downsize the number of decorations and baubles. We considered Katie's new room, ideally situated directly across from the nurses' station, a significant improvement over the recent lackluster PICU room assignments.

The two women initially assigned to Katie's care eased our trepidation regarding our new surroundings. We knew Katie's admission nurse from the PICU, where she worked a couple days the previous week. Dawn, the tech assisting the nurse with Katie's admission, quickly became one of Katie's favorites. And then we met the physician.

A fit, young doctor appeared at the door as we unpacked. He extended an energetic hand, introduced himself, gave Katie a quick once-over, and took a seat on the couch. The doctor told us he reviewed Katie's chart but wanted to hear the medical background from the parents' perspectives. He did not have to ask twice. Krista gave him the unabridged version of Katie's life over the course of an hour. He followed the story intently, taking notes and asking questions. Ecstatic to have a physician who freely gave so much of his time, Krista asked the doctor when we would see him again. He said, "You won't. I only have 45 minutes left at St. Vincent. I'm transferring to a hospital in Virginia. This is my last shift." Just our luck.

I initially found the Peds staff somewhat standoffish, a rough first impression. Speaking in generalities, the nurses and techs possessed the hardened demeanor of people who routinely work with the general public. The buzzer doors at the entrance did not help. More times than not, a person obviously annoyed by the distraction grilled me regarding why I wanted to enter. Having worked with ballistic nuclear weapons, I have some experience with and appreciation for security. That said, whatever security the main doors provided, they did so at the cost of alienating families and guests.

Admittedly, the PICU spoiled us because we had, at times, the sickest kid and most complicated patient. That earns one a significant level of attention. On the Peds floor, Katie was initially just "Patient Number 7174," although that changed as she worked her magic. While we would grow very close to the staff during Katie's stay, we did not know that upon admittance. We also did not know that the happiest chapter in Katie's life was just beginning, in no small part due to those people.

Over the next two days, a score of doctors and nurse practitioners assessed Katie. Her vitals remained stable, and the rapid respirations persisted. Blood oxygen saturation levels fluctuated between the high sixties and low nineties. The physical and occupational therapists noted that Katie slightly favored her left side and worked to improve movement in her right arm. I feared this indicated some degree of cerebral palsy, but I often failed to see the fine line between legitimate concern and paranoia. Katie also preferred to keep her head turned to the left, a new development. Her skull showed signs of flattening as a result, so we tried to keep her head in a neutral position or facing to the right. She hated and fought manual manipulation, but became accustomed to positions that naturally kept her head from turning left. Katie fussed during some of her examinations and treatments, but she loved the attention and thrived with the new stimulation.

The respiratory therapists (RTs) gained new prominence in Katie's treatment on the Peds floor. A therapist administered Katie's 30+ minute breathing treatments at 9:00 a.m. and p.m. The treatment consisted of Katie inhaling medicated vapors through a mask on her face. None of the physicians and few nurses outside the NICU ever held Katie. Now, two therapists held Katie for extended periods daily. Some would watch television with her while others read books or just talked. She generally disliked the procedure, but enjoyed the time cuddling with RTs. The treatments fostered bonds between Katie and the RTs unlike those with any other caregiver.

Katie sporadically ran temperatures since entering the PICU in early December for unknown reasons. Her fever of 102 degrees late in the afternoon of New Year's Eve, therefore, did not surprise us. Katie's temperature began to fall after the nurse administered Tylenol, dipping to 98 degrees as daylight ebbed. Krista and I stayed with Katie until she fell asleep around 10 p.m.

Spirits high after overcoming yet another bump in the road, we ventured to a nearby steakhouse to celebrate the end of a trying year. Our relationship had thus far withstood the crushing stress of a sick child. Looking back on the many challenges we overcame, I felt proud of our success. Neither of us drank alcohol that night, so we toasted with iced tea and Dr. Pepper. "Here's to a better 2014," I said over the sound of clinking glasses.

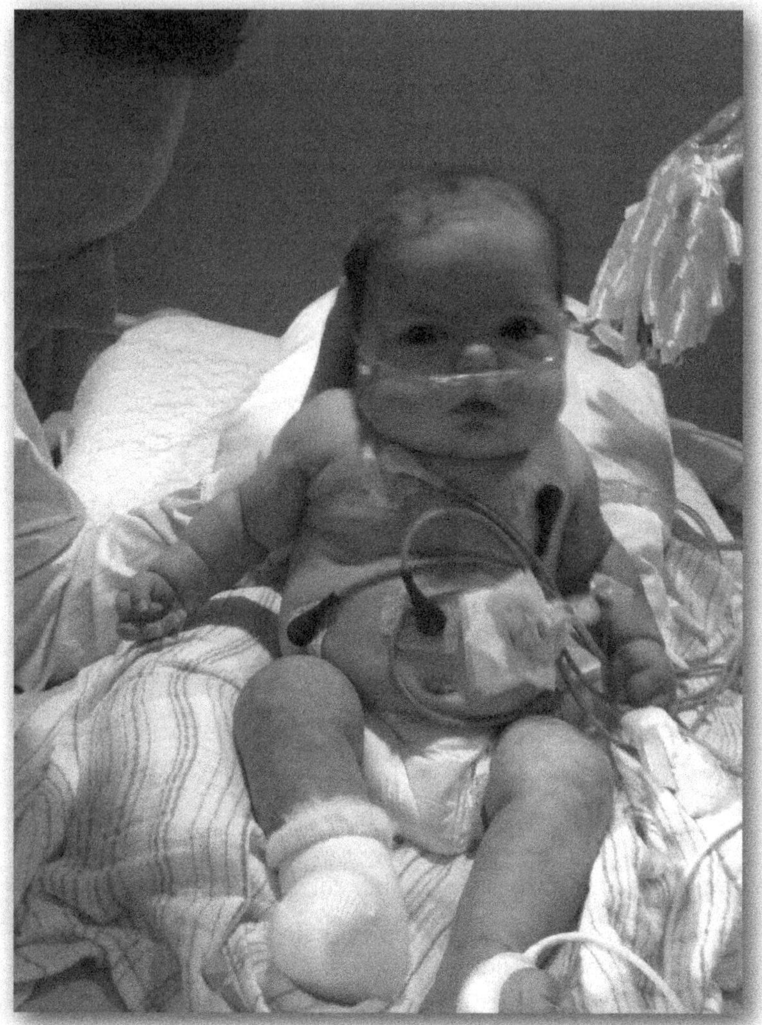

Katie on New Years Eve.

Midnight approached as we left the restaurant. The nurse informed me Katie was sleeping soundly when I called the hospital. Satisfied that Katie was getting some well-deserved rest, we returned to the house. Sleep came easy as we looked forward to a happy and healthy new year.

CHAPTER 19

Friends Old and New

KRISTA AND I BRIMMED WITH optimism as we entered the Peds department in the early hours of New Year's Day. We gave the staff in the nurses' station a bubbly greeting before entering Katie's room. Katie slept peacefully despite the glaring lights. Her nurse leaned against the counter with a pensive expression and told us Katie was running a fever of 103 degrees. No more than a few days passed without an escalated temperature over the past month, so the news neither surprised nor concerned me.

"Oh, okay," I said flatly.

The nurse replied with more than a touch of concern, "She doesn't have a line."

"Why?" Krista exclaimed. "What happened?"

The nurse knew only that someone had removed the IV on the overnight shift. After she excused herself to find the doctor, my focus turned to Katie. Krista, already at the crib, listed a litany of observations with an intensity only a mother could muster. She wasted her breath, as Katie's problems were self-evident. Her disconcertingly pale face contrasted sharply with her mottled arms and legs. Katie was not sleeping; she was nonresponsive.

The hospitalist arrived no more than a minute later and told us Katie had developed a low-grade fever in the early morning hours. The doctor working the overnight suspected an infected IV line. Unfamiliar with Katie's history, he removed it. This textbook response, appropriate for almost everyone, presented a significant risk to Katie, a notoriously difficult "stick." Establishing another access point would be critical if the fever persisted.

Not only did the fever persist, it escalated. Without an access port, Katie could not receive medications or fluid. Lacking our familiarity with Katie and not appreciating her distress, the staff felt no urgency in placing another line.

I immediately went downstairs to the PICU. Two of the unit's best nurses welcomed me at the nurses' station with New Year's greetings. With civility low on my priority list, I ignored the salutations and got straight to the point.

"Who's on today?"

"[Intensivist] Dr. Abraha," one replied as her expression immediately grew concerned.[7] "Why?"

"Is he around?"

"I think he's in the back. I'm not sure. What's wrong?"

"Katie popped a fever last night, and the doctor pulled her line. She's running a temp of 103 [degrees], and we have no access."

"We'll let him know."

With my message delivered, I headed for the door. I met another nurse outside the patient's elevator and repeated the previous conversation. She had not seen Dr. Abraha, either. Locked doors blocked access to the stairs, so I hit the "up" arrow spastically and waited for the doors to open.

I threw the Peds floor doors open once the tech buzzed the lock. I turned the corner to see Krista in the hall outside Katie's room.

"What's going on?" I asked.

"They're trying to get a line."

I looked over Krista's shoulder and immediately recognized the two PICU nurses with whom I had just spoken. They beat me upstairs to Katie's room. I sensed movement behind me and turned to see Dr. Abraha round the

---

7 Pronounced "uh-bra-hah," Dr. Abraha's name differs significantly in pronunciation from that of Dr. Abraham. The similarity in spelling caused confusion in many who read my updates.

corner in intense conversation with the Peds physician. The intensivist and nurses had taken it upon themselves to leave the PICU to check on Katie. Dr. Abraha stopped only long enough to tell us the lack of IV access gravely concerned him.

After the nurses failed to find a vein in two attempts, Dr. Abraha arranged for the on-call surgeon to surgically insert a line stat. The Peds physician, now fully on board with Dr. Abraha's plan, stayed with Katie while Dr. Abraha worked the phone. When the OR notified the unit the surgeon had arrived, Dr. Abraha, the Peds physician, and the PICU nurses personally pushed Katie in her crib to the main hospital's pre-op unit. The surgeon quickly rattled off a now familiar list of risks, and I signed the consent form without reading it.

Krista and I sat in a deserted waiting room for more than an hour before a nurse informed us the surgeon finished the operation. Another thirty minutes passed before he came to see us. He explained that the new line entered at the jugular vein and proceeded down into the right superior vena cava. He encountered no problems and thought Katie handled the procedure well. We saw Katie briefly in the recovery room and trailed the nursing staff as they escorted her to the PICU.

Dr. Abraha admitted Katie to the PICU for her post-op recovery and ordered fluids and a new regimen of medications. Not only was Katie back in the PICU, she returned to the very same room that we had vacated just three days earlier. Krista and I moved all of her possessions once again, placing her statuettes and box of treasured items on her bedside table and the "Smile" album in the window. We were getting far too much experience decorating hospital rooms.

Despite the New Year's Day drama, Katie fighting off whatever caused the fever without suffering acute respiratory distress pleased the intensivists and pulmonologists. They hoped this success indicated successful pulmonary hypertension treatment. In the short term, Krista and I planned to bring Katie home within the week.

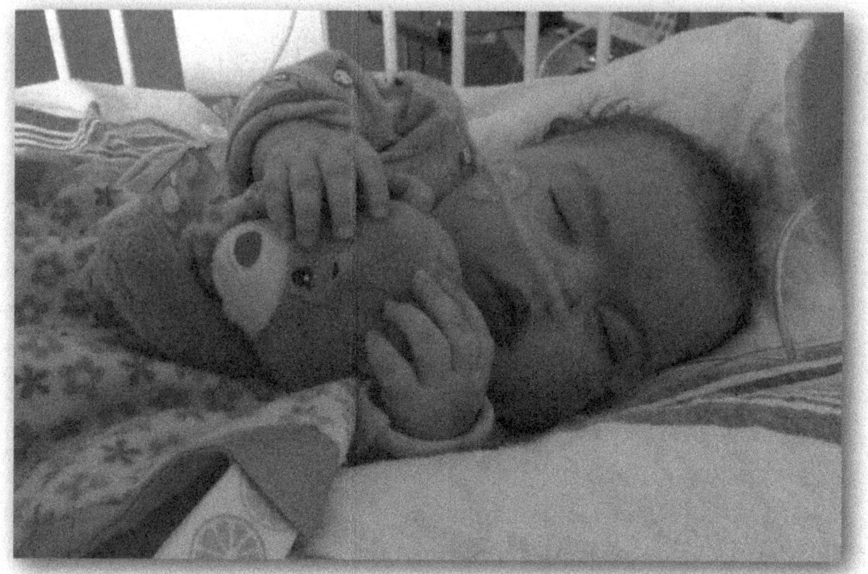

Katie resting after a long day of therapy.

Satisfied with Katie's recovery, the intensivist transferred Katie back to the Peds floor on January 4. Management placed Katie in Room 1, the unit's "Baltic Avenue." The room boasted the furthest distance to the nurses' station and shortest distance to an exit, a double whammy. Krista and I worried that the staff would not hear Katie crying from the nurses' station. Krista also worried that the proximity to the exit subjected Katie to a higher risk of kidnapping. This marked one of the few occasions we disagreed about Katie. Kidnapping did not make my list of concerns. Katie was connected to more alarms than the Crown Jewels, plus three torso leads, a neck IV, a pulse oximeter on her foot, and nasal oxygen. Fortunately, the issue was moot since the location in relation to the nurses' station alone warranted a move.

The nurse manager welcomed us back to the Peds floor while we once again unpacked and decorated Katie's room. She asked if we needed anything. Krista seized the opportunity and requested a room closer to the nurses' station. We transferred back to Room 4, the "Boardwalk" of the third floor, the following day and decorated yet again.

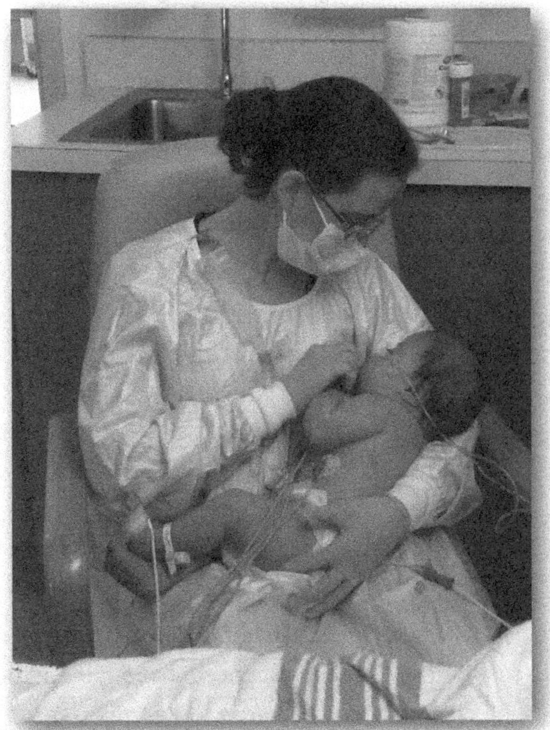

Katie and her mom.

The Beach Boys continued to provide the soundtrack to Katie's hospitalization. I added discs containing their first six studio albums to Katie's rotation in December. As days in the hospital turned to weeks which turned to months, those discs kept spinning. While still unknown to the staff on the Peds floor, I overheard two nurses walking out of Katie's room during changeover. One said, "If she starts fussing, turn on The Beach Boys. That calms her."

The Peds unit on the third story of PMCH primarily houses kids with cancer and cardiac ailments. I met many families battling cardiac issues in the PICU, but I never saw an oncology patient until Katie transferred upstairs. Knowing some children suffer with cancer is nothing like witnessing it firsthand.

An affable five year-old girl staying down the hall from Katie often made laps around the unit. She always stopped at Katie's door. I do not know whether regulations generally permitted patients to enter another patient's room; Katie's isolation measures prohibited such activity. The little girl nonetheless loved to "check on the baby," watching Katie from the hall. I presumed that she was a fellow cardiac kid. One day, I asked her dad about a tube peeking out from beneath her gown. He explained it was the port used for chemotherapy. She was days away from finishing treatment. On the day of her discharge, she gave Katie a beautiful flower bouquet that had decorated her room.

We lost touch with the family after her discharge. In the midst of hospital drama, I rarely thought to collect contact information before the patient and his family disappeared. HIPAA prevents the staff from relaying other patients' progress. Thus, friendships forged with other families in the hospital usually ended with unknown outcomes and everlasting hope.

We did witness the happy conclusion to one oncology patient's battle. Doctors diagnosed Maddy with a rare cancer at the tail end of her senior year of high school. The treatable cancer had a low remission rate if caught early enough. Maddy suffered through a long period of chemotherapy that robbed her of strength and hair. We often walked with Maddy and her mom to the cafeteria. Hearing her perspective on life and plans for the future revealed a maturity far beyond anything I had known in someone her age. She finished her treatment in February and returned home to attend nursing school, hoping someday to help other sick kids.

Krista and I were busy dressing Katie one day when the sound of a boisterous toddler in the hallway drew our attention. A mother pulling her three-year-old son in a cart stopped outside our door. The boy wanted to see his new neighbor. Krista introduced herself and walked into the hallway while my attention returned to Katie. I heard fragments of their conversation, enough to learn he was one of Dr. Abraham's patients. My mind wandered until a sentence snapped me to attention: "Eli had the Fontan last year." The Fontan, the third surgical procedure Katie required, completes the process of creating a one-ventricle heart. I had never met someone who completed all three operations. I joined Krista at the door. The boy before me looked perfectly healthy, a t-shirt hiding the surgical scar. Nothing indicated that he had a major heart defect. He looked normal, and I saw in him what I so wanted for Katie.

Eli suffered with a congenital heart defect known as hypoplastic left heart syndrome (HLHS). The structures comprising the left side of his heart failed to develop normally. The burden falls on the right side of the heart, designed to propel blood through the lungs, to pump blood through the entire body. Although Eli and Katie had different underlying conditions, they shared a similar surgical treatment course. Encouragingly, Eli thrived after all three operations.

Eli's latest ordeal began on Christmas when he awoke vomiting. Once he recovered, his parents noticed a slight limp. They hoped for a sprain, but an orthopedist could not find a cause. The cardiology team admitted Eli to PMCH on December 30 for observation. Tests revealed a staph infection of an unknown source. The infection did not respond to aggressive pharmaceutical intervention. The infectious disease physician hypothesized that germs had colonized a small tube connecting Eli's inferior vena cava and his pulmonary artery. The only remedy was to remove and replace the tube, which required Dr. Abraham to repeat the Fontan procedure. Adamant that the tube was not infected, the cardiologists argued against putting Eli under the knife once again. The infectious disease doctor and a cardiologist engaged in a loud and heated exchange over the matter outside Katie's door one afternoon.

Dr. Abraham ultimately removed the tube, which tests later confirmed as the source of infection. Arresting the infection came at great cost. Eli suffered serious complications, including seizures, weakness in his left arm and leg, and a stroke. He was still early in his recovery when we left the Peds floor weeks later, but Eli continued to fight and made a remarkable recovery.

Stories of inspiration were not limited to the patients. Erin, Katie's favorite physical therapist, put her little patients through their paces using a prosthetic hand. After a random accident, she lost her hand at the age of five. She turned tragedy into a calling, dedicating her professional life to helping sick kids. With three beautiful children, a loving husband, and countless kids who will enjoy increased physical abilities due to her care, she personified courage, determination, and faith.

The temperature plummeted into the single digits in the waning days of 2013. We measured accumulated snow, which had no opportunity to melt, by the foot. January 6 set the record as the coldest day in Indianapolis' recorded history. Krista and I spent more than an hour shoveling out the driveway upon which the friendly neighborhood plowman dumped an additional few feet of snow. Sam came out to help, but fell in the snow and refused to get up. When times got tough, Sam laid down and played dead. After finally getting the SUV onto the road, I carried my canine popsicle into the house. Sam was not our only dependent that the weather affected.

Krista and I feared that inclement weather could delay, if not prevent, us from getting the seven-month-old Katie to the hospital in an emergency. The snow fell so heavily at times that the driveway required more than an hour of shoveling, one reason we felt no rush to bring Katie home. Weather concerns notwithstanding, I scoffed at Krista's suggestion that we replace my thirteen year-old Rav4 with a more reliable vehicle.

The rancid smell of an overheated engine polluted the crisp evening air outside the main terminal at the Indianapolis airport on Thursday, January 9. As I waited for my Aunt Elaine, who had just flown from Syracuse to spend two weeks with Katie, the engine began smoking. I turned off the ignition when I saw the temperature indicator spiked as far as it would go. The smell overwhelmed me when I opened the door. I am still amazed that the car overheated in sub-zero weather. We lumbered one exit north before pulling over at a restaurant where Krista rescued us an hour later. An inch of snow had already blanketed my car except for the sizzling hood.

The mechanic called the next day with the dim diagnosis. The estimated repair cost matched the car's optimistic replacement value. But for Katie, I might have kept the old girl going a few more years. Krista was right; we needed reliable transportation and bought a new vehicle that Saturday.

I sat on the edge of our bed after returning from the car dealership, nauseated by the thought of the money we just spent. We did no research whatsoever, uncharacteristic for both of us. With bigger concerns at play, we did not have the time or inclination to shop around. My mind swirled contemplating the recently incurred debt nonetheless when Krista entered the room and interrupted my thoughts:

"I'm pregnant."

CHAPTER 20

Ticket to Ride

PMCH AND THE AVERAGE JUNIOR high school differ in one significant respect: gossip spreads much, much slower at a junior high. A respiratory therapist arrived to administer a breathing treatment the day after Krista's revelation. No longer alone with Katie, I struck up a conversation. I must have looked beaten down given her subsequent line of questioning.

"How are you guys holding up?"

"Okay, I guess. You know, a lot going on."

"I can imagine."

"It's frustrating. We don't know why [Katie] keeps having fevers. We don't know when the next cath will be. And I don't know what we're going to do when Katie goes home, and I go back to Rock Island. Krista's expecting, so she can't give the [pulmonary hypertension medication] Bosentan. The visiting nurses aren't there in the evening, and we have no one to give it. I don't know what we're going to do about that."

"Krista's pregnant?"

"Yeah," I said dismissively. "But it's really early. I don't know how we're going manage the Bosentan."

My point was that I would not be available during the week to administer Katie's pulmonary hypertension medication. The drug may cause birth defects if handled by pregnant women, so Krista could not do it. Not a single person in the hospital ever broached the Bosentan issue thereafter. I could not say the same for the pregnancy.

Not an hour later, Dr. Kumar interrupted me as I updated three nurses on Katie's status at the PICU nurses' station. "So I hear congratulations are in order," he said in front of the nurses. Initially too surprised to respond, I turned to the women to tell them the news, but one spoke first. "We're really happy for both of you." Her eyes flittered to her coworkers sitting behind the desk as they nodded in agreement.

How word traveled from the therapist to the nursing and cardiology staff so quickly remains a mystery. Krista was nonplussed that I let the word out. And out it was. Word reached the physician, nursing, therapy, cleaning, and chaplain staff before sunset.

The gossip network apparently did not include Dr. Abraham. A month after the announcement heard around the hospital, the surgeon stopped by Katie's room after checking on another patient. He stood next to me in the doorway and casually asked Krista, "How is everything going?"

"Aside from a little morning sickness, I'm doing okay," she replied.

An expression of shock supplanted Dr. Abraham's characteristically stoic demeanor. Stupefied, he asked, "You're pregnant?"

"Yes," Krista answered. "It's very early."

His gaze darted from Krista to me. I could read the unstated thought in his expression: "In the midst of all this, you are having another baby? Are you crazy?" I managed a cross between a grimace and a smile and nodded in affirmation.

Dr. Steinberg and two pediatric hospitalists discussed discharging Katie on the morning of January 9. Krista and I were in no rush to take the seven-month-old home, and the news put me on edge. Our focus was getting Katie in the best possible health for the cardiac cath tentatively scheduled for

February 5. The staff, particularly the cardiologists, had the expertise and resources to identify and address changes in her condition, an ability Krista and I simply could not match. Not only could we not adequately respond to a critical emergency, weather could delay getting Katie the help she needed. Despite the risk of catching a hospital bug, Krista and I strongly believed Katie was safer at PMCH.

My protestations fell on deaf ears. Katie's temperature had remained stable for a week, so the doctors could not justify her continued hospitalization. I left the three physicians to discuss timing and aftercare to check on my daughter. I turned on the light and said, "Good morning, Hunny Bunny." A lethargic Katie looked at me and managed a weak smile. I popped my head out into the hall and asked Katie's nurse for the last temperature reading. After a quick glance at the chart, she responded, "98.1 [degrees]." Puzzled, I returned to Katie's crib and gave her another once-over.

With mottled extremities and a pale face, Katie did not appear healthy. I took the thermometer from the wall, slipped a plastic sleeve over the probe, and placed it under Katie's arm. The device beeped when finished and displayed a large "98.1" on a dull green screen. On a hunch, I replaced the plastic sleeve, reset the device for an oral reading, and placed the probe under Katie's tongue. She normally fought the thermometer, but lacked the energy today. The thermometer beeped and displayed "102.5." I repeated the process and received the same result. I carried the thermometer to the ongoing physician huddle in the hall.

The doctors were operating under the false impression that a week passed without a fever. A little investigation revealed that the staff had been taking Katie's temperature under her arm. Katie's extremities were cooler than her trunk because of her less than optimal circulation, making axillary temperatures unreliable. The two contemporaneous measurements differing so significantly destroyed any reliability in the earlier readings. Lacking a temperature record confirming the absence of fevers, the doctors reluctantly postponed discharge. Dr. Steinberg failed to hide his disappointment. The cardiologist obviously wanted Katie to go home with her family, a sentiment Krista and I appreciated. However, believing Katie remaining at PMCH improved her chance of qualifying for the next operation, we were pleased when he cancelled the discharge.

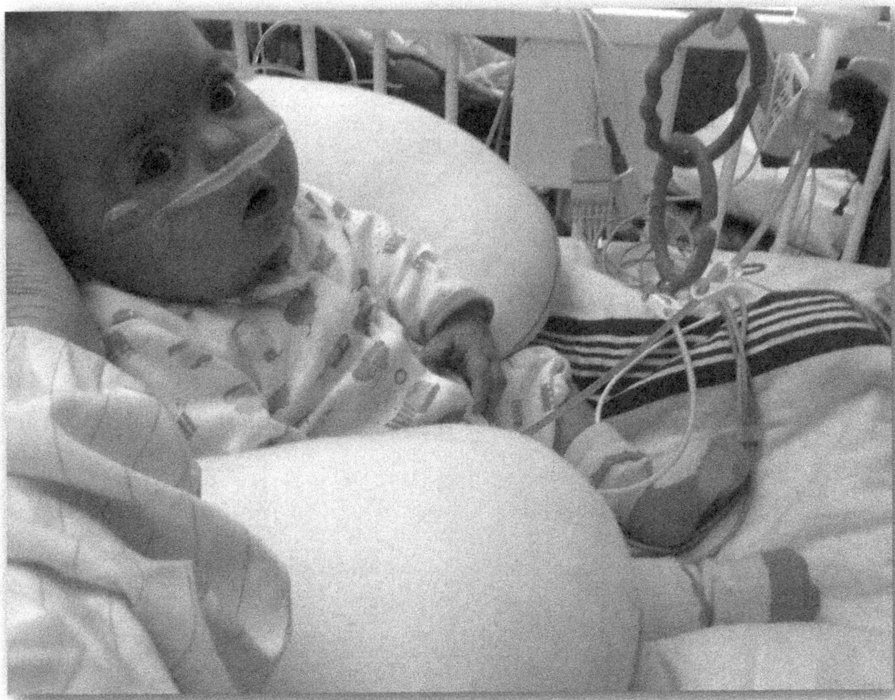

Katie relaxing between therapy sessions.

Dr. Steinberg was not the only party who wanted Katie out of the hospital. Soon after the thermometer incident, our insurance provider refused to cover additional hospitalization. Dr. Steinberg called the company's medical advisor and explained Katie's condition, including two additional fevers since the nurses started taking oral temperatures. The insurer reversed its position in less than a few minutes. This incident constituted the first and only time that our health insurance carriers refused or questioned any charges.

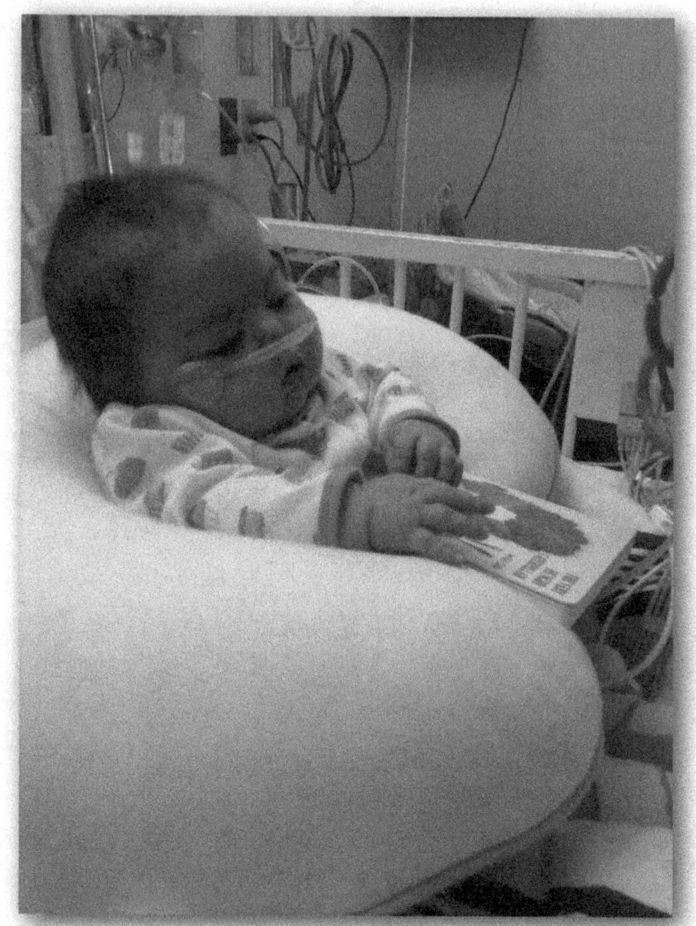

Katie reading in her room on the Peds floor.

A hospitalization does not relieve parents of their responsibility to care for a sick child. Katie grew increasingly cranky one afternoon, prompting me to inspect her medical equipment. In the three months since the G-J placement, I became quite familiar with Katie's feeding tube configuration. The MIC-KEY consists of two tubes, one line delivering formula directly into her intestines and the other allowing her stomach to vent, i.e., burp. I discovered a nurse had transposed Katie's tubes. For at least seven hours, the formula drained into Katie's stomach instead of the small intestines. The MIC-KEY balloon and G-J tube blocked the formula from passing into the intestine.

Krista caught the same error a few days later. While the mistakes did not put Katie at significant risk, they increased our vigilance. I hoped the staff was a little more discerning with the oral and rectal thermometers.

Katie made significant gains developmentally on the Peds floor. She initially received occupational and physical therapy three times weekly; however, her progress prompted the physician to order daily therapy similar to Katie's NICU and PICU treatment:

- Physical therapists focused on improving Katie's range of motion, especially in her neck and shoulders, increasing her tolerance for handling and touch, and rebuilding lost strength.
- Occupational therapists worked on restoring Katie's fine and gross motor skills to an age-appropriate level, introducing cognitive and sensory experiences, and standing.

Both disciplines tried to loosen Katie's neck muscles. She had developed a habit of turning her head to her left, perhaps because of previous IV lines in the right side of her neck. This left Katie prone to plagiocephaly, a flattening of her back and the side of her head from lack of movement.

Therapy aided Katie's emotional and mental well-being in addition to her physical health. The therapists stimulated her mind and forced Katie to push the boundaries of her physical capabilities. Despite occasional stubbornness, she accomplished feats, such as standing with assistance, beyond imagination just weeks earlier.

A friend from the Guard and her fiancé visited Katie on Saturday, January 19. Katie surprised her guests from Chicago by her high spirits and playfulness. They told me Katie was much happier and living a "more normal" existence than expected.

Katie and her favorite stuffed animal.

I tried as best I could in the score of e-mail updates to capture Katie's situation. Gavin and Maria's reactions indicated my efforts were, at best, partially successful. Changes in Katie's medical condition, usually for the worse, prompted me to send updates. Katie enjoying an uneventful week at home made for thin gruel in an e-mail. I made a mental note to emphasize positive aspects of Katie's life in subsequent messages.

Why a baby selects one toy amongst many as her favorite is a mystery. Maria and Gavin gave Katie a stuffed animal before leaving. The dog entranced Katie as soon as Maria placed it in the crib. She immediately grabbed it and caressed its soft fur. The light brown pooch had a dark brown front torso, floppy ears, and nose. A field of pink adulterated with scattered brown and pink dots decorated the underside of its soft ears. The dog's tilted head sported a large smile with two round patches at either end of its mouth, one pink and the other red. The bottom of the paws also alternated red and pink. The dog's left eye peered out from a dark red heart patch. Maybe the animal's anthropomorphic expression resonated with Katie. Whatever the reason, Katie loved that canine, and it never left her side.

On February 1, two days shy of her eigth-month birthday, Katie reached the milestone of spending two straight months at Peyton Manning Children's Hospital. The following day, the Seattle Seahawks crushed Manning's Denver Broncos in the Super Bowl, 43-8. The Broncos gave up a safety on the first play, which set the tone for the remainder of the game. The Child Life Department hosted a party in the Peds floor Family Room to watch the event. Katie could not attend because of the isolation precautions, but Krista and I stopped by briefly to socialize and grab some food before retreating to Katie's room.

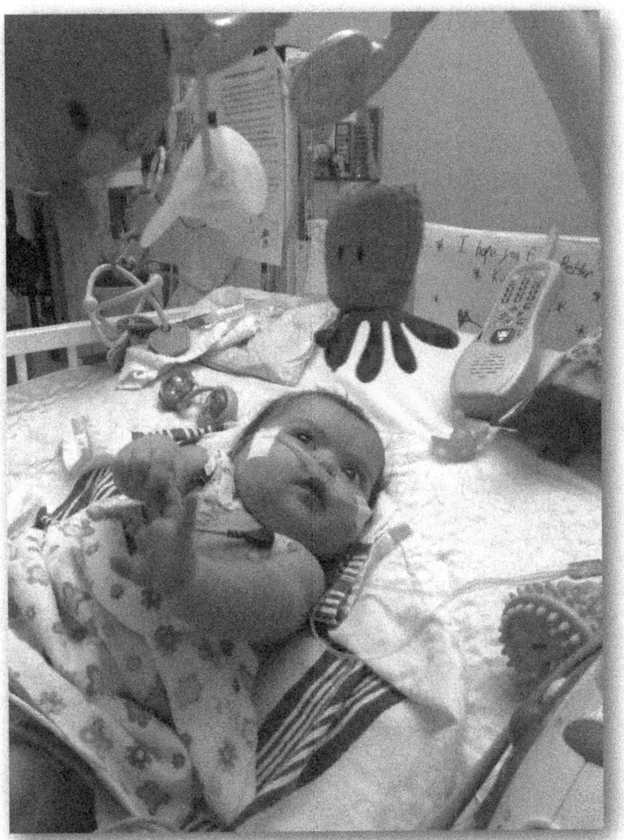

Katie watching her mobile.

What started as an acute infection in early December had turned into a prolonged series of sporadic fevers interrupting periods of surprising normalcy.

The number of nurses assigned to Katie narrowed to a small cadre of women who loved and knew her well. All of us celebrated Katie's first tooth appearing two days after the big game. Meanwhile, Katie's aggressive pulmonary hypertension treatment continued.

Dr. Kumar scheduled the cardiac catheterization for February 5. Katie developed a fever in the early morning of the big day, so Dr. Kumar cancelled the procedure. The cardiologist planned to leave town for an extended vacation exactly a week later, so we kept our fingers crossed that Katie would have another opportunity before his departure. The stars aligned two days later. A five year-old girl hospitalized for chemotherapy treatment brought Katie roses before the test. Someone had given them to her a day prior, but she told her parents that she wanted Katie to have them for good luck.

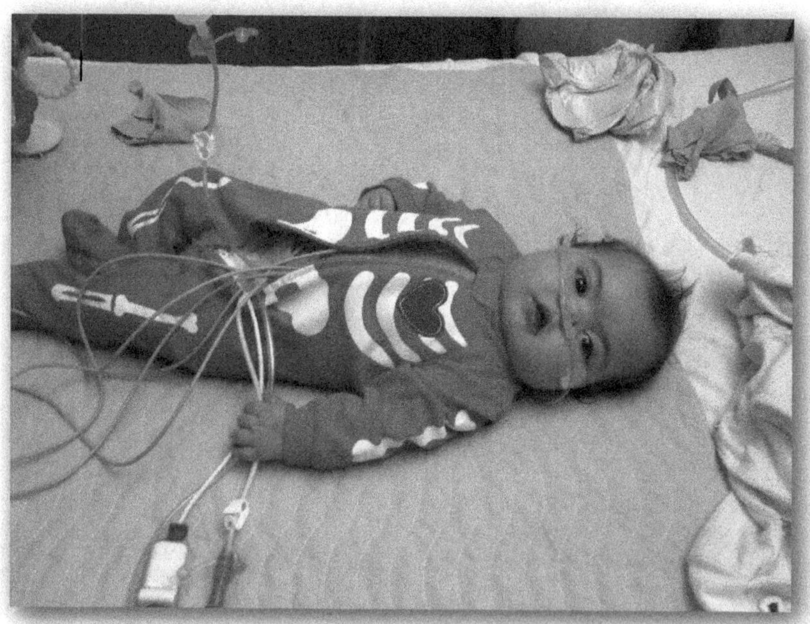

Katie reminding her doctors where her heart is the day before her February catheterization.

The transport team invited Krista to sit on the gurney and placed Katie in her lap. I escorted them to the cath lab in the main hospital. Trapped in her room for more than a month, the new sights and sounds mesmerized Katie. She had the expression of a kid in a toy store. When we arrived, a surgical nurse took Katie from Krista while another nurse directed us to a small waiting room dedicated to the cath lab. We had waited through many procedures before, but this was particularly excruciating. I could not shake the vivid memory of the kid who died from complications during a cath a few months earlier. More than an hour passed before a nurse informed us Dr. Kumar had finished the procedure and would meet us in the PICU Family Room with the results. Katie sailed through with no complications. With Katie now out of the woods, our focus turned to the test results.

Dr. Kumar entered the Family Room with a neutral affect. After joining us at the table, he told us Katie tolerated the procedure well and revealed the test results. Katie's pressure decreased from 27 to 16 mmHg, a reduction of forty percent. Although pleased with the pressure drop, Dr. Kumar remained concerned.

The pressure inside Katie's lungs had to be less than that of her cardiovascular system for the new heart configuration to work. This "negative pressure" would draw the deoxygenated blood into the lungs. If the pressure were too high, blood would pool in the veins, deprive organs of needed oxygen, and force the heart to work harder. He and Dr. Abraham told us repeatedly that the highest acceptable pressure for the Glenn procedure was 15 mmHg. Lacking a good alternative, Dr. Kumar recommended proceeding with surgery the following week nevertheless. In contrast to Dr. Kumar's stoicism, Krista and I were elated at Katie's eligibility for surgery, which I christened her "ticket to ride." The surgery at least afforded Katie the opportunity to fight the next battle.

I ran into Dr. Abraham in the hall on the third floor later that day. Still ecstatic from the conversation with Dr. Kumar, I asked him if he heard the results. He replied in the affirmative with a somber voice that made Dr. Kumar sound like a carnival barker by comparison. The response surprised me, and I dismissed it as the doctor having a bad day. I was wrong.

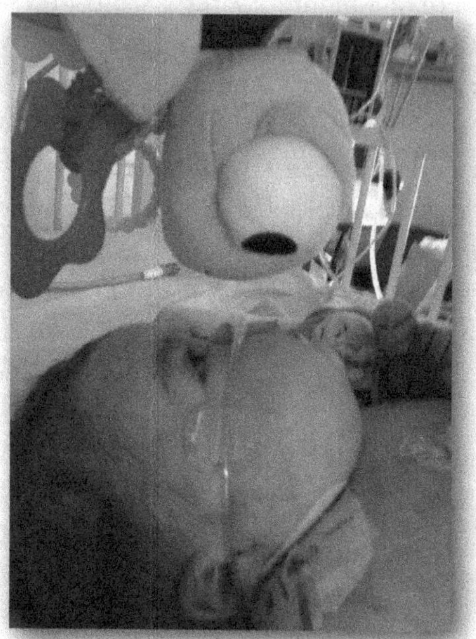

Katie losing a staring contest.

Like the captain of the *Hesperus*, I failed to heed warnings from the experienced men around me. Katie's pulmonary hypertension had indeed improved, but even with an aggressive regimen of drugs, oxygen, and breathing treatments, the pressure failed to reach the highest acceptable pressure limit. Katie had no margin for error. Even the slightest pressure increase could prove fatal.

Dr. Abraham scheduled Katie's surgery for February 12.

CHAPTER 21

Calamity

I CREPT INTO KATIE'S ROOM just past 5 a.m. on the day of her surgery. Playing with a stuffed turtle and zebra suspended above her, a huge smile crossed her face upon realizing she had visitors. Krista turned on the lights, and Katie's eyes darted to the door where her mom and aunt stood. Krista's sister, Amy, flew in from Denver for the surgery. She smiled broadly upon seeing them. The surgery transfer team ran an hour behind schedule, giving us more time with Katie and allowing the oncoming dayshift staff to visit. Two of Katie's favorite aids along with numerous nurses and physicians stopped in to wish Katie well.

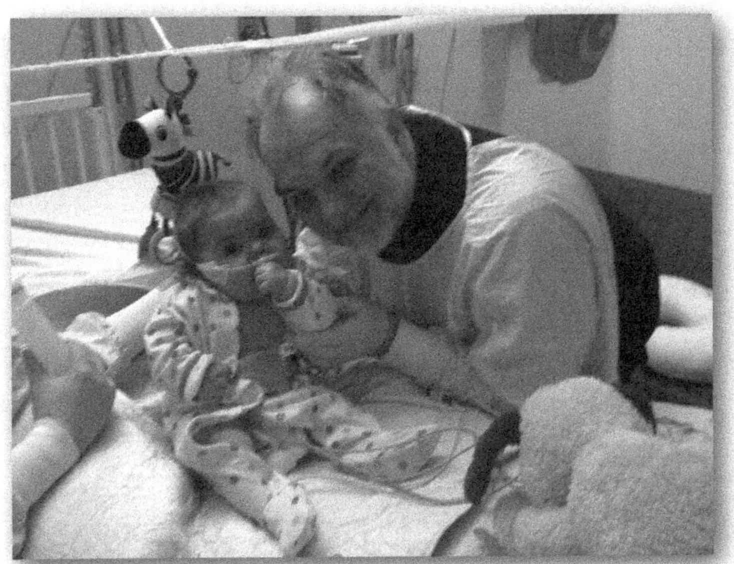

Fr. Jim visiting Katie the day before the scheduled Glenn surgery.

My excitement for Katie overshadowed any feelings of sadness associated with leaving the unit. In mere hours, she would be a step closer to finishing her surgical treatment. Breathing closer to, if not at, a normal rate would prevent common respiratory illnesses from necessitating hospitalization. I spent countless hours imagining all the experiences we would share. First, however, Katie had to overcome this hurdle.

When the transport team arrived, Katie's night nurse sat on the full-size gurney. Another nurse disconnected Katie from the monitor, lifted her from the crib, and placed her in the coworker's lap. Katie wore a tiny floral gown. After a few pictures and another round of kisses, the team wheeled Katie and the nurse to the OR. Katie once again gazed at her surroundings in wonder as she passed through the hall. The room felt cavernous without her.

Breakfast was our next priority. Krista recommended that we first stop by the PICU to see Katie's room assignment and possibly request a change. After three cumulative months in the unit, we certainly had room preferences. I thought it a great idea, so we took the elevator one flight down to the second floor.

I outpaced Krista and Amy after the receptionist buzzed the double PICU doors, turned left at the end of the main hall, and passed through the second set of double doors into the PICU proper. I strategically stopped at the southeast corner of the nurses' station. From this vantage point, I could look down two of the three halls with rooms 6-8 and 9-15. That the rooms closest to the nurses' station, 6-10, were occupied slightly disappointed me. Krista, waving her hand emphatically from the window between the nurses' station and the main hallway, caught my attention. Thinking she was futilely still trying to work a good room assignment, I motioned I would be over after I said "hello" to a nurse. Krista persisted, so I walked back into the main hall. Krista and Amy were visibly upset.

"What's wrong?" I asked.

"Amy can't come in," Krista replied.

"Come in where?"

"In the PICU. They won't let her in the PICU."

I looked at the receptionist who explained further: "Only parents and grandparents are allowed. That's the visitation policy."

Perplexed, I countered, "That isn't what the sign says. 'No visitors under the age of eighteen.' That's what the sign says."

"No, only parents and grandparents."

"But that isn't what the sign says."

"The policy is only parents and grandparents."

A wise senior enlisted man once told me never to take "no" as an answer from someone lacking the authority to say, "yes," so I asked for the nurse manager. We knew her quite well from Katie's prior hospitalizations. In another bad break, she had just started maternity leave. I asked to speak with whomever replaced her. The receptionist left us alone in the hallway while she sought the manager. Krista, already on edge, wasted no time voicing her protestations. With no doubt this problem would easily resolve, I thought Krista was overreacting and told her not to worry. Not a minute later, the double doors opened and the receptionist reappeared with an unfamiliar middle-aged woman clad in scrubs.

"I'm sorry, but only parents and grandparents are allowed in the PICU due to the flu season," she said with her head cocked slightly to her side and hands clutched at her midsection.

"But that isn't the policy," I retorted.

"I'm sorry."

"Wait, wait, wait … That isn't the policy. The policy is posted all over the hospital – 'no one under eighteen,'" I paraphrased. "We flew Amy in from Denver for this surgery, and now you're saying she can't see her niece, who is having heart surgery?"

"That's the policy," she said as though telling a customer at Burger King that they do not serve Big Macs.

> Trying to reason with her, I continued, "We have no family here … nobody. The closest grandparent is two states away. No one else is coming, just Amy. She's it, she's all we have."

After another half-hearted apology, Krista pled her case to no avail. I listened to the repartee without comment. This woman made no effort to console a scared mother or even ask about our daughter, who spent more than three months in her unit. Nothing. My initial indifference over the underlying issue gave way to contempt.

Recognizing the futility of further appeals, I suggested to Krista that we let it go for now and get something to eat. She agreed. The three of us left the PICU quite agitated. After the main PICU doors closed behind us, I stopped to read the sign and shook my head: "No visitors under the age of eighteen permitted."

We sat in a booth in the basement cafeteria and pondered our predicament. I could do nothing at that point for Katie, but I could try to resolve the visitation issue for Krista. We needed a patient advocate, a hospital employee whose responsibilities include handling patient complaints and questions regarding treatment or health care providers. Unfortunately, I did not know such a position existed until long after our tenure at PMCH ended, and Krista and Amy did not think to mention it. My only contact outside the PICU was Risk Management. Not knowing any other option, I devoured some eggs and walked over to the administration building.

The Risk Management receptionist greeted me pleasantly. When I told her I wanted to speak to someone regarding the PMCH visitation policy, she sternly informed me that the facility permitted no visitors under the age of eighteen, period. I told her my concern did not involve minors. After taking my information, she told me someone would meet us in the OR waiting room and wished Katie well.

I did not know Risk Management offices in large hospitals often fall within the legal department. "Risk management" sounds so benign. After all, who does not want to mitigate risk? I merely raised an issue, or so I thought. My innocuous concern prompted a reaction similar to that of a root canal minus the Novocain.

I found Krista and Amy in the surgical waiting room just as two women approached us. I recognized the woman trailing the first as the acting PICU nurse manager. The person leading the duo, a petite woman in her fifties with sharp features, extended her hand for what would be a curt handshake. She introduced herself through gritted teeth by name and title, but I caught neither. I did note, however, that she had some upper management position at PMCH. She presented an unmistakable aura of hostility, which initially rattled me. Not knowing her name, I gave her the moniker of "Nurse Ratched," a character from Ken Kesey's novel, "One Flew Over the Cuckoo's Nest." I am not sure the woman was a nurse, but the name fit regardless. I admit the term may be a bit strong given the situation, but temperance is for better men than I am. A hospital employee approaching parents of an infant undergoing open-heart surgery with such disdain appalled me. I knew within seconds that this interaction would be both futile and unpleasant.

"Do you want to talk about this here or in a meeting room?" Ratched asked Krista.

I interjected before Krista could respond. "No, let's do this here." Ratched entered this discussion in a dominant position, i.e., she had the authority to grant our request. I was not about to cede the additional advantage of location.

Ratched condescendingly lectured us on the importance of the visitation policy, which we conceded, before she and I went back and forth on the policy's logical faults and the inconsistent application thereof. With me dressed in jeans and a PMCH t-shirt, she probably did not anticipate an attorney questioning her. She proved a hostile witness.

"For the safety of all the children, we limit visitors to grandparents only."

"That isn't what the sign says."

"I just told you the policy."

"Which isn't what the sign says. Where is it?"

"Where is what?"

"The policy. Where is it written down? Where can I, as a parent, see the policy so I know the rules." She did not have an answer. I pressed on.

"Why isn't that the policy for the entire hospital?"

"It is."

"Amy spent more than an hour with Katie on the third floor this morning before surgery. No one said anything."

"Well, that was wrong."

"The nurses didn't object. The doctors didn't object."

"They must not know the policy."

"If the staff doesn't know the policy, how are we supposed to know it? We flew Amy in from Denver knowing that the only prohibited visitors were those under eighteen."

Thinking she found an exit from my line of questioning, Ratched pounced. With exaggerated shock, Ratched said she would not allow Amy admission because planes are germ incubators. No one could argue that planes are anything but petri dishes with wings, but I did not relent.

"Is that in the policy?"

"What?"

"That people who've recently flown can't visit?"

"No."

"What if a grandparent had recently flown? Would you let a grandparent in?"

"Yes."

"Why is it less dangerous for a grandparent to fly than an aunt?"

She stumbled for a plausible response. Having made my point, I fell silent as Krista and Amy took over using a more conversational approach. The hostility Ratched directed at Krista stupefied me.

The meeting ended when Sarah appeared and asked to speak with the family. Ratched did not relent on the visitation issue. I never saw her again, for which both of us are probably thankful. While we did not achieve our objective, I found some solace in knowing we stood our ground.

Sarah ushered the three of us into a small conference room adjacent to the surgical waiting room. Sarah paused for a long moment after we took our seats: "There's been a change of plans. There won't be a surgery today." I initially thought another patient required Dr. Abraham's attention, thereby pushing Katie off the schedule. Sarah's face, however, hinted otherwise. She continued, "As Dr. Abraham prepared to make his first incision, Katie de-sated," meaning her oxygenation level fell, "and he cancelled the surgery." Krista asked why it fell. Sarah shook her head side to side and pursed her lips together tightly before admitting apologetically, "We're not sure." She gave us some words of encouragement before escorting us to the PICU Family Room where Dr. Abraham would meet us.

While en route, Sarah told us that Ratched was allowing Amy to join us in the Family Room. I do not know whether Sarah knew the backstory to that comment, but I shook my head in disgust. Exterior to the unit's entry control point, nothing prevents someone from accessing the Family Room. The phrase "thanks for nothing" literally applied. Ratched could not resist a parting shot, which turned my simmering anger into a white-hot rage. I did not respond as bigger concerns took precedence.

We waited for Dr. Abraham for forty-five minutes. I paced. I sat. I paced some more. Disappointment, fear, and apprehension colluded to put us in mental stasis. None of us knew what to say. The doctor, in his white coat and carrying a cup of coffee, entered and joined us at the table without greeting. He wasted no time getting to his point: "Well, as you know, things didn't go as planned."

As Dr. Abraham lowered the scalpel to Katie's sternum for the first incision, Katie's oxygenation had plummeted from the mid-80s into the 40s. The surgical team immediately administered 100 percent oxygen and nitrous oxide. Katie's oxygenation climbed back to the 60s. Dr. Abraham determined Katie was clinically unstable; therefore, he cancelled the procedure and returned Katie to the PICU where she remained sedated and intubated. After a painfully long pause, he said, "I just don't know what happened. I've never seen anything like this."

Katie now required far more breathing assistance than anyone expected. She had been breathing on her own for seven months. Just a few hours after leaving the Peds floor, she needed significant respiratory support. It did not make sense. Dr. Abraham speculated that Katie experienced a sudden pulmonary hypertensive event. The pressure in her lungs skyrocketed, which decreased blood flow to the lungs and subsequently prevented blood from replenishing its oxygen supply. When asked for the cause, the surgeon did not know. Dr. Abraham alluded to trying the surgery again in a couple of days, but, for now, we needed to stabilize Katie. After apologizing for his inability to give us a more definitive answer, Dr. Abraham left us to check on our daughter.

We rehashed our conversation with Dr. Abraham until a nurse informed us that we could see Katie. By "us," I mean Krista and me. Leaving Amy alone in the Family Room, we walked alongside the nurse to the outer PICU doors. I asked for Katie's room number. The nurse replied, "She's in Room 2," one of the ECMO rooms. She should have just punched me in the stomach. Although Katie did not currently require a heart-lung bypass machine, they wanted to be prepared should she take a turn for the worse.

Wearing only a diaper, Katie lay unconscious in her crib. The blue marker guideline for Dr. Abraham's incision glared against her otherwise pale chest. In sharp contrast to the smiling baby on the nurse's lap just hours earlier, Katie looked fragile, so very fragile. Krista and I stood on either side of the crib. Krista caressed Katie's cheek while I snaked my fingers through the wires and tubes to hold Katie's hand.

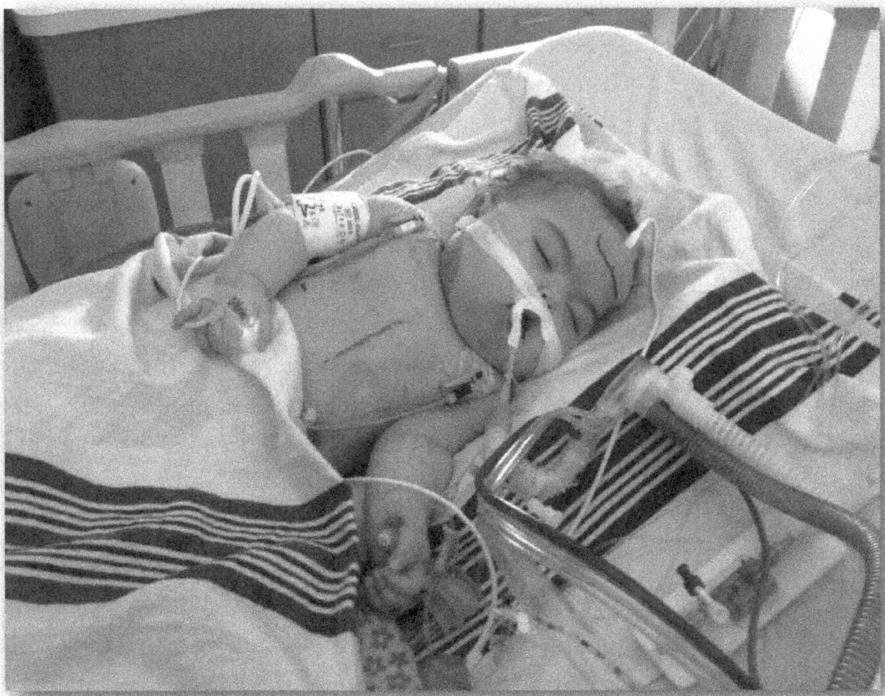

Katie after the aborted surgery on February 12. Note the guideline for the surgeon remaining on her chest.

In mid-afternoon, Krista left me with Katie and the nurse to visit Amy in the Family Room. I sat at the end of the couch in silence, trying to process the day's events and giving the nurse space to work. We experienced many unforeseen obstacles over the prior eight months, but nothing this devastating. The aborted surgery put our entire surgical plan in question. We waited, prayed, and hoped for this day, only to meet absolute failure.

Dr. Bob stopped by to check on Katie. Evidently satisfied, he sat at the opposite side of the couch and asked how I was "holding up." Still seething from our meeting with Nurse Ratched and the amorphous visitation policy, I laid into Dr. Bob over the visitation policy and the staff's treatment of Krista.

He responded diplomatically if not convincingly. Like a boxer who went two rounds too many, I had no fight left in me and let it go for the time being. Conversation turned to family and, of all things, caring for patients following a Glenn procedure.

We talked for the better part of an hour with only passing allusions to the day's events. Dr. Bob remained positive and reassuring, as though talking me off a ledge. I suppose that was his intent. He probably sensed the depths of our disappointment and engaged in conversation to keep me from stewing in frustrated despair. His attempt to distract me worked even though I saw through the ruse, and I welcomed the hour of mental respite. That he took the time with a parent in such circumstances evidenced that he was not only a good doctor, but also a good man.

I watched Katie's nurse, Heather, ply her trade as Dr. Bob and I bantered. She completed the tasks associated with Katie's transfer from the OR to the PICU with military precision. She rotated from crib to counter to computer repeatedly while securing lines, administering meds, and checking monitors. I found her absolute concentration reassuring.

I returned to the crib after Dr. Bob departed. As Heather caught up on charting, I inspected her handiwork. When I last saw Katie, she was lying on disheveled linens under a chaotic jumble of wires, tubes, and cords. Katie's crib was now in perfect order. Any nurse who took such great pains to ensure the little things were correct would catch any big issue. Trusting Heather with Katie's care, I stopped worrying about immediate emergencies for the first time since Sarah delivered the terrible news this morning and turned my attention to the question of where we go from here.

After holding Katie's hand for a while, I joined Krista and Amy in the Family Room. I had barely sat down before Dr. Kumar entered. I invited him to join us at the table. He took a step forward before reconsidering. "Why don't we move to the Conference Room?" I had no illusions he would give good news, but his request to relocate struck me hard. Save the cardiologist and the three of us, the room was empty. No doctor has ever delivered anything but bad news after relocating to "where we can speak more privately."

The cardiologist did not break with precedent. The operating theory was that Katie had a "pulmonary hypertensive event," meaning the pressure in the lungs' blood vessels skyrocketed. No one knew why. Such an event would cause almost certain death in one who had the Glenn operation. Dr. Kumar's language indicated the incident was far more critical than Dr. Abraham and Sarah led us to believe. I inferred that, but for the quick response and expertise of the surgical team, Katie would not have survived.

Dr. Kumar believed Katie was no longer a good candidate for the Glenn surgery and recommended a heart transplant. Without either procedure, Katie's heart would not support her growing body much longer. The only question was when, not if, a stroke or cardiac arrest ended her life. Dr. Kumar would not speculate as to how long Katie's heart could function, but, when Krista pressed, he said any guess should be framed in months, not years. Dr. Kumar suggested running blood tests to ascertain whether Katie met basic eligibility requirements for a transplant.

Krista and I had discussed heart transplants generally with some of the staff already, more out of curiosity than any other reason. PMCH did not have a pediatric heart transplant program. Riley Children's Hospital in downtown Indianapolis had the only such facility in the state. Some doctors and nurses with previous training or work experience at transplant centers spoke of the procedure in mixed terms. Living with a heart transplant is not as simple as taking a few pills every day. Kids lucky enough to receive a donor heart face persistent challenges, including constant monitoring, blood draws, biopsies, dietary restrictions, kidney dysfunction, and side effects from numerous anti-rejection and cardiac drugs. Moreover, a transplanted pediatric heart does not last forever, at most a couple decades, requiring yet another transplant.

Dr. Kumar told us that, as the liaison with the Riley transplant team, he would contact them on our behalf. Then another hammer dropped: Dr. Kumar was leaving town Friday for a few weeks. Thus, PMCH's heart transplant specialist would be unavailable while we deliberated over seeking a new heart for Katie. The doctor left us in the conference room after expressing his condolences. We awoke that morning expecting Dr. Abraham to splice Katie's SVC with her pulmonary artery by noon. By 3 p.m., we were instead discussing a transplant.

I began pacing the room after Dr. Kumar departed, and Amy took my seat on the couch next to Krista. The room's size restricted me to no more than three steps. I kept saying, "I can't believe this." Krista and Amy consoled each other. A knock at the door caused the room to fall silent. A young woman dressed in business attire opened the door and asked if she could join us. Krista invited the woman in, introduced her to me, and explained that the two worked together on a committee at the hospital. The woman and I each took one of the remaining two empty chairs. She then gave me her job title, which I assumed was PMCH upper management, and turned to Krista.

"Is there anything I can do for you?"
"They say Amy can't see Katie. She's from Denver. She's the only family we have here. Is there anything you can do?"
"I'm sorry, no."

Her response startled me. I cannot believe she had not heard of our encounter with Nurse Ratched. During Katie's 179 days in the hospital, this woman had never visited Krista, not once.[8] Just hours after our clash with Nurse Ratched, she asks whether Krista wanted anything, knowing that she would refuse the one thing Krista was sure to request. Amy asked the next question in trembling voice.

"What if Katie is … dying … Can I see her?"

Her question met stone-faced silence. The sisters broke into sobs after they absorbed the answer. Incredulous, I told the woman we wanted to be alone. She must have recognized my intense animosity and quickly made for the door. Before leaving, she asked if we wanted her to escort Krista and me to

8 I kept a running tally on various metrics, including the length of Katie's hospitalizations and intubations, and always knew the current statistics.

Katie's room. With my hand on my crying wife's shoulder, I did look at her when I responded coldly, "We know where it is."

We remained in the room until Krista and Amy gained their composure. Krista and I resumed our vigil at Katie's bedside. Meanwhile, Amy spent the rest of the day in the Family Room alone.

Throughout the evening, my mind kept going back to a framed poem my grandmother hung on her wall. The allegorical piece, known as "Footprints," tells the story of a person walking on a beach with God. Their footprints represented various stages throughout the person's life. The person asked God why, during times of strife, he only saw one set of footprints, implying God had abandoned him. God explains that "[d]uring your times of trial and suffering, when you see only one set of footprints, it was then that I carried you." I hoped He would carry us through this trial.

Katie remained stable as midnight approached and her parents succumbed to emotional and physical fatigue. With a top-notch nurse dedicated solely to Katie, we felt comfortable going home. Even after the day's calamitous events, Krista and I did not waiver from Katie's nighttime routine. I made the sign of the cross on Katie's forehead before we prayed, "Our Father, who art in Heaven...."

CHAPTER 22

The Decision

Katie struggled Thursday in the aftermath of the aborted surgery. Her numbers remained terrible, and she required significant ventilator support. She did not rebound as everyone expected. The question persisted, "From what did she not rebound?"

Krista and I left the hospital Wednesday night thinking we had two options: heart transplant or no heart transplant. Dr. Parikh checked on Katie Thursday morning and agreed with Dr. Kumar that we needed to decide whether to pursue a heart transplant; however, the cardiologist recommended we "go for the Glenn" before that drastic step. Dr. Abraham added another perspective a few hours later. The surgeon disagreed with Dr. Kumar's transplant recommendation and wanted to try the Glenn again once Katie recovered. He was not convinced that pulmonary hypertension caused Katie to de-sat on the OR table. Unfortunately, the demands of the PICU made meeting with the surgeon, an intensivist, and a cardiologist simultaneously impossible.

All hands were on deck for rounds on Friday morning; however, the lineup changed slightly. Dr. Halczenko replaced Dr. Bob, who finished his scheduled four consecutive days on Thursday. Dr. Parikh represented cardiology. Residents and nurse practitioner students augmented the normal collection of specialists. Katie was not the sole cause for the assembly. I gathered from the frequency of physicians visiting Room 1 that her neighbor was gravely ill.

I anxiously waited with the still unconscious Katie while the team "rounded" on the other infant. A resident examined Katie as the team collected outside Katie's door. She was in the PICU for a cardiac rotation during

Katie's June hospitalization, so I knew her well. We engaged in superficial conversation as she examined Katie. I stopped speaking when she placed a stethoscope against Katie's chest.

"Hmmm," she said.

"'Hmmm,' what?" I asked.

"That's strange," she said more to herself than me.

"What's strange?"

"I can't hear the shunt."

"Do you normally hear the shunt?"

"Normally. Sometimes it's hard to hear. I haven't heard it since Wednesday."

"Last Wednesday? Two days ago?"

"Yeah."

"Before or after the surgery?"

"After."

"Is it odd that you couldn't hear the shunt after the OR fiasco?"

"Not really. The shunt's hard to hear. Sometimes you can't hear it."

I could not argue that point. If I had a dollar for every time a nurse offered me a stethoscope to listen to the odd sound of Katie's heart beating, I could have paid for an hour of Katie's stay in the PICU. In my many, many attempts, I never heard a strange heartbeat. I was lucky to hear a heartbeat at all, let alone the "whoosh" of blood passing through a shunt.

The resident's comment unsettled me. The consensus was a spike in pulmonary pressure of unknown origin caused Katie's duress on the operating table. Perhaps the shunt was somehow to blame for the crisis. When Krista returned from talking with Amy in the Family Room, I quickly summarized the resident's statements as we walked to the door. The NP started rounds before Krista could respond, but I could see the wheels spinning in Krista's eyes.

The group listened as Anthony recited Katie's vitals and brief history. The day's intensivist, Dr. Halczenko, then asked questions of the various specialties and raised the issue of Dr. Abraham wanting to try the Glenn procedure again. Dr. Parikh, who voiced Dr. Kumar's opinion that transplant was our only option, also advocated first trying the Glenn. Then in walked the only member of the cardiology group who had yet to weigh in on Katie's situation.

Having just returned to Indianapolis after an extended absence, Dr. Steinberg joined the conversation with a fresh perspective. He listened for a minute or two, his face a mask of concentration, before throwing out a thought: "What if the shunt is blocked?" His comment met fierce resistance, but he persisted. "What if she threw a clot, and her shunt is blocked?" He asked Dr. Parikh whether anyone saw blood passing through the shunt in echocardiograms since the aborted surgery. Dr. Parikh answered in the negative, caveating his response by adding, "It's very hard to see … very small. We don't always see it." Dr. Parikh spoke authoritatively on the subject as he specialized, in part, in echocardiograms and had difficulty seeing the shunt in a December echo.

Like a dog with a bone, Dr. Steinberg would not let go. "So how do we know it wasn't a clot?" The two cardiologists subsequently engaged in a contentious exchange. Although reluctant to interrupt, I wanted them to know what the resident told me.

> "A couple of minutes ago, she couldn't hear the shunt," I interrupted while motioning towards the resident. "She said she hasn't heard it since Wednesday."

Dragged into a conflict of which she obviously wanted no part, she elaborated on my statement. After throwing fuel on the conflagration, she and I remained quiet as the cardiologists debated. They had not reached agreement before the intensivist led the group to the next occupied room. Krista and I stood speechless in the hall.

"What just happened?" I asked.

Stupefied, Krista shook her head and replied, "I don't know."

Dr. Halczenko returned to our room after concluding rounds. He wanted to discuss the conflicting theories as to what happened on Wednesday and what those theories meant to our future course of action. With the doctor present, the nurse took the opportunity to step out.

"Before we start," I said, "would you mind moving out to the Family Room? Krista's sister is out there, and we'd really like her to hear."
"Sure," the doctor replied in his characteristically soft voice. "Is she out there now?"
"Yes," Krista interjected.
"Why doesn't she just come here? I can wait until you get her."

I hesitated, fearing interference from the PICU's Praetorian Guard. And then Dr. Helzcenko solved the problem:

"Would you like me to get her?"
In a very slow and sincere voice, I said, "We would *love* for you to get her."
"Her name is Amy, right?"
"Yes."
"I'll be right back."

With that, he left Krista and me alone with Katie. For the first time since Katie's aborted surgery, we both grinned. True to his word, Dr. Halczenko escorted Amy into Katie's room a minute later.

We lost every battle but ultimately won the Visitation Policy War. The victory was not without cost. Fairly or not, the callousness with which a few administrators treated my wife during those three awful days forevermore tainted our feelings toward the unit. After allowing ourselves a few seconds of silent celebration, we turned our attention to Dr. Helzcenko.

The four of us stood around Katie's crib as the doctor began speaking. His message was neither long nor complicated: Krista and I needed to make a decision regarding the direction of Katie's treatment in the very near future, i.e., within days ... if not sooner. Katie remained heavily dependent on the ventilator, an unsustainable situation. We had to either try the Glenn surgery again as Drs. Abraham and Parikh recommended or pursue a heart transplant as Dr. Kumar advised.

We asked Dr. Halczenko what he thought happened in the OR. He hypothesized without much conviction that something may have caused Katie's pulmonary pressure to elevate. When pressed for what that "something" was, he gave a vague, circumspect answer. I knew no one could explain with certitude what happened two days earlier, but I would have been remiss not to at least ask. I did, however, want an answer to my next question: Assuming pulmonary hypertension was responsible for the current complications, how would it impact a transplanted heart?

> "The new heart won't fix the pulmonary hypertension," he said, "but, ideally, it would be strong enough to overcome the pressure and maintain positive blood flow. Ideally."

Dr. Halczenko spent five minutes describing a myriad of other transplant issues Katie may encounter before returning to his original point: The Glenn and transplant were each fraught with grave risk, and the hour to decide was fast approaching.

The nurse returned during our conversation. Seeing the doctor discussing Katie's care with the three of us, she did not object to Amy's presence. Her position was not uniformly adopted. Within an hour after Dr. Halczenko left, the nurse in charge of training visited us. She said our family had been the subject of great debate amongst management. Amy was now allowed in Katie's room provided Krista or I escorted her, which struck me as an odd accommodation. After all, the basis for denying her entry was limiting exposure to germs. Having either of us in the room with her did nothing to address that concern. Satisfied that Amy could visit Katie, we accepted the terms.

For the first time since her anesthesia, Katie woke up later that afternoon. Krista and Amy stood at opposite sides of her crib, holding Katie's little hands. The misery was evident in Katie's face. Katie tried to cry, but the ventilator rendered her mute by preventing air from passing over her vocal cords. She fought the ventilator tube by making silent coughing motions to no avail. We did what little we could to comfort her. Katie's mom and aunt held her hands, stroked her hair, and talked to her in reassuring tones. I would have given anything for Katie to be as happy as she was just two days earlier.

Katie fell back asleep before another visitor appeared with a large contraption on wheels. The possibility of a blocked shunt continued to haunt Dr. Steinberg, so he decided to look for himself. He brought with him a portable echocardiogram machine, which has a large color monitor, a control panel, and hand-held scanner resembling that of a grocery store clerk. An image of Katie's heart appeared on the screen when he placed the scanner on Katie's chest. I stood on the opposite side of Katie's crib and watched the moving

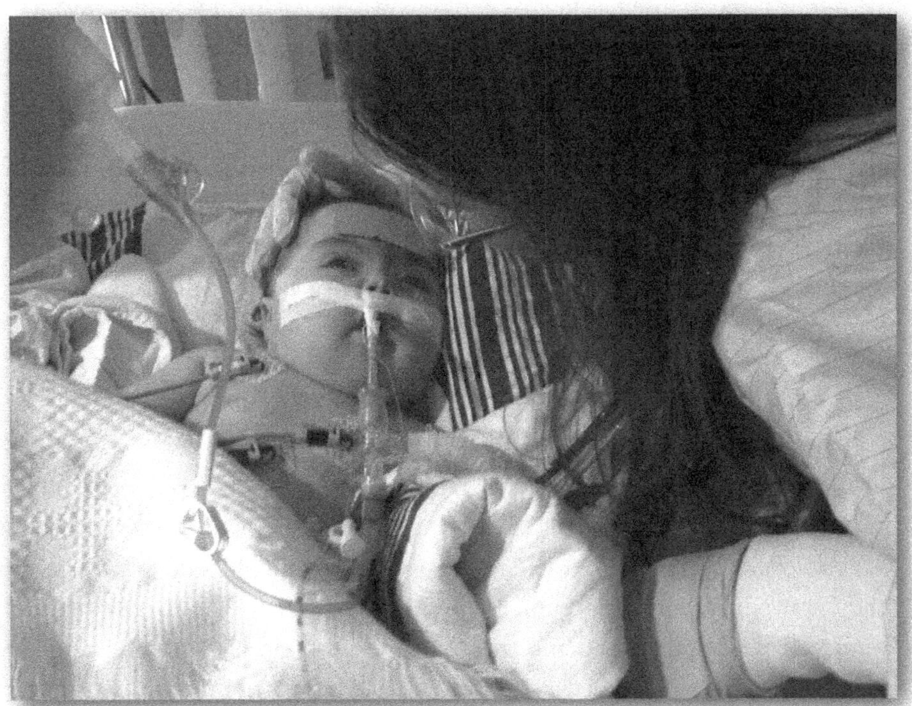

A miserable Katie comforted by her mom.

image. Blotches of red and blue repeatedly appeared and disappeared, indicating oxygenated and deoxygenated blood flow, respectively. Dr. Steinberg searched in vain for the shunt. Either the shunt's position blocked it from view or no blood flowed through it.

My misgivings about the "acute pulmonary hypertension event" theory turned into deep skepticism following Dr. Steinberg's test. Neither Drs. Steinberg nor Parikh could detect the shunt on an echocardiogram since the aborted operation. The resident had not heard the shunt since before the operation. Perhaps a clot formed within the shunt, thereby preventing blood flow. If so, the cardiovascular flow Dr. Abraham established during the first surgery, upon which Katie relied for survival, no longer existed. That would explain why Katie remained critically ill. If Dr. Steinberg were correct, Katie probably did not have a hypertensive event and was therefore still eligible for the Glenn procedure.

Dr. Kumar's absence left us without a connection to Riley Hospital; therefore, we spent the remainder of Friday frenetically searching PMCH for and questioning people with pediatric heart transplant experience. We missed Dr. Kumar's voice in the discussions. As Katie's primary cardiologist who had performed both of her catheterizations, he was adamant on Wednesday regarding Katie's ineligibility for the Glenn procedure. We wanted to know whether Dr. Kumar would have a different conclusion given the new information and differing opinions, but he was frustratingly absent from the conversation.

In the midst of discussions, debates, and arguments Friday evening, I introduced myself to the mother of the baby in Room 1. I had seen Kimberly in passing over the previous two days. We were never close enough to speak, and I was admittedly preoccupied with our own issues. The twenty-year-old woman looked both scared and frail. I happened upon her standing alone in the hall and approached her. Her last week had been a nightmare. Living just this side of the Ohio border, she went into labor two months early. The local hospital sent her to St. Vincent via ambulance when she and the baby experienced complications. She gave me a cursory description of her son's medical problem, generally that some of Hayden's organs developed in the wrong location. I did not press for further details. The staff, particularly the nurses, treated Kimberly with tremendous kindness. The attention Hayden garnered from the staff indicated he was fighting for his life.

I told Kimberly to let us know if we could do anything for her and returned to Katie's room. I presumed she would be too shy to ask, but hoped she would find some measure of solace in knowing two more people cared for her.

We went home that night having not yet made a decision. The day's discussions swirled in my head. Unable to sleep, I joined Sam on the couch for some brainless television. While flipping through the stations, I saw a local news preview about a pediatric oncology patient. Intrigued, I sat through the entire show before the anchorwoman introduced the segment. Family and friends had thrown a surprise party for a local high school graduate after she finished her last dose of chemotherapy at PMCH. I immediately recognized Maddy from the Peds floor. She appeared exhausted, but her prognosis was excellent. Fatigue did not prevent her from smiling at the people gathered in the Family Room on the Peds floor at PMCH, including two Indianapolis Colts players who came to support one of their biggest fans. In the gloom and despair of the past few days, seeing Maddy's triumph was both an inspiration and a blessing.

The news crew interviewed Maddy and took a tour of Maddy's hospital room. She and her family had personalized the otherwise bland décor over the past three months. Watching the familiar images, I thought back to Nurse Ratched giving Amy permission to join us in the Family Room. Two days later, the hospital authorized a party in the Family Room one floor above. The visitor policy was not so strict as previously led to believe. As the camera panned across the room, a thought occurred to me: PMCH administration banned my sister-in-law during Katie's major heart surgery due to infection concerns, yet two days later allowed a cameraman and news reporter access. I turned to Sam. Taking his lower jaw in my hand, I lifted his head off the couch until our eyes met. "What are the odds that camera guy is her grandparent?" He did not answer, and I went to bed.

Krista, Amy, and I spent most of Saturday watching Katie sleep. Intensivist Dr. Williams and Dr. Parikh visited us mid-afternoon to (1) inform us the blood tests revealed Katie was eligible for transplant, (2) frame our options, and (3) impress on us the need to make a decision. Dr. Parikh expressed his opinion that the Glenn procedure was high risk, but he believed Katie had a *chance* of a good outcome. His opinion differed from that of Dr. Kumar, but the latter did not have the benefit of information garnered since his departure. Dr. Williams was more circumspect, focusing more on fleshing out the options and revealing a previously unknown complexity.

If Katie did not fare well after the Glenn surgery, a transplant was the only alternative treatment. In that scenario, the intensivist would place Katie on a bypass machine to await a donor heart. If Katie were at Peyton Manning, the closest transplant hospital that would accept her was in Cincinnati. The transplant center at Riley Children's Hospital in Indianapolis does not take kids on bypass machines. I asked why we could transport Katie two hours away but not twenty minutes. Dr. Williams explained that Riley did not have a transfer team capable of moving a baby on a bypass machine. Regardless of the reason, if we wanted to ensure Katie's treatment remained in Indianapolis, we had to transfer Katie to Riley now and allow the Riley physicians to perform the Glenn surgery. Even if we transferred Katie immediately, the Riley staff would take time, maybe days, to determine its preferred course of treatment. Each day brought greater risk of infection, respiratory crisis, and shunt failure.

Dr. Parikh emphasized that the Glenn procedure and transplant were our only options. He described some technology available for patients with valve defects on the left side of the heart that would not work for Katie. Amongst the tools included an external device that serves as a portable bypass machine. Dr.

Parikh said that his practice has used such devices on many patients. Krista asked the cardiologist about their success rates. Dr. Parikh apparently misunderstood her question, saying as he shook his head violently, "Oh, they fail miserably." The answer shattered the tension in the room. The nurse pinched the bridge of her nose, closed her eyes, and shook her head. Dr. Williams buried his face in his right hand. Krista, Amy, and I broke out in laughter.

Dr. Williams closed the discussion by listing our alternatives before he and Dr. Parikh left us alone to deliberate. After recapping the information the intensivist and cardiologist provided with one of our favorite nurses, the family retreated to a hole-in-the-wall creole restaurant on the east side of town to evaluate the options:

- Forgo further treatment, hope that Katie can get off the vent, and bring her home to enjoy the time she has
- Wean Katie off the vent, keep her in the hospital, and hope that she avoids complications and grows stronger for a later surgery
- Proceed with the Glenn surgery at PMCH and transfer Katie to Cincinnati should she fail afterwards
- Proceed with the Glenn surgery at PMCH and not seek additional treatment should she fail
- Transfer Katie to Riley Hospital for the Glenn surgery and proceed with a transplant should she fail
- Transfer Katie to Riley for the Glenn surgery and not seek a transplant if she fails
- Forgo the Glenn surgery and pursue a transplant at Riley

Before leaving the restaurant, Krista and I decided against a transplant. The odds of receiving a heart are slight due to the very few donors. Katie could very well languish for months or maybe even years at Riley while waiting. Moreover, as she outgrew her shunt, Katie would become increasingly susceptible to illness. If she were lucky enough to get a heart, the odds of rejection at her age were high. That could mean a miserable existence waiting for the end. If Katie did not reject the heart, she would require constant invasive testing.

The pharmaceutical regimen would be brutal. While transplant presented a small chance of a positive outcome given Katie's situation, a life of pain and limited quality was significantly more likely.[9]

Concluding a successful Glenn procedure would give Katie the best chance at a relatively normal and rich life, we decided to proceed with the surgery at PMCH as soon as possible. Dr. Abraham was the dispositive factor in our deliberation. As the only person who saw and handled Katie's unique heart, no one had greater knowledge of the organ. Although Riley Hospital had a more robust cardiac program, we had great confidence in Dr. Abraham and the PMCH staff. They knew Katie's idiosyncrasies. Moreover, after 184 days of hospitalization, the relationship between many of the staff and Katie transcended that of simple patient-caregiver. Should the surgery not go well, we wanted Katie surrounded by friends rather than strangers in a new hospital.

When we returned to the PICU that evening, I stopped by the nurses' station to speak with the intensivist. A nurse informed me he was currently in another patient's room. I asked her to deliver a message for me: "Please tell him we're going to do the Glenn here." She nodded in understanding, and I returned to Katie's room. We made our decision and left the rest to Providence.

In the midst of the PICU chaos on Friday, I had the sickening realization that my left ring finger lacked a grey steel band. Having removed my purple rubber gloves repeatedly throughout the day, I was convinced my wedding ring came off with one. I tore the room apart searching without success. I retraced my steps in the hospital. Nothing. Amy helped me search the path to my car

9 Since our discussions in February, 2014, I have read articles and seen many television profiles on children living rich lives with a transplanted heart. No one presented us with the possibility of such a positive outcome. We based our decision on eight months of experience caring for Katie and the limited information on transplants we gathered; therefore, I am in no way qualified to speak to the merits of heart transplants, pediatric or otherwise, under any other circumstances.

in the parking lot, complicated by six inches of partially melted snowy sludge. Still nothing. I returned home and tossed the house like a rogue television cop executing a search warrant. All I had for my effort was a handful of loose coins. To be fair, that I managed not to lose my ring for more than three years bordered on the miraculous. I could not have picked a worse occasion: Valentine's Day.

The search continued through the weekend. Wanting Katie to hold my wedding ring before the next surgery, I gave up hope Sunday afternoon and went shopping. Amy and I drove across town to the family jeweler where I had purchased the ring. The business was not open Sundays, so we walked to a national chain store next door.

The store bustled with activity, which struck me as odd two days after Valentine's Day. I suspected more than a few of the customers failed to meet expectations on the holiday and were trying to make amends. Amy and I scanned ring cabinet for ten minutes before a saleswoman approached. Admittedly, I was not looking my best. The lack of sleep and stress turned my eyes red and complexion sallow. In a pair of jeans and a well-worn blue PMCH T-shirt Krista bought me in December, I was not your typical jewelry shopper.

I told the bubbly saleswoman that we were interested in a wedding band. The store did not carry anything resembling my original ring. Lacking the luxury of time to search elsewhere, I chose a basic band and asked about the return policy. The startled saleswoman answered my question while sporting a puzzled expression. I imagine not many wedding ring shoppers ask about returns. Amy briefly explained our situation, which prompted the saleswoman to ask about Katie. I gave her the two-minute biography. A mother of five children, she fought to hold back tears. She called out as we left the store, "God bless your family and little Katie."

Amy and I parted ways back at the hospital. Amy took Krista to dinner in the cafeteria while I visited a family on the third floor. The sun had set by the time I returned to Katie's room thirty minutes later. When I rang the buzzer for PICU entry, the receptionist said someone left a package for me. We did not get many visitors during this period and no company delivers on Sunday evenings, so I was perplexed. Light from the hallways and monitors barely illuminated Katie's otherwise dark room, but I could see a huge cardboard box resting on the couch with the name of the jeweler stamped prominently on the side. I found a piece of paper with a message from the saleswoman taped to the top of the box:

"These are for Katie and her friends in the PICU. God Bless."

I reached inside the box until plush material filled my hand and pulled out a large white bear with a green knit cap. I fished out another stuffed animal and then another, sixteen identical bears in all. After placing a bear in Katie's crib, I gave the remaining bears to the other kids in the PICU. The first bear given away went to Hayden.

CHAPTER 23

The Undiscovered Country

Dr. Abraham scheduled Katie for the first available slot in his schedule, the morning of Tuesday, February 18. The temperature hovered around freezing as we arrived at the hospital before sunup. Amy rescheduled her return flight to support us through yet another surgery. We each gave Katie individual encouragement before saying an "Our Father" and "Hail Mary." I briefly slipped my new ring onto one of Katie's fingers, just in case I would not have another chance. The happy, energetic Katie from the morning of her last surgery was nowhere to be seen. Aside from respirations and occasionally biting down on the intubation tube, Katie lay motionless.

Our goodbyes before Katie's eighth trip to the OR contrasted with the earlier procedures. While the stress and fear accompanying surgery did not change, the fact we chose this procedure weighed on me heavily. I felt confident we made the *best* decision based on the available facts. As I watched Katie's transport team wheel her past Hayden's room and down the hall, I hoped we made the *right* decision.

We spent the morning in the waiting room. Krista and Amy conversed. I tried to read, but an affable elderly gentlemen sitting across from me kept interrupting with questions. I eventually gave up on the book, and the two of us talked until his daughter's hernia operation ended two hours later. A lifelong resident of an Indianapolis suburb, he told stories of life in the county before the urban sprawl. Miles of crops separated Indianapolis from its northern neighbors of Carmel and Zionsville when he was a young man. Wheat and corn gave way to strip malls, restaurants, apartments, and, fortunately for us, the St. Vincent Hospital complex.

Our pager buzzed not long after the man's departure, alerting us that our daughter's surgery was complete. I turned in the pager, and an energetic nurse led us into a patient consultation room. One of our favorite nurses from Katie's first PICU stay joined us, filling in for the vacationing Sarah. Not having the normal staff present made me uneasy.

The nurse explained that Katie was out of surgery and doing well. Using vague terms, she informed us that the surgery did not go as planned. When we started asking questions, she said Dr. Abraham would meet us in the PICU Family Room to explain. Possibilities swirled in my mind as we walked the five minutes to PMCH, but only one thought kept repeating: "Why can't Katie get a break?"

Dr. Abraham joined us at the same table as he had just six days earlier. "Well," he said, "I wasn't able to do the Glenn." The superior vena cava (SVC), not pulmonary hypertension, was the culprit for today's change of course. The deoxygenated blood returning from the head, upper torso, and arms passes through the SVC before entering the heart. Due to an anomaly affecting 10 percent of patients with congenital heart defects (as opposed to 0.3 percent in the general population), Katie had two SVCs.[10] They should gush like a red geyser when severed. Dr. Abraham explained that the SVCs "didn't bleed" when he cut them. He saw "a few little drops [from the right SVC], nothing out of the other [SVC]." He rubbed his left thumb and forefinger together as though still in the OR and said, "They didn't feel right." After pausing for a moment, he pinched the skin on the top of his hand and said, "It felt like a tendon, not a vein." He might as well have told me they felt like unicorn hair whetted by leprechaun's tears. His analogy meant nothing to me; I just knew it was bad.

The surgeon next explained why so little blood flowed through the SVCs. The SVCs were "fractionally clogged by a mixture of partially calcified fibrous tissue." He felt reasonably certain this material originally formed around the

10 "Double Superior Vena Cava," Albay, Cankal, Kocabiyik, Yalcin, and Ozan; Morphologie. 2006 Mar; 90(288): 39-42.

many central lines used over the past few months and remained after their removal. Dr. Abraham also found evidence of blood clots. The damaged SVCs could not provide the blood flow needed for the Glenn, so Dr. Abraham sewed them back into their original position. I asked how the blood that should have flowed through the SVCs returned to the heart. He explained that Katie's body generated a network of smaller veins to compensate for the damaged SVCs.

Shifting from the SVCs to the shunt, Dr. Abraham confirmed Dr. Steinberg's theory that blood or other matter almost, if not entirely, blocked Katie's shunt. He removed the ineffective 4 mm shunt and replaced it with a 6 mm version, thereby increasing the blood flow capacity by 125 percent. Assuming the shunt remained open, he hoped the increased blood flow would support Katie for at least another year, possibly two or three. Dr. Abraham left her incision open and ribcage somewhat expanded to facilitate shunt manipulation over the next couple of days to "tweak" blood flow.

The damaged SVCs made both the Glenn procedure and transplant impossible. Unless we could rehabilitate them, Katie would have, optimistically, a few years to live. Dr. Abraham hoped that, with time, the troublesome blockages would resolve and make another attempt at the Glenn procedure possible. The pulmonary hypertension issue that bedeviled us for months fell to a secondary concern.

Our attention now turned to preventing more clots. We were fortunate to have discovered the blocked shunt during the previous week's aborted surgery. The blockage would have been fatal had Katie not been on life support. The staff was considerably surprised she survived it anyway.

After apologizing for not having better news, Dr. Abraham left us to wait for the "all clear" to see Katie. We did not wait long. Bloated from surgery, covered in prick marks and bruises from repeated attempts to get IV access, disfigured in shape by the unnatural rib cage position and an open midline incision, Katie was a tough sight to see. Even with some experience in such things, I struggled with the scene best described as, in a word, gruesome.

I always included pictures with my e-mail updates, but her condition made a dignified and respectful photograph of Katie almost impossible. Her right hand was the only presentable part of her. A pulse monitor in her right palm glowed bright red. I positioned Krista's diamond cross necklace in Katie's hand and slipped my ring over her thumb. The red backlighting reflecting off her skin made an ethereal image.

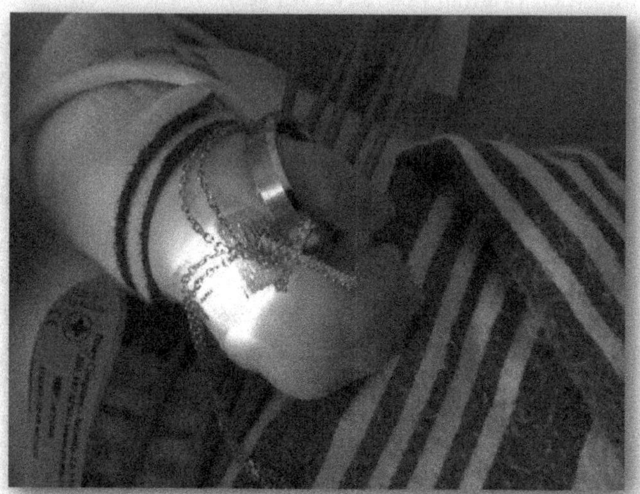

Katie's hand with her mom's cross and her dad's replacement ring.

Beyond the blood, bandages, tubes, and alarms, one monitor clearly showed that Katie's cardiac function was very strong. Albeit at a high price, Katie made progress that day.

Katie progressed steadily following her previous surgeries. After the latest operation, however, Katie endured a grinding recovery. Katie once again became dependent upon heavy sedatives and pain medications. Her muscles atrophied after weeks in the crib. The open chest wound limited what OT and PT could do. In the days following the operation, Katie contracted a couple of infections that kicked off another round of fevers. She was also extremely bloated and undernourished. The doctors had stopped feedings in the early morning of February 12, six hours before the canceled surgery. Anticipating another procedure in a day or two, the intensivists did not restart feedings until after the second Glenn attempt six days later. Katie's poor liver function prevented TPN nourishment. The eight-month-old did not return to her pre-surgery caloric intake for almost a week after surgery.

Dr. Abraham tested various blood flow rates by crimping the shunt prior to closing Katie's chest on February 21. He ultimately decided to maximize flow with a fully open 6 mm shunt. We could only hope the increased blood flow into Katie's lungs would enable stable cardiovascular function.

Extubation was the next big step, and the risks were substantial. We did not know whether Katie could breathe independently given her new cardiac configuration. Complicating matters, we had to wait long enough for Katie to recover from surgery, but not so long that she became too deconditioned to breathe on her own. If Katie failed extubation, the swollen throat caused by the previous intubation may have made placing another ET tube impossible. An emergency tracheostomy is the only alternative in that scenario, which itself presents a significant risk of oxygen deprivation.

The intensivists originally planned to extubate Katie on February 21; however, she was too bloated. The doctors aggressively tried to reduce Katie's fluid levels. Katie grew increasingly deconditioned as we delayed extubation day after day, making the wait evermore excruciating.

Katie moved to Room 4 on Sunday, February 23. A terribly ill cardiac baby with a higher probability of needing the ECMO equipment bumped her from Room 2. We packed Katie's belongings and carried them thirty yards down the hall. After five days of *de minimis* improvement wrought with fevers and frustration, moving to a standard PICU room felt like a little progress. Any joy derived from the transfer was short-lived. Katie's former neighbor in Room 1, Hayden, died later that evening. Katie's replacement in Room 2, whom we did not meet, died three days later.

I returned to Rock Island on Monday after more than a month away, passing the baton to my mom who had arrived the previous day. Krista and

I discussed a long-term employment strategy and concluded I needed to return to the office. Katie could spend the next year or longer in the hospital. An indefinite absence from work was just not feasible. My supervisor had again distributed most of my outstanding projects, limiting my value to the office. My mom, on the other hand, was the advocate Katie needed at the hospital.

The Monday through Thursday dayshift intensivist repeatedly delayed extubation despite my mom's protestations. He held that re-intubation following a premature extubation presented far more risk to Katie than prolonged intubation. Watching Katie fight the tube day after day in a haze of sedatives, our family grew increasingly more aggressive and accepting in terms of risk. Admittedly, we viewed the issue through an emotional prism. I texted mom for updates with high hopes of extubation only to have those hopes dashed.

I also struggled with the distance separating me from Katie. She never left my mind, nor did the thought that maybe, just maybe, I could do something for her were I in Indianapolis. Returning home late Thursday night, I resolved that, after my Air National Guard training that weekend, I would never leave Indianapolis again with Katie in the hospital.

I spent Friday, February 28 at the hospital with Mom. The intensivist again cancelled the extubation scheduled for that morning. After four days trying to reduce Katie's excess fluid, Katie was now dehydrated. Our inability to keep Katie's system in balance unsettled me. Why were we still struggling to manage her fluid levels? The reasons for Katie's fluctuating fluid level remain a mystery. Helpless in regards to extubation, I took the opportunity to address another facet of Katie's care during rounds Friday morning.

Some of the nurses did not reposition Katie throughout their twelve-hour shifts. Mom noticed the practice during her week at PMCH, asking one nurse why she did not move Katie. "Oh, she's comfortable," the nurse replied, which struck a bad chord with my mom. Leaving a patient in one position too long invites ischemia and tissue damage. As the intensivist concluded rounds on Katie, I interjected.

> "Just one more thing: Can you instruct the nurses to reposition Katie throughout the day?"
>
> The intensivist gave me a withering look and stated indignantly, "She is repositioned every two hours."
>
> "No, she isn't. I sit in there all day. She isn't. My mom was with her this week. She wasn't repositioned."
>
> The intensivist dug in, flatly repeating the previous statement. "She *is* repositioned every two hours."
>
> "Do you check that? Do you know that personally? I'm telling you ... I'm in the room. I'm *in* the room. *All day.* She isn't moved."

The intensivist did not respond, which I interpreted as disbelief. Rather than debate the point, I proposed what I considered a mutually agreeable solution: "Can you write an order for [Katie] to be repositioned every two hours?" The intensivist agreed. After all, if the nurses were in fact repositioning Katie, no harm could come of ordering what they were already doing. I do not know whether the doctor actually wrote the order, but the nurses repositioned Katie every two hours thereafter. A small win to be sure, but sometimes a small win is the best for which one can hope.

The failed Glenn surgery on February 18 marked a turning point in Katie's treatment. From our first meeting with Dr. Abraham on the day of Katie's birth, Krista and I operated under the framework of Katie either undergoing three operations to salvage her heart (the shunt, Glenn, and Fontan) or pursuing a transplant. We chose the former route and processed everything else, including infections, tachypnea, compressed airways, cerebral bleeds, pulmonary hypertension, and GI and feeding issues, under that framework. As long as the SVCs remained damaged, the planned surgeries and even the transplant were impossible.

In his "To be or not to be" soliloquy, Hamlet compares what one finds after death to exploring a mysterious and unknown land, an "undiscovered country." Unmoored from the original surgical plan, Krista and I found ourselves adrift. The definitive goals by which we compared all progress and setbacks were gone. We had entered our own undiscovered country.

CHAPTER 24

Bump in the Night

WITH KRISTA ON KATIE DUTY for the weekend, I left for Air National Guard training late in the evening of Friday, February 28. Krista promised to keep me informed of any changes in Katie's condition. Although I hated to leave, I could make the drive from Springfield, Illinois within a few hours should the need arise.

I reported to drill Saturday with every expectation that the intensivist, Dr. Halczenko, would extubate Katie that morning. Regulations prohibit cell phones in the facility in which I work, so I joined the smokers outside every fifteen minutes to check for texts from Krista. The news was no better than the smoky air. Dr. Halczenko had discontinued Katie's strongest meds Friday evening. Katie did not handle major change well. Predictably, she looked awful the next morning, and the doctor once again postponed extubation. I tried my best to mask the crushing disappointment. With so many opportunities to practice, I was becoming an expert in the art.

I continued to check my phone throughout the day. Just before three o'clock, I opened a text from Krista stating,

"They are going to extubate."

Scrolling to the next message, I read,

"Extubated. She's doing well."

In my excitement, I fumbled to type Krista's number so I searched for her in my contacts. The phone rang for what seemed like eternity before Krista answered. She told me that, although Katie's vitals improved throughout the day, new lab results forced Dr. Halczenko's hand. Katie's ET tube tested positive for infection and had to come out. With no choice but to extubate, Dr. Halczenko decided to give Katie the opportunity to breathe on her own. Krista reported that Katie was struggling somewhat, which we expected after her ordeals of the past two-plus weeks. I would have given anything to be with my wife and daughter at that moment. Mother Nature fortunately intervened.

A group of Guardsmen passing by interrupted my call. A captain told me the commander wanted to see everyone in the auditorium. Weather forecasters were predicting a huge blizzard would sweep through the plains of Iowa before slamming central Illinois that evening. The commander gave permission for those who lived outside of Springfield to leave immediately to beat the storm. I was the first one out the door and did not stop until I arrived at PMCH.

I found the hospital deserted upon arriving after sunset. For the first and only time since Katie's surgery on June 5, I did not wear a PMCH shirt at the hospital. Dressed in my uniform, the squeaks of combat boots against the polished tile floors reverberated in the empty hallways. I found Krista sitting with Katie and holding her hand in the dark. Katie's oxygen saturation hovered steadily in the high 80s, well within the desired range. Her respiration rate remained in the seventies, but the intensivist expected it to fall as she grew stronger.

Krista and I sat with Katie for hours, listening to The Beach Boys as our daughter rested. Nurses and respiratory therapists visited infrequently, as though they did not want to disturb us. God's presence in that little room was palpable as a serene calm replaced the ever-present asphyxiating tension and fear since the aborted surgery. I would soon yearn for that feeling of peace again.

Katie's breathing grew increasingly labored throughout the night. Intensivist Dr. Abraha ordered an X-ray in the early morning hours on Sunday. Her lungs looked, in the doctor's technical medical jargon, "absolutely terrible." Fluid of unknown origin flooded the organs, which appeared in the film as two dark storm clouds bracketing Katie's large heart. The doctor posited that the fluid could be blood from the shunt expanding the blood vessels, water, mucus, or a combination thereof. Dr. Abraha so feared Katie failing that he ordered the nurse to place an intubation kit outside the room.

Dr. Williams, Katie's primary pulmonologist, visited Katie later that morning. He shared Dr. Abraha's concern over Katie struggling to breathe. He once again brought up the possibility of a tracheostomy. The pulmonologist said he would have to discuss Katie's situation with Drs. Abraha (intensivist) and Abraham (surgeon), perhaps during a "care conference" later in the week. This set off two red flags. First, if Katie were in danger of failing at any time, we could not wait until later in the week. Second, "care conferences" are all but mythical.

A "care conference" is a gathering of all treating physicians at one time to discuss a case. We had one in 198 days of hospitalization in which a single NICU hospitalist and nurse attended. The odds of a "care conference" are similar to that of someone voluntarily paying extra taxes. I am sure it happens, but I have never seen it personally. In reality, the intensivist speaks to each specialist individually and devises a plan.

We had seen Dr. Abraham's car parked outside the hospital entrance that morning. Reasoning that Dr. Abraham was in the PICU, Krista suggested to Dr. Williams that the three physicians discuss Katie's treatment now. Shockingly, it worked.

Dr. Abraham delivered the consensus almost an hour later. Unfortunately, the consensus was that no one knew why Katie's lungs looked so bad. Dr. Abraham stood at the foot of the crib and observed Katie in silence for a minute. His forearms rested on the crib railing while his hands, the hands that had operated on Katie's heart, dangled limply above her feet. He broke the silence, saying, "Look at how much she is struggling to breathe. I give her a 1 in 4 chance of remaining off of the vent."

The dire pronouncement surprised me in part because Dr. Abraham was the only physician who consistently fought to give Katie the chance to breathe on her own. Krista and I respected the straight shooting Dr. Abraham greatly, which made his pronouncement very difficult to hear. Moreover, Katie did not appear in such a perilous state in my eyes. Katie appeared much healthier now than she did prior to her only failed extubation. She worked hard to breathe, as if someone put an invisible three-pound weight on her chest, but her color was good. Given everything Katie had been through in February, I clung to the hope that she would improve. I knew Katie was a fighter. If independent respiration were anatomically possible, she would do it.

Katie woke for short periods throughout the day. We held her hand. We prayed. And we waited. Katie remained stable as midnight approached. Ten hours had passed since Dr. Abraham's dire speculation, and the fighter continued to fight.

A stack of mail met me when I returned from the hospital. After Krista retired for the night, I sorted the envelopes into stacks of bills and junk mail when a half-page advertisement fell onto the desk. The image of a large brick church adorned with gold crosses on its many steeples caught my eye. I picked up the advertisement and read "Saint Meinrad Archabbey" in large cursive lettering. I flipped the advertisement over to the reverse side. The text stated that the monks support the Indiana Abbey by manufacturing handcrafted wooden caskets. I stared at the caskets long enough to register that my grandfather, a skilled woodworker, would have appreciated their elegant simplicity before flipping to the front of the flier. I glanced once again at the beautiful Abbey before setting it aside. Road trips were rather low on the priority list, but I made a mental note to show Krista someday.

Katie continued to fight into the morning of Monday, March 3, not the ideal way to spend one's nine-month birthday. Adding insult to injury, she also experienced sedative withdrawal. Katie was awake and alert, but uncomfortable. Her latest X-ray indicated some improvement.

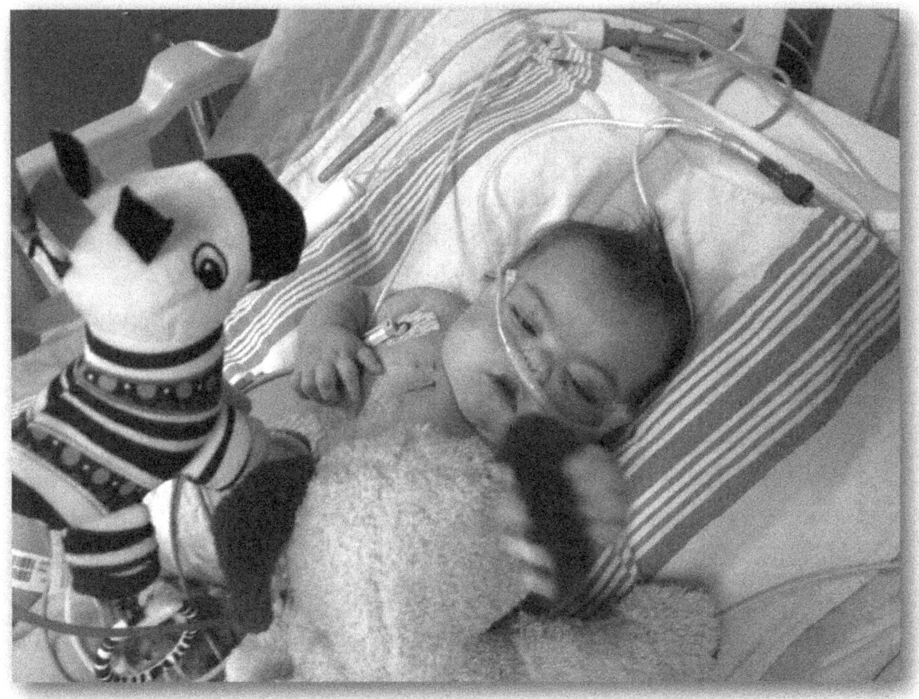

Katie playing with her stuffed animals after extubation.

The intensivist used all the tools available to help Katie in her struggle. He continued diuretics to remove any remaining excess fluid in Katie's system and started weaning Katie from the pulmonary hypertension medications that opened the blood vessels in her lungs. With such a large shunt, those vessels may have been letting in too much blood. The intensivist hoped the increased pulmonary pressure would reduce the amount of blood in the lungs. After five months battling pulmonary hypertension, our new hope for increased pressure demonstrated how radically the treatment plan had changed.

Respiratory therapy began treatment to break up the foreign matter in Katie's lungs. They beat her about the upper torso with a plastic cup. It sounds brutal and looks even worse, but Katie, like most babies, seemed to enjoy it.

Katie improved slightly by Tuesday morning. While the disappointed doctors fretted that her lungs were still so wet, they were also surprised Katie remained off the vent. No one could deny her grit. Katie's relief at being free from the ventilator was evident. Though she struggled to breathe and endured withdrawal, she played with her toys and hugged her favorite stuffed dog. My confidence that she would overcome this latest obstacle grew with every passing hour.

As I read a book to Katie that afternoon, I noticed a bump on her chest. I put the book down and lowered the side of her crib. Dropping my head to the level of Katie's torso, I confirmed a slight protuberance the size of a nickel in diameter just above her incision. Katie had worn only a diaper since the staff transported her to the OR on February 12, so I quickly examined her from stem to stern and found nothing else abnormal.

Returning to the mysterious bump, I stared at it from different angles to ensure my eyes were not playing tricks on me. I walked to the nurses' station and asked Katie's assigned nurse whether she had noticed a bump. She had not and followed me back to Katie's room. The bump did not bother the nurse, who dismissively said such things were common after surgery. I remained fixated nonetheless. I later beckoned Sarah, Dr. Abraham's nurse practitioner, as she walked by and asked for her opinion. She agreed with Katie's nurse that pooling blood underneath the skin caused the bump, a byproduct of Katie's blood thinning medication. Their explanation did not quell my concern. Once alone again with Katie, I photographed the bump from multiple vantage points and sent the photos to Krista and my mom. They were equally perplexed.

The bump grew to the size of a quarter by the time Krista came over after work. We asked the intensivist to inspect it, and he, too, told us that it was likely pooled blood. It would dissipate, but he would monitor for possible infection. We got the same response from the night intensivist and nurse.

Everyone, including Krista and I, fixated on Katie's lung X-rays, yet the bump unsettled me. I remained with Katie through the early morning hours on Wednesday and chatted with her nurse. She promised to keep an eye on Katie's chest and encouraged me to get some sleep. With Katie in good hands, I took her advice.

The Wednesday morning X-ray again indicated that her lungs had cleared a little more in the prior twenty-four hours. Katie progressed by inches, but at least she was progressing. Meanwhile, her bump had swollen to the size of a half-dollar. Again, the staff thought little of it.

After a quick visit home to walk and feed Sam, I returned to the hospital late Wednesday afternoon to discover an all-star crowd in Katie's room. Dr. Abraham, the intensivist, and an assortment of nurses, therapists, and technicians bantered casually. The surgical scrubs worn by some of the staff and large, clear plastic equipment containers stacked at the foot of Katie's crib contrasted with the jubilant atmosphere. The unmistakably positive aura in the room dispelled my initial concern. Dr. Abraham approached me and explained the recent drama.

Katie's growing bump caused a small portion of the chest incision to separate. Blood spurted and then, after some time, flowed steadily. The nurse called for the intensivist. Sarah, serendipitously in the PICU, rushed to the room. The three managed to stem the flow of blood. Dr. Abraham arrived and drained the remaining pooled blood until the bleeding subsided. The doctors concluded that a pressure bandage would stop the benign bleeding. Dr. Abraham did not say what they initially feared had occurred, but I deduced they had been gravely concerned. Each person in the room wore a look of profound relief. The disaster turned out to be a minor issue. Even Dr. Abraham departed from his normally stoic demeanor.

I called Krista from the hall to report on the latest happenings. As I relayed the story, Dr. Abraham walked out of Katie's room, waving with a smile as he started toward the PICU exit. I covered the phone with my hand and called out,

"Calling it an early day?"

"Yes. Lost two patients," he said.

"Lost?" I said and paused. "What do you mean 'lost?' What kind of 'lost?'"

Dr. Abraham stopped and turned toward me with a perplexed expression. His countenance brightened as he realized my interpretation of his words. "Went home. Went home. They went home," said the surgeon with a slight smile. I laughed as he left the unit. PICU humor can be a little dark at times.

Krista joined me on bandage duty for the rest of the evening. No blood flowed while Katie rested; however, blood oozing from the incision saturated her bandage in minutes while she was awake. After a crash-course in dressings from the nurse, Krista and I took turns applying bandages. Blood flow ebbed with each passing hour. Krista changed the bandage for the last time that evening after Katie had fallen asleep. The cloth remained unstained virgin white for the better part of an hour, indicating that the bleeding had decreased dramatically if not stopped altogether. We left for the night optimistic that Katie was improving.

Once again beating the odds, Katie continued to breathe on her own. Her lungs, far from perfect, had improved. Katie was not out of the woods, but she was making progress. And then she walked into another forest.

CHAPTER 25

Blindsided

The State of Indiana requires attorneys to attend continuing learning courses every year to keep their license to practice law. I cancelled my training the previous year because it coincided with Katie's hospitalizations. With the deadline to satisfy the requirement quickly approaching, I rescheduled for March 6. Spending a morning away from the hospital to feed the bureaucratic machine made me more than a little bitter.

I stopped by PMCH before my course. The night shift nurse reported that Katie's incision resumed bleeding, forcing her to repeatedly change the dressing. The bleeding did not concern her or the intensivist. Before I departed, she promised to let me know of any status change. I texted Krista as I walked to the car:

> Very little bleeding while Katie is asleep, but moderate when awake/agitated. Nurse asking Dr. Abraham to readdress today whether need stitches. [sic] I asked if they need to culture drainage. Needed 4-5 dressing changes on night shift.

The fluid on Katie's lungs remained my primary concern. Katie still struggled to breathe, but not so much for us to fear failure.

I joined a few dozen attorneys in a large ballroom a block from Monument Circle, the heart of Indianapolis, for a morning of presentations. I took a seat in the last row of tables and watched the latecomers trickle into the room. The first presenter, a balding man approaching fifty, managed to breathe some life into an otherwise painful overview of new case law. His entertaining delivery kept my attention for twenty minutes before my phone vibrated on the white tablecloth. I acknowledged and read the text message from Krista:

> Intubating, need to do an MRI, may have to go to OR, think it might be an aneurysm. I'm leaving [work] ASAP.

I stuffed my belongings in my briefcase and left the room, dropping my registration papers at the front desk without breaking stride.

Back at PMCH, I found Krista alone in the Family Room. She explained the events that transpired since my visit two hours earlier. Dr. Abraham called Krista after he examined Katie, telling her the bleeding had increased to the point of necessitating a transfusion. Dr. Abraham and a hematologist concluded that something was leaking inside Katie's chest, hypothesizing an aneurysm at the base of the shunt. The intensivist intubated Katie in preparation for a CT scan. I arrived as Krista awaited the results.

Dr. Abraham returned to inform us that the shunt looked fine and he could not identify the source of blood. He subsequently performed an echocardiogram. Again, he could not see the source of the leak; however, the shunt appeared to function properly. Dr. Abraham told us the blood flow had to be stopped. The only way to determine the source was "visual inspection," shorthand for another open-heart operation. He gave us the standard list of now familiar surgical risks, but added a caveat: The riskiest time to have open-heart surgery is 2-6 weeks after another open-heart surgery. Our lack of other options obviated Dr. Abraham's reticence to proceed. Katie went to the OR for her second surgery in less than three weeks.

Krista and I sat in the silent Family Room for two hours before Dr. Abraham returned. In a practice now all-too-familiar, the surgeon joined us at the white table. Dr. Abraham discovered the problem immediately after opening the skin: The staples holding Katie's sternum together since the last surgery ripped through the cartilage, thereby allowing it to separate. He attributed the sternum separating to (1) Katie breathing too hard because of her wet lungs and (2) malnourishment due to poor liver function.

We peppered Dr. Abraham with questions. My question of whether he had ever seen a sternum separate before received a negative response. I then asked if he had ever heard of such a thing happening, and again he shook his head solemnly and said, "No."

Krista changed the direction of conversation to Katie's status. While the chest was open, Dr. Abraham visually inspected Katie's heart and associated vessels, concluding everything "looked good." He then wired the sternum together and sent Katie back to the PICU. Getting an arterial line, which the PICU staff had removed just two days earlier, took longer than the actual surgery. Dr. Abraham ordered a special vacuum dressing to keep the wound clean and facilitate healing. He wanted Katie intubated until the incision healed so as not to strain the sternum, which meant another ten to fourteen days of Katie on a ventilator.

Dr. Abraham advised against extubation even if Katie's wet lungs cleared and nourishment improved. He now believed Katie's recurring infections and recent struggle to breathe tipped the risk scale in favor of a tracheostomy. This would not get Katie extubated any earlier. The distance from the chest incision to that of the proposed tracheostomy was about two inches. With many of the same bacteria found in the human mouth, a tracheostomy hole presented a major infection risk. We could not proceed with a trach until the incision healed.

Krista and I proceeded to Katie's room following Dr. Abraham's departure. Katie slumbered peacefully in her crib. My apprehension that the vacuum dressing would be gruesome was unfounded. A black disk no more than two inches in diameter sat in the middle of Katie's chest incision. A tube connected the disk to a mechanism that gently and silently suctioned fluid from Katie's chest and deposited it in a container below the crib. A sheet of clear material resembling cellophane covered Katie's chest to hold the disk in place. Katie looked much better than she had following the last surgery, as though resting after a long day. Katie's stuffed animals, which a nurse had lined up alongside the crib, watched their playmate sleep.

The unfairness of such improbable misfortune striking Katie twice shook my faith. For the first time, I felt anger. I never asked God to heal Katie's sick heart miraculously. I never asked, "Why Katie?" from the point of her diagnosis through the subsequent trials and tribulations. Katie fought harder to breathe than anyone expected or even thought possible under normal conditions, let alone with a broken sternum, all the while suffering withdrawal. Potent sedatives again coursed through her veins as the ventilator breathed for her. All of Katie's hard work was for naught. This turn of events was not merely unfair; it was cruel.

I sulked on the couch the rest of the day. When a nurse or doctor stopped by to check on Katie, I managed to fake a positive attitude. I retreated into my misery once alone again with Krista and Katie. Krista and I did not speak much, each processing the latest setback independently. Too self-involved to offer any words of comfort, I kept to myself. Moreover, I did not know which words, if any, would have made a difference.

A few hours of sleep did wonders for my attitude. We could pontificate over the theological and philosophical reasons for Katie's setback later. Katie needed us to focus on getting her healthy again, at least as healthy as possible. I returned to the hospital in the morning of Friday, March 7 with renewed determination.

Dr. Abraham stopped by to check on Katie after rounds. Other than saying both she and her numbers looked good, he had little to offer. I asked him how long Katie would need the vacuum dressing. His reply, "ten to fourteen days," made me cringe, for that was the same estimation from the day before.

Following the emergency surgery, Krista and I again considered a tracheostomy. For eight months, I tried to save Katie from the device. Now, after a terrible month of surgeries and infections, to deprive her of it seemed heartless. The trach would relieve Katie's little body of the burden of breathing and, we hoped, allow her to use all of her strength to recover. That she would never need the sedation that intubation required presented a potentially huge quality of life improvement.

Katie woke for the first time after the sternum operation on Friday afternoon. Her eyes, teary and bloodshot, searched the room in confusion and exasperation. I sensed that she understood her predicament: She had fought so hard to get that tube out of her mouth, yet the implacable foe had returned. An incredible sadness filled her eyes, a depth of sadness one so young should not be capable of feeling. Severe sickness ages kids beyond their years and, along with their hardships, gives them a wisdom few who live well into old age achieve. Looking into Katie's black eyes was like looking into the depths of space: one could see, but not truly appreciate.

The nine-month-old progressed minimally over the next couple of days. A "wound team" consisting of two nurses changed the vacuum dressing daily. The painless process took no more than a few minutes. I asked the nurse every day about Katie's progress.

"How does the incision look?"
"It looks a little better. She's doing great."
"How much longer before it heals?"
"Ten to fourteen days."

We repeated that exchange day after day after day. The intensivists, nurses, and members of the wound team consistently said Katie's incision was improving, but the projection as to when the wound would finally heal never changed.

Dr. Abraham returned to examine Katie on Sunday afternoon. He again rested his forearms on the railing as he did the week before. I asked how much longer Katie would need the vacuum dressing and got the now familiar response, "ten to fourteen days." Dr. Abraham then broached the subject of a tracheostomy. After briefly recapping the numerous respiratory infections and complications, he stated circumspectly, "I may have been wrong [not to trach in June]." I doubt many cardiovascular surgeons make a practice of admitting fallibility. Notwithstanding Dr. Abraham's humility, I disagreed with his statement. Given the risks associated with a tracheostomy, Krista and I never questioned that we made the correct decision. We chose the option with the highest probability of success. Even if we did not get the desired outcome, our decision was still correct.

Krista returned to work on Monday, March 10 after giving me one mission: arrange a care conference. Understanding the value of speaking with experts from various disciplines simultaneously, Krista constantly tried with little success. Now that Katie's treatment plan had completely gone off the rails, Krista wanted a group huddle.

Rounds were uneventful that morning since Katie remained stable on the ventilator. When I asked how much longer for the wound to heal, I got the same answer: "Ten to fourteen days." As Dr. Williams concluded rounds on Katie, I interjected, "One more thing ... Krista really wants a care conference." I received a cool reception, so I expounded a bit. "She wants everyone in the same room at the same time to figure out where we go from here." After getting a noncommittal response, the staff moved on to the next patient.

Using a "good cop, bad cop" strategy, I informed every doctor, nurse practitioner, nurse, and therapist I could find that Krista adamantly demanded a care conference. I may have exaggerated her temperament regarding the request slightly. Regardless, my persistence paid off. On Wednesday, Sarah informed me she scheduled a care conference for 12:30 on Thursday, March 13.

Katie remained sedated day after day as we waited for the chest incision to heal. Despite the discomfort of intubation, she stroked her animals and held their paws. Family and caregivers spoke and sang to Katie and caressed her with gloved hands. Katie occasionally looked at me pleadingly. "Please get me off of this machine; please take these drugs away," I imagined her imploring through teary eyes. Of course, I could do neither, nor could I explain that to her. I continued to put on a happy face as inwardly I slid into depression.

Numerous acts of kindness broke the enervating monotony in the PICU. Fr. Jim continued to update the congregation on Katie's plight during Sunday mass. On the Sunday before Katie's second attempted Glenn surgery, he asked for a moment of silent prayer on her behalf. In decades of attending mass, I

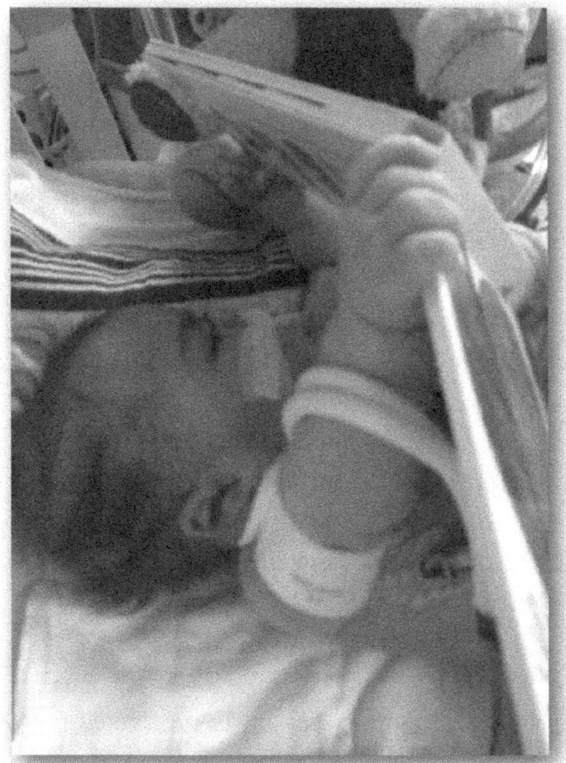

An intubated Katie catches up on her reading.

had never seen such a gesture. Standing unrecognized in the midst of hundreds of people praying for Katie moved me deeply. In the weeks that followed, students at the church's elementary school sent cards with words of encouragement. One first grader told Katie she would serve as her "big sister" once she started school. Another student informed Katie that her class prayed for her every morning. Mothers from the school delivered homemade dinners to the PICU. I brought all the mothers in to meet Katie, and they left inspired by our little fighter.

Our church supporters were not limited to St. Pius X parishioners. I walked out of the house late one Saturday morning on my way back to the hospital only to find three people approaching my porch. They introduced themselves as Jehovah's Witnesses and asked if they could share their message with me. I briefly explained my situation, pointing to my grey PMCH shirt as though I needed to substantiate my explanation for declining their request. They asked a few questions regarding Katie's condition. After I answered, they promised to pray for her. I thanked them and left for the hospital. After a brief detour to check on another family, I discovered two balloons emblazoned with "Get Well Soon" anchored to a beautiful bouquet of flowers on the table at the foot of Katie's crib. I recognized the names on the card as the three Witnesses who visited the house an hour earlier.

Katie's supporters extended far beyond Indianapolis. Friends, family, and strangers alike sent words of encouragement in e-mails, texts, cards, and letters. Krista and I passed many evenings reading the messages aloud. Try as I might, I cannot express the depths of my appreciation for these expressions of support, and I hope these wonderful people understand how much their kindness lightened the burden of our situation.

The day after Katie's sternum operation, Fr. Jim asked me via text whether I wanted a second opinion. Unsure whether he meant a physician or a saint, I was open to both. He put me in contact with one of his friends, a physician who worked in pediatric cardiology at Riley Children's Hospital. At her request, one of the top pediatric cardiologists at Riley, Dr. Robert Darragh, agreed to review Katie's case. I gathered Katie's records on Monday, March 10 and hand delivered them to Riley.

Dr. Darragh called us Tuesday night and spent more than an hour discussing Katie's situation. He agreed with Dr. Abraham's initial position that infants with certain cardiac issues, including Ebstein's Anomaly, should not have a tracheostomy. Given Katie's recent difficulties, however, he believed the risk of not having a tracheostomy now outweighed the risks associated with the cardiac defect. I asked whether he had any experience with a sternum separating following surgery. Not only had he never seen that personally, he never heard of such an occurrence. Most importantly to us, Dr. Darragh confirmed we could not pursue the Glenn procedure or a transplant without rehabilitating Katie's superior vena cavas.

The cardiologist offered to assume responsibility for Katie's care if we transferred her to Riley. Krista and I thanked the doctor profusely, but declined his offer. Laser focused on the tracheostomy, we saw no benefit in having the procedure at Riley as opposed to PMCH. We asked if we could contact him again once Katie had improved sufficiently for the next surgical procedure. He told us we could call him anytime. The conversation ended after we thanked the doctor for his generosity and kindness.

Krista and I spent the next hour dissecting every word Dr. Darragh said. The doctor only differed with the PMCH medical team on two points. First, Dr. Abraham intended to perform the Fontan procedure after the Glenn. The Riley physicians eschewed the Fontan in severe Ebstein patients. Second, the Riley physicians avoid using the SVC for an IV line if possible to prevent damaging the vein. On the first point, we would address the need for the Fontan only after a successful Glenn operation. On the second, Katie's veins were already damaged, making the difference moot. Dr. Darragh eliminated the little doubt remaining that Katie needed a tracheostomy and affirmed our treatment decisions to date.

A young woman stopped me in the hall outside Katie's room late in the afternoon of Wednesday, March 12 and asked me for subjects to discuss at the care conference. I did not recall her specialty, maybe a nurse or social worker. She surprised me with the request, and I wished Krista could have fielded the question. Thinking on my feet, I did the best I could. I rattled off a few topics, including a tracheostomy, Katie's new surgical course, and preparations for Katie's homecoming. She thanked me and disappeared down the hall.

Krista took a few hours of vacation time to attend the case conference on Thursday, March 13, one week after the sternum repair surgery. We walked to a large conference room off the main hall in the PICU a few minutes shy of 12:30 p.m. The staff generally kept the door open; however, we found the door closed and waited outside patiently, at least at first.

"You think they're in there already?" I asked.

"Yes."

After a pause, "Do you think they're talking about Katie?"

"Oh, yes, definitely," Krista said nodding her head. "*This* is the discussion I wanted to hear."

"Me, too."

Knowing the direness of Katie's circumstances, neither Krista nor I wanted sanitized opinions. I would have given anything to hear the discussions inside that room. I will not admit that I lowered myself to eavesdrop. I can say, however, with certainty that the solid wood door is practically soundproof even with one's ear pressed tightly against it. The door finally opened at 1:15 p.m., and Sarah beckoned us inside.

Krista asked for a care conference with the full team, and she got it. The only two open chairs sat at the table's end closest to the door. Krista took the chair at the corner, leaving me at the head of the table. I sat and surveyed the brain trust before me. On my left sat Krista, Drs. Abraham (surgeon), Steinberg (cardiologist), and Williams (intensivist). Drs. Abraha (intensivist) and Williams (pulmonologist), Sarah (nurse practitioner), and Soni (a favorite PICU nurse and nurse practioner in training) sat to my right. Another nurse and the young woman who asked for subjects the day before sat directly across from me. I expected someone to speak, but all eyes locked on me. I turned to Krista, expecting her to take the lead. She looked away as though something at the far end of the room suddenly caught her attention. I turned back to the professionals assembled before me and realized they expected us to run the meeting. When I stammered, Dr. Abraham mercifully stepped in.

Dr. Abraham had the questions I gave the woman typed on a piece of paper. He started with the tracheostomy issue. Dr. Abraham simply stated that, given all we had seen over the past few months, the procedure presented the best course of action. Krista agreed, stating she jettisoned her reticence after "the debacle of the last surgery." Dr. Abraham chimed in with a wry smile, "I'm not used to hearing my work referred to as a 'debacle.'" That evoked chuckles from the group and broke the tension. Krista then fired off a barrage of questions covering topics such as resuscitating the SVCs, nutrition, home monitoring, infection avoidance, and the long-term harm of heavy sedation that intubation required.

Krista and I made a good team. The room turned silent after she posed her questions until the awkwardness prompted someone to speak up. I then took over, asking another doctor by name what he thought of the answer. After he answered, I asked a third physician or a nurse whether he disagreed with anything his peers stated and so forth. Using the strategy learned during military training, I ensured we heard the few minor contrasting opinions. We broke after an hour having finally decided to press forward with the tracheostomy once Katie's chest wound healed. Krista also successfully petitioned for weekly, smaller care conferences to reassess strategy.

The meeting was somewhat anticlimactic. We faced a long list of alternatives when we made what I termed the "Big Decision" after the aborted surgery, i.e., whether to pursue the Glenn or a transplant. In contrast, our current decision mattered little. With the many complications Katie now faced, extubating or proceeding with a trach immediately presented so much risk as to be irresponsible. Thus, our decision did not translate into any immediate action.

Krista and I did feel more comfortable knowing members of the various disciplines were on the same page. Something the intensivist Dr. Williams said, his concern evident in his voice, affected me more than anything else mentioned. Specifically, we did not know the long-term effects of so many drugs on Katie's brain. That thought kept me awake many a night, hoping that she would not suffer long-term consequences. I appreciated hearing one of the intensivists echo the same concern.

I updated my mom with the latest news after the care conference. She had news of her own; my grandmother was "actively dying." Unfamiliar with the phrase, I asked what that meant. Parkinson's disease had stripped my grandmother of quality of life years before, but the organs responsible for keeping her alive continued unaffected as she approached her ninety-seventh year. My grandmother's body had finally started to shut down. She no longer ingested food or water. I asked how long the process would take. Mom did not have a firm answer, giving a wide range of hours to two weeks.

The last six years of my grandmother's life were fraught with pain and suffering. That she would finally find peace was cause for thanks, not sadness. Knowing that Gram would never meet Katie saddened me nonetheless. I know nothing would have brought her more joy than meeting her then-youngest great-granddaughter. I accepted the reality that the two would never see each other once I realized the severity of Katie's illness months before, although I clung to a glimmer of hope. News of Gram's imminent passing extinguished that hope. As the eldest member of the family slowly released her grasp on this world, the youngest member fought to keep hers.

CHAPTER 26

Losses

I TOOK SAM FOR A walk on the first nice day of the year. We barely reached the end of the block before Sam turned around to go home. Sam would typically walk forever if given the chance. Over dinner that night, I told Krista, "We need to walk Sam more often. He's really deconditioned." She agreed, but walks with Sam grew shorter, not longer. He struggled getting up on the couch. I bought some lumber to build a small set of stairs to aid him in climbing on the furniture, but the unfolding PICU drama distracted me from the project. He managed, although sometimes with a helpful boost. After watching Sam exhaust himself climbing atop the loveseat on Friday, March 14, I scheduled an appointment with the veterinarian the following day. I hoped that a shot of steroids would loosen his joints.

Krista spent Saturday morning with Katie while I drove Sam across town to our veterinarian. Sam needed my help to get out of the car and struggled to walk the short distance from the parking lot to the office. The practice consisted of two veterinarians along with support staff. We loved the female veterinarian who normally treated Sam, in part because she referred to the portly yet distinguished foxhound as "Handsome." She was not working that day, so I waited with Sam in the examination room for her counterpart.

Lying next to Sam on the floor, I noticed he looked old in the glare of fluorescent light, as though he aged five years over the past week. When I stroked his neck and small tufts of hair came out in my fingers, I realized we were dealing with more than arthritis. The veterinarian came in and knelt next to my pal. He ran his hands down the length of the dog from snout to tail, searching for abnormalities. Sam always enjoyed attention and panted pleasantly. I could see the veterinarian's eyes squint as his hands fell on Sam's ample stomach. "It feels like a lot of fluid in there." He excused himself and left us alone again. Sam was never svelte, but, now that the vet mentioned it, I could see the dog's belly bulging even more than normal. The vet returned with an ultrasound machine. Passing the scanner over Sam's stomach, he showed me an accumulation of fluid on a grainy screen. Without further testing, he could not definitively diagnose the problem but speculated Sam had cancer.

The vet presented me with two options. First, admit Sam to an animal hospital for further testing and treatment. Second, leave Sam with him for the next forty-eight hours for testing. Either way, Sam would spend most of that time caged in isolation with very little human contact. I presented a third option: Take Sam home to live the remainder of his days in comfort amongst family. The vet agreed that, given Sam's age of twelve years, my option was most appropriate. I asked him to speculate as to how much time Sam had to live. He could not say without additional testing, but speculated weeks, possibly months. Wanting to spare Sam the pain and discomfort of testing, I told the vet we would make the best of what time Sam had remaining.

I always gave Sam a treat after a visit to the vet, and this occasion was no different. I pulled into a fast-food restaurant down the block from the clinic and bought Sam a sausage biscuit. Sam went crazy when his hound nose picked up the scent long before I got back to the car. He took it enthusiastically. I again helped him out of the car when we arrived back at the house. To my dismay, half of the sausage patty remained on the back seat.

Sam's strength drained from him like water running through a sieve. After walking off the back patio to relieve himself Saturday evening, his back legs quivered and gave out as he turned to come back to the house. I lifted his hind end so he could get his legs under himself. He could stand, but faltered when trying to walk. Lifting him slightly by the back hips, the two of us ambled the twenty feet across the patio. After Sam took a long drink from his bowl, I picked him up and placed him gingerly on the couch, as gingerly as a seventy-two pound dog will allow.

We were fortunate to have help that weekend since Sam was too weak to leave unattended. The hospital lifted the visitor restrictions on March 1, and my Aunt Elaine had returned to Indianapolis a few days later. Between the three of us, we managed full-time coverage with both Sam and Katie.

Sam's breathing slowed and grew labored as midnight approached on Saturday. He struggled so much that I did not expect him to last the night. Thinking this was the end, I stayed by Sam's side. He shared Katie's resiliency, though, and his breathing improved by 3:00 a.m. We spent the remainder of the night fighting for space on the couch as we had so many times before.

Sam continued struggling to ambulate on Sunday. While Krista and my aunt tended to Katie at the hospital that afternoon, I took care of the dog at the house. Sam failed to transverse the patio before relieving himself and then collapsed, covering his hind legs and paws in filth. I brought him into the kitchen where his legs again gave out. I retrieved a bucket, soap, and water from the garage and bathed him on the floor. Sam did not like having his paws touched, yet I cleaned every crevice without protest. He looked away, disconnecting himself from my activities. Dogs are proud animals, and the circumstances mortified him. I recounted the ordeal to Krista when she returned from the hospital, and we discussed options. The only responsible decision was self-evident.

I called the vet first thing in the morning on March 17, St. Patrick's Day. The woman who answered sounded surprised to hear Sam had declined so quickly. I set an appointment for 5 p.m. and headed to PMCH. After attending rounds, I returned home to relieve my aunt on Sam duty while she replaced me at the hospital. Sam barely touched the fast food breakfast sandwiches I purchased for him on the way home. Unable to walk on his own, Sam needed me to carry him outside so he could relieve himself. He no longer wanted to be on the couch, preferring instead to stretch out on the floor. My phone rang as Sam and I were in the middle of the living room just after one in the afternoon. When I answered, my mom told me my grandmother had passed away.

Parkinson's disease had robbed my grandmother of meaningful quality of life years before, so death came as liberation from the imprisonment of a woefully sick body. That she was no longer with us made the world a lesser place. Gram was a devout Catholic who lived her faith. Coming of age in a poor coal mining family during the Great Depression, she possessed a wisdom and appreciation for life one can only glean from a hardscrabble existence. After illness robbed her of the ability to speak and express herself, we could not determine how much she could process. By the end, we thought dementia prevented her from comprehending her surroundings. Her last act was to die almost to the hour exactly twenty-eight years after her husband passed away. I cannot believe that was coincidental.

I helped Sam walk out to the garage and lifted him into the car two hours after losing my grandmother. Krista joined Sam in the cargo space after I picked her up from work. She comforted him on the forty-minute trip to the veterinary clinic. Once we arrived, I carried Sam from the back of the car to the yard outside the clinic's front door. He loved visiting the vet and tried his best to walk to the entrance. His legs repeatedly gave out on him, so I again lifted his back hips to aide his walking. Once inside the office, he strained to walk to the examination room, but did so under his own power. The staff had placed a fuzzy red blanket in the middle of the room. Always a blanket aficionado, Sam plopped down on it with satisfaction.

The vet who had diagnosed Sam two days earlier came in to explain the procedure, which consisted of a single injection. He then left us alone with our dog. We laid down next to Sam as he panted happily, obviously feeling no discomfort. I knew where the staff kept treats and peanut butter, so I prepared a little snack. Sam took a couple licks of the peanut butter, but showed no interest in the treat. A healthy Sam would have devoured both. I took his refusal as confirmation that we made the correct decision.

The vet returned and knelt by Sam's tail. Without warning, he inserted a needle in Sam's left hind leg and slowly pressed the plunger. Sam closed his eyes and gently rested his head between his front paws. The syringe still held half of its fluid when the vet stated, "His heart has probably already stopped." He finished the injection and withdrew the needle. My pal was gone. Krista and I said our last goodbye, and left Sam lying peacefully on the blanket in the examination room.

Krista and I stopped at a restaurant to collect ourselves before going to the hospital. We later joined Katie and my aunt for a quiet evening of reminiscing.

I planned to return to my hometown for my grandmother's visitation and funeral. Having failed to visit her for the last year of her life because of Katie's illness, I felt compelled to attend the services. I hoped to depart late Tuesday morning after rounds and return after the burial on Thursday, a forty-eight hour trip. Krista arranged for a coworker to sit with Katie in my absence. Blinded by grief, I selfishly put my need to cope with my grandmother's passing over Katie's need for me at the hospital. My grief also blinded me to the symptoms that foreshadowed the disaster to come. Katie developed a low-grade temperature on St. Patrick's Day just as she had so many times before. I thought little of it.

The PICU bustled with activity when I arrived at the break of dawn on Tuesday. Katie's fever persisted through rounds early in the afternoon. Katie had always responded well to Tylenol, which quickly quelled previous fevers. That the drug had no discernable effect befuddled Dr. Williams, the intensivist on duty. I just considered it yet another fever. I decided to sit with Katie until the fever broke. Hours passed with no improvement. As five o'clock approached, I pushed my departure back until Wednesday.

After checking the night schedule at the nurses' station, I returned to Katie's room to find Dr. Williams standing a few feet from the foot of the crib. The lights were off, leaving only the ambient light from the hall and the dusk sky to illuminate the room. A blue windbreaker draped over his folded arms. Lines of concern etched his face as he stared intently at Katie. He said nothing as I entered. I broke the silence, joking about him overstaying the end of his shift. The intensivist's expression remained pained.

"I don't have a good feeling. Something's going on here, and I don't know what it is."

The sixth sense developed over decades of caring for critically ill children bedeviled him. Like searching for a specter, Dr. Williams could feel its presence and the chill of close proximity, but could not quite put his hands on it. I completely disregarded his concern.

Two days after my grandmother and Sam died, I reported to the hospital before leaving for Pennsylvania. Katie's temperature remained steady at 100.2 degrees. I sat with her for a couple hours waiting for rounds. Wanting to attend the visitation, I kissed the sleeping Katie good-bye as noon approached, asked the nurse to call me should Katie's condition change, and left Indianapolis. I had just crossed the Ohio border when my phone rang. Seeing Krista's name appear, I accepted the call.

"Hey, babe. What's up?"

"Katie's temperature is 106.2," Krista said.

"What? What happened?"

"I don't know, but I'm on my way to the hospital now."

I called my mom to report the latest crisis and asked her whether I should continue to Pennsylvania or return to Indianapolis. She responded, "What would your grandmother do?" I had no doubt as to the answer. I hung up, turned around at the next exit, and slammed the accelerator against the floorboard.

CHAPTER 27

Crisis

I ARRIVED AT ONE O'CLOCK in the afternoon and found two technicians performing an ultrasound on Katie's belly. No one bothered to turn on the lights, which made the atmosphere even more somber. I asked the women if they found anything. Knowing they would not answer never stopped me from asking a technician if she saw something abnormal. I always received the same response: "The radiologist has to read the films," as though she knew nothing. You could ask a technician x-raying a decapitated man if her patient were dead, and she would refer you to the radiologist. The technicians kept their lips sealed, an admirable, if not frustrating, practice.

Krista soon returned from speaking with Dr. Williams and updated me on Katie's status. Infection had overtaken her system. Katie's fever skyrocketed to 107.0 degrees. Aggressive medication knocked her temperature down a few degrees, but the fever still raged. Katie's kidneys and liver were shutting down.

The doctors suspected necrotic bowel, i.e., insufficient blood flow to the intestines causing oxygen-starved tissue to die. No one knew the cause definitively. Since Katie's birth, a few doctors speculated that Katie's defective heart might have been unable to furnish other organs with sufficient oxygen in utero. Consequently, these organs were not as resilient as one would expect in a child with the benefit of a normal gestation and may succumb to disease much faster.

The technicians spent two hours with Katie, turning her limp body like a bag of sugar. No more than twenty minutes after leaving with their machine, they returned with the radiologist. The doctor could not detect what would cause Katie's liver and kidneys to shut down from the initial scans, so she decided to search for herself. Absorbed in her work, the physician said nothing to us. Not wanting to interfere, Krista and I observed silently.

Dr. Abraham walked in, stood at the far end of the room, and watched the radiologist examine Katie. A few minutes passed without any movement from the surgeon. I took a position beside him as we stared at Katie. My patience eventually gave out, and I asked, "What do you think?" Dr. Abraham continued to stare at Katie for a long moment. "Something very bad is happening here." He then excused himself, saying he needed to confer with a general surgeon.

The radiologist identified only some minor inflammation in the intestines. She speculated this indicated dead tissue. Only visual inspection could confirm or determine what, if anything, was happening in Katie's belly. As if on cue, a general surgeon arrived and curtly introduced himself before examining Katie.

The surgeon slumped in a tall rolling chair when he finished. "There's nothing I can do," he said. The surgeon did not think Katie would survive an operation in her deconditioned state. Even if she did, she lacked the physical reserves to withstand the demands of recovery. He delivered his opinion matter-of-factly, which I appreciated. I needed information, not sentimentality. He left without any words of sympathy or comfort. With exploratory surgery no longer an option, we lost our best, and maybe only, remaining tool to identify what had gone so horribly wrong.

The doctors and technicians who had monopolized our daughter all afternoon left us alone with Katie. We held her limp hands as she lay unconscious in her crib. Shock overcame me. I expected and prepared for heart issues. I expected and prepared for lung issues. I expected and prepared for brain issues. I never, not in my wildest dreams, imagined that an abdominal problem would threaten Katie's life, yet I could not deny the magnitude of this setback and the almost certainty of death. Nausea struck me when two staff members erected yellow room dividers outside Katie's door. The staff used the dividers to give privacy to a patient during an in-room procedure or a family to grieve.

Dr. Williams returned in the late afternoon with the working theory on Katie's deteriorating condition. He sat in the same chair the surgeon had used not an hour earlier, sitting backwards and crossing his gangly arms on the backrest. Blood cultures failed to establish the presence of infection, let alone the source of infection. The tests did confirm, however, that Katie's kidneys and liver were failing. Her urine output had dropped precipitously, and Dr. Williams predicted complete failure soon. X-rays revealed sizable pockets of air in Katie's large intestine, indicating dead tissue. If the large intestine were not dead, it was actively dying.

> "We get to the point when we have to ask ourselves, 'Are we doing things *for* Katie or *to* Katie?'"

Even if he could convince the surgeon to operate, Dr. Williams said the procedure and recovery would be very painful with little chance of survival. Dr. Abraham, Dr. Williams, and the general surgeon recommended we make Katie comfortable and let nature run its course. Krista and I did not ask for privacy to discuss options. We did not request another opinion. We clearly understood Dr. Williams' message: Additional treatment would only lead to pain.

> "Okay," I said in a defeated voice before turning to Krista. "Are you okay with this?"

She nodded and sobbed quietly, unable to speak. After a respectful pause, Dr. Williams proffered a clipboard. Krista showed no intention of taking it, so I did. Through wet and unfocused eyes, three words atop the page jumped out at me: "Do Not Resuscitate" (DNR). I had no interest in reading the particulars. I knew signing meant denying Katie the help of the people and technology available at PMCH. As the pen lowered to the paper, Krista found her voice.

> "Can we remove the nasal thermometer and discontinue her anticoagulation shots?"

An advocate to the end, Krista tried to make Katie as comfortable as possible. Dr. Williams nodded his approval. I signed the DNR with a cheap ballpoint pen.

Krista and I never planned for such circumstances. I suppose the thought so abhorred us that we never broached the subject. We sent a flurry of text messages to our family. We did not think they could travel to Indianapolis in time to see Katie, so we made no arrangements. I also e-mailed a brief update and an invitation to friends:

> I'll write more later, but I need to pass the word that an infection has overtaken Katie's system. Multiple organ systems are failing. Any attempt to stem the tide would require extremely invasive and high-risk abdominal surgery. Doctors think such attempts are futile and would cause her great pain. Therefore, we are letting this process run its course.
>
> If you would like to visit, be advised that she has hours to days if we leave her on life support. We welcome anyone. Katie has touched many people in her short time here. I leave to you whether you want to see her. Your presence will be welcome.

I did not expect anyone to take me up on my offer, but, given the bond many had formed with Katie over the past nine months, I did not want to deprive someone the opportunity of saying goodbye.

After a day of constant activity, Katie's room fell silent as evening approached. The throng of doctors, nurses, and therapists dissipated once we agreed to the DNR. Nurses kept a respectful distance while Katie fought for her life flanked by her parents.

Krista and I spent the evening praying for, reading to, and, more than anything, talking to Katie. We told Katie we loved and were so very proud of her. I am not one to show emotion in front of others, but the circumstances erased all inhibitions.

Around 8 p.m., Katie's hands and feet began twitching. The initially sporadic movement increased in frequency and severity over the next thirty minutes. Katie's fingers opened and closed into fists. Her feet, clad in socks that resembled blue ballet shoes, kicked ferociously as if performing a morbid dance. I held Katie's right hand and foot still, while Krista held their counterparts. We fought the reflexive movement, as though somehow helping.

Dr. Metz, the overnight intensivist, checked in periodically. He continued Dr. Williams' strategy of intense pharmaceutical treatment as a Hail Mary to arrest the infection. For the first time since Katie's birth, I stopped following the particulars of Katie's care, choosing instead to spend the remainder of Katie's time with Katie, not her doctors.

Katie continued to decline throughout the evening. The nurses lowered the room temperature and placed cooling pads over Katie's body in hopes of breaking the fever. Katie's distended stomach felt hot to the touch in stark contrast to her ice-cold extremities. Her pulse grew so faint that the nurses could only detect it with a Doppler in her ankles. Meanwhile, Katie's heart rhythm became increasingly erratic as her potassium continued to escalate.

Katie's tremors stopped just before 11 p.m., and her heart rate rebounded. Krista and I had expected Katie to fail at any moment. Now that the tremor episode passed, we planned for the possibility of a slower decline. One of us needed to be with Katie at all times, so we decided to take shifts. I offered to stay with Katie overnight, while Krista tried to rest in one of the PICU's family sleep rooms. I wanted Krista rested in the event Katie survived until the relief staff arrived the following morning. Extremely reticent to leave Katie, Krista agreed only after I placed my cell phone in the crib at Katie's feet and promised to call if Katie took a downturn.

Krista left me at Katie's crib with the nurse keeping her post on the other side of the room. Danielle had cared for Katie on a few previous occasions, but we had not spoken much. Watching her interact with doctors and her fellow nurses, she struck me as fiercely bright with little patience for those who did not meet her standards. I felt fortunate that she cared for Katie on this most unfortunate night. She visited Katie's bedside when needed, but otherwise left Katie and me alone.

Katie resumed her twitching, albeit not as severely, soon after Krista left. At 1 a.m., Danielle informed me that Katie's potassium exceeded nine, the highest value her machine can register. This explained, at least in part, Katie's erratic heart rhythm as excess potassium affects cardiac function. Danielle notified Dr. Metz, who appeared in the room to discuss the process of removing life support. I listened, but said little. I could not bring myself to broach the issue with my wife. I repeatedly looked at my phone sitting at Katie's feet and wondered whether I should call Krista. I kept thinking, "Give it another five minutes." The doctor apparently noticed my reluctance to talk and did not press the issue. Dr. Metz ordered a massive amount of insulin in an attempt to lower her potassium before leaving me with Katie.

I spent countless hours over the past nine months encouraging Katie, telling her to keep fighting, to keep pushing. Not wanting Katie to suffer, I rested my forehead to hers and delivered a new message.

> "It's okay, Bunny. You don't have to fight anymore. You fought so hard. Now you can rest. We are so proud of you, Bunny. Rest. You can let go."

She did not listen. The insulin kicked in, and Katie miraculously stabilized. I spent the next couple of hours watching Katie rest.

In the agony of watching Katie struggle in expectation of imminent death, I needed to talk to someone. Whether for the distraction or to work through my thoughts, I do not know. Danielle obliged, and we passed the night hours discussing Katie's history, our families, careers, money, religion, and just about everything else. Emotionally raw, I opened up to the nurse, a practical stranger, to a degree I would not consider with many of my closest friends. I do not know how I would have weathered those gut-wrenching hours without Danielle.

Katie's potassium and temperature receded and heart rhythm normalized by 5 a.m. With Katie now stable, I decided to catch some sleep on the couch in Katie's room. Completely exhausted, I apologized to Danielle. She encouraged me to get some rest and promised to wake me should anything change. Someone had deposited a set of linens on the seat cushions. Rather than use the foldout bed, I collapsed on the couch, faced the backrest, and fell asleep using the linens as a pillow. The next sensation was a hand gently shaking my shoulder. "Jack, everything is fine. My shift is over, and I'm going home." So tired that every muscle screamed when I made the smallest movement, I managed to raise my open left hand in the air. I felt Danielle's fingers wrap around mine. Squeezing her hand, I said, "Thank you," and fell back asleep.

The feeling of someone towering over me jolted me awake on Thursday morning. I looked up to see Dr. Williams' back as he examined Katie. I groggily scanned my surroundings. Even without my contacts, I could see dramatic changes from the previous day. The room dividers outside the door were gone. The room buzzed with activity as doctors, nurses, and RTs tended to Katie. In the thick of it all, Krista conversed with a cardiologist. I could tell from her posture that she was in "advocate mode," not "mourning mode." Like Dorothy waking from her dream in the "Wizard of Oz," I was in a familiar, albeit completely different, world.

Krista updated me on the latest events as I ran water through my hair to tamp down an acute case of bedhead and slipped contacts on my bloodshot eyes. Katie started to turn the corner Thursday morning. Her large intestine, although terribly sick, had not died. If it had, she would have followed within hours. It remained, however, terribly sick. Defying all expectations, her kidneys continued to function to some degree. Dr. Williams joined the conversation, telling us that the kidneys were producing urine, but he did not know whether they were cleansing the blood of toxins. Similarly, Katie's liver barely functioned, but it did not shut down. Dr. Williams said he would continue the antibiotics and diuretics and restart wound care and anticoagulation treatment. Although Katie remained critically ill, death was no longer imminent. Katie appeared to have once again defied expectations. The physicians could not explain her rebound. We had no idea what sent her spiraling and would probably never know. Katie's turnaround was the closest thing I had ever seen to a miracle, and we rejoiced accordingly.

Krista and I had company in our celebrations. In addition to some local friends, my mom, sister, and one of my aunts drove out immediately after my grandmother's funeral that very morning. John, my best friend and the best man at our wedding, flew in from Florida, and a law school buddy made the three hour drive from South Bend. After a week of loss and apprehension, we celebrated Katie's stunning turnaround in complete euphoria. Krista remained engaged with the treatment team, but I remained aloof. In the midst of Katie's struggle the night before, I turned off thoughts of treatment and concerned myself with her comfort moment by moment. Part of me did not want to assume the yoke of responsibility for her care again, and I spent some time away from the hospital with my friends.

My hiatus from the treatment team ended Friday morning when I joined Krista and my mom for rounds. Lab results indicated minimal kidney and liver improvement. The wound team resumed changing the dressing on Katie's chest incision. Eight days after the operation, they still estimated the wound needed another "ten to fourteen days" to heal. An X-ray of Katie's intestine showed slight improvement, but the organ remained very fragile. Complicating matters, we had difficulty managing Katie's wildly fluctuating potassium.

Katie needed nutrition to rebuild her strength, heal, and avoid another infection. We did not know how much food Katie's intestines could tolerate, assuming they could tolerate any at all. The intensivist tried very limited feedings measured in milliliters, not even a tenth of what she required. Her lab results indicated that she did not tolerate even that small amount of food. We found ourselves in a feeding catch-22: Katie's intestines could not heal until she received proper nutrition, and she could not receive proper nutrition until her intestines healed. The doctors planned to increase feedings slowly, careful not to overload her system, while we hoped Katie had the reserves to endure the process.

I returned to the hospital after running errands Friday afternoon to find a law school classmate waiting for me in the Family Room. Emily and I had not spoken for almost five years, our paths diverging as our careers veered in different directions after graduation. She had followed Katie's story from the beginning. I hugged Emily and escorted her back to Room 6.

After helping Emily don her gown and gloves, I introduced her to the assembled friends and family before guiding her to the crib. Few things gave me the joy of watching someone meet Katie for the first time; however, Katie's appearance startled me. Bloated almost beyond recognition, the swelling obscured her facial features.

Krista told me Katie began rapidly retaining fluid that afternoon. By 7 p.m., Katie had swollen to such a degree that the nurse could not open Katie's eyes to check her pupils. The pressure of retained water in her legs caused the injection points from the coagulation therapy to seep clear fluid. The kidneys still functioned, but they were not excreting enough fluid from her system. As much as I appreciated the company, I perseverated over Katie's bloating and the underlying kidney issue.

The kidneys, although still "sick," managed to shed the excess fluid over the next forty-eight hours. Katie's color and temperature returned to normal by Sunday, March 23, and she appeared healthy, even radiant. Her abdominal x-rays showed significant improvement. We ended a week of unrelenting hits and losses, undoubtedly the nadir of our PMCH experience thus far, with a glimmer of hope.

After six days of waiting, Katie finally woke on Monday. I was elated. Playing with Katie made our hospital existence tolerable. I jumped when I saw her clear, black eyes, rushing to her crib to welcome her back:

> "Look who's awake! Hi, Bunny! I missed you. We all missed you so much!"

She stared straight back at me as I stroked her thick brown hair.

> "Do you want to play with your dog? Let me get your puppy."

As I stretched to reach Katie's favorite stuffed animal at the far end of the crib, I glanced back at my little girl. She continued to stare, her gaze fixed where my head had been seconds before. I moved back into her line of sight and looked directly in her eyes. I slowly moved to the left and then the right. Her eyes remained looking straight ahead. She was not tracking.

CHAPTER 28

A Pyrrhic Victory

I COULD NOT BRING MYSELF to speak of Katie's inability to track, acting as though I failed to notice anything wrong. Krista broached the subject with Dr. Halczenko before mentioning it to me, her words speckled with a twinge of dismay but no sign of the dread I felt. He speculated that Katie's sick liver and kidneys were unable to process the heavy doses of drugs Katie received over the past week. Therefore, Katie was and would remain in a state of heavy sedation until her system could rid itself of the medications. I found relief and rekindled hope in the doctor's reasoning.

The tracking issue constituted just one of a growing number of concerns. Katie's large intestine could still only tolerate a fraction of the food she needed to live, let alone heal. Much to the staff's surprise, Katie's liver and kidneys continued to slowly improve. Despite the progress, the ordeal left the organs terribly vulnerable to another infection. The wound team reported that Katie's chest incision was slowly healing, but still estimated "10 to 14 days" before healing completely. Katie's body simply lacked the nutrition to rebuild her damaged cells. Finally, Katie's prolonged intubation, 32 of the past 38 days, risked infection and breakdown of the airway tissue. The latter could cause fatal bleeding. As we focused on these issues, Katie's failure to track was the elephant in the room.

We hoped Katie's tracking would improve over the next two days as the drugs lost their sedative hold. Seeing no change, Dr. Halczenko ordered a battery of neurological tests. Technicians started with an ultrasound on Katie's head, searching for indications of a bleed. They then attached small electrodes to Katie's scalp to measure brain waves. Once completed, they transferred Katie to the first floor for an MRI. Again, the technicians would tell us nothing, so we waited for the neurologist's assessment. In the meantime, Krista discovered another problem.

Not long after returning from the MRI, Katie's heart rhythm became erratic and her skin grew mottled. Always the pharmacist, Krista checked Katie's drug pumps and discovered a nurse had forgotten to restart the milrinone, a drug used to improve cardiac function after heart surgery. The medicine, administered via IV, increases the force with which the heart pumps and decreases venous pressure. Krista identified the mistake, and the nurse started the drug pump.

Doctors had tried to wean Katie off the milrinone for more than two weeks, but her heart could not function adequately without it. The inadvertent cold-turkey test hammered that fact home. The amount of milrinone in her system when the nurse removed the pump should have lasted approximately four hours before symptoms of heart failure became apparent. Katie started exhibiting signs of failure almost immediately. Intended for short-term use, Katie could not depend on the drug indefinitely.

A PICU resident called Krista at work the following morning to inform her of an elevated lactate. Krista told her that was expected given the milrinone medication error. The resident had not heard of the issue. This is but one example of the family bridging communication gaps amongst the staff.

The neurology report arrived late Thursday afternoon. The neurologist saw absolutely nothing to explain Katie's failure to track. That outcome exceeded my most optimistic expectations, but did little to assuage my concern. Lacking resolution from the last battery of tests, Dr. Halczenko ordered another test for Friday, March 28 to determine whether the infection and resulting fever of the previous week damaged Katie's optical nerves. In other words, Katie might be blind.

That I found the prospect of blindness not completely devastating evidences the degree of Katie's setbacks over the previous six weeks. The seemingly endless stream of bad news somewhat inured us to even this devastating possibility. Nine months earlier, the thought of the incision scar on Katie's chest pained me. Now, I preferred blindness to severe neurological deficits. The degree of sorrow to which one can become acclimated over time is staggering. Moreover, I thought blindness improbable. Katie no longer petted her fuzzy stuffed dog or held hands. Blindness could not account for that.

We did not have to wait long for the results: Katie's optical nerves functioned normally. She could definitively see. The question remained whether she could process the image. Based on previous tests and unfounded optimism, we continued hoping that Katie would recover after her kidneys and liver cleansed her body of sedatives.

The tracking issue began to consume me, sapping my optimism and leaving a well of foreboding in its place. The weekend consisted of anxious waiting made tolerable only by visits from friends. The distraction of a visitor gave me a break from the constant worry now plaguing me. My law school friend, Micah, drove up from Nashville to spend the weekend with us at the hospital.

Saturday afternoon found Krista, Micah, Krista's Aunt Pat, who recently returned to Indianapolis to help with Katie, and I sitting in Room 6 watching Katie sleep. Micah had the idea of taking me to a movie, which Krista wholeheartedly endorsed. I begrudgingly acquiesced, and Micah drove us the quarter mile to the theater. With me completely out of touch with the outside world and knowing nothing currently playing, Micah chose a picture billed as an "action/drama." I allowed myself to get lost in the film. I realized its mediocrity after seeing it again some months later, but, that afternoon in Indianapolis, down the street from PMCH, I loved every minute of it.

Micah left Sunday morning just before another law school friend, Meghann, and her husband, Chris, arrived. For the first time, the thought of someone visiting Katie filled me with trepidation. We kept Katie's tracking difficulty a closely held secret. I sent my last email update prior to Katie waking from the crisis event. Katie's life to that point was an open book. Something, perhaps pride, prevented me from sharing this latest development.

If drugs were not preventing her from tracking, I considered the only alternative explanation too horrid to accept. Meghann and Chris obviously enjoyed meeting Katie; however, that they did not experience the Katie I knew so well saddened me.

Dr. Bob started a four-day stretch on Monday, March 31 and injected a renewed sense of urgency into Katie's treatment. He listened with grim concentration as the team updated him on Katie's status. Returning after a seemingly long absence from the PICU, he told those attending rounds that Katie's minimal progress deeply troubled him. The intensivists had pushed as much formula into Katie's stomach as she could handle. On her best day, she tolerated a third of the required amount of nutrition. She remained dependent on milrinone, and the wound team held to their estimate of yet another "ten to fourteen days" for Katie's incision to heal. Dr. Bob rattled off a series of changes to Katie's drug regime, which I jotted down in preparation for my update call to Krista, and moved on to the next patient.

I succeeded in completely confusing Krista with my interpretation of Dr. Bob's drug changes. I mangled the pronunciations, which I spelled phonetically. I still have to stop and remember where the "u" belongs in "restaurant," so "succinylcholine chloride" is a bit above my pay grade. Drug names are all Latin to me, which, then again, they mostly are. While I did not hesitate to ask a clarification question during rounds, I was not about to ask the doctor to spell every drug he mentioned in front of a half-dozen or more doctors and nurses. Having failed in my mission to report on rounds, I told Krista I would ask Dr. Bob to call her.

As soon as I ended the call, Dr. Bob appeared in Katie's room. Standing across from me at Katie's crib, Dr. Bob admitted his concern that Katie suffered permanent neurological damage during the March 19th crisis, marking the first time anyone directly voiced the fear everyone felt. To emphasize his point, Dr. Bob raised his right arm straight out, holding it steady directly above Katie's feet. I inferred what he intended to do. Instinctively, my right hand shot up and seized his wrist firmly. "We don't need to do that," I asserted sternly. He was going to quickly move his hand toward Katie's face to demonstrate she would not flinch. I did not doubt she would fail the test. With the outcome known, I saw no reason to subject Katie to the indignity. Dr. Bob withdrew his hand, understanding for perhaps the first time that I appreciated the seriousness of Katie's condition.

Dr. Bob went on to explain what happened during rounds. We needed to know the level of Katie's cognitive ability; therefore, he was withdrawing Katie's sedatives. If Katie did not improve neurologically, we would have big decisions to make. After waiting day after day for any progress, I just wanted action. Even though I understood the plan, I asked the doctor to call Krista, which he did.

Krista and I met with Dr. Bob and Anthony in the Doctor's Office later in the day for a mini-care conference. The conversation merely repeated that between Dr. Bob and me earlier in the day, but with a different tone. I perceived that Krista had much more hope for a recovery than I did, a perception I inferred Dr. Bob and Anthony shared. I sensed they were gently trying to prepare Krista for a negative outcome. I still could not bring myself to raise that possibility with her. Dr. Bob reminded us that Katie's brain was slightly smaller than normal given all she had endured, so she did not go into the abdominal crisis with a completely healthy organ. He offered to bring up the film of Katie's head on one of the large computer screens behind him.

> "Is it any different from the X-ray before the fever?" I asked.
>
> "No," said Dr. Bob.
>
> "Then we don't need to see it. Her brain was that size when she was looking around and playing, when she was being Katie. To look at it now is just…." I trailed off, searching for a word. "Macabre."
>
> "That's a good word," replied Dr. Bob as Anthony nodded in agreement.

From the moment we learned of Katie's heart defect, I had no fantasies that Katie would split the atom using a toothbrush, thumbtack, and an old issue of *Boy's Life* in the basement at age thirteen. She would almost certainly experience some delays. But every person fortunate enough to interact with Katie saw her curiosity and playfulness. I wanted that Katie back. I did not care what any x-ray depicted; knowing Katie was all the proof I needed.

We observed no changes in Katie's condition over the next two days, but not for lack of trying. Krista and I scrutinized everything Katie did, wondering if each act signaled an emergence from the fog.

> "Did you see that? Her hand brushed against the stuffed turtle. Did you see that? I think she was reaching for it. I'm not sure. I think I saw it. Did you see it?"

After a few minutes, that these acts were not meaningful or intentional became evident. Every time, our hopes would rise a little less and our disappointment would sink a little lower.

Sitting dejectedly on the chair in Katie's room as her nurse checked equipment on Wednesday afternoon, I rambled on about Dr. Bob's latest gambit while staring blankly out the window. I stopped speaking when I sensed the nurse staring at my back. I turned to face her as she said,

> "You know." Then, after a pause, she repeated herself, "You know, don't you?"

She inferred from my ramblings that I knew Katie would not regain her previous neurological function.

> "I know," I admitted, and turned back to the window.

Now it was my turn to infer. The staff had no hope of Katie recovering, but they were waiting to tell us until exhausting every possibility. This was a conspiracy, albeit an informal one. I did not blame them as I counted myself among the conspirators. I shared my concern over Katie's prognosis with only this nurse, not even my wife.

A sliver of hope broke through the darkness that evening. Since Katie's aborted surgery on February 12, I stayed with Katie later and later into the night. I loved being with Katie in the stillness that enveloped the PICU during the early hours of the morning. This night was no different. Katie's nurse, Danielle, interrupted our alone time to perform her examinations. She said, "Hi, Katie," as she approached the crib, and Katie's eyes opened and turned toward her. Katie then looked at me standing opposite the nurse, then back at Danielle before falling asleep. "That looked purposeful to me," Danielle said, and I agreed. I left the hospital with a small burning ember of hope that Katie was indeed coming back to us. I woke Krista when I got home to share the news. I should have interpreted Krista's measured response as her having a more realistic grasp on the situation than I previously thought, but I was too elated.

A wave of ice-cold water extinguished that ember of hope Thursday morning. I rushed to Katie when she awoke before rounds. Putting my face six inches from hers so that we looked eye to eye, I exclaimed, "Good morning, Bunny! I missed you." She looked back at me with those large black eyes. I moved slightly to her right. Her eyes did not move. I moved even further; her eyes remained fixed. I grabbed her favorite stuffed animal and shook it frenetically beside her left shoulder while talking in a high-pitched voice. Looking off into space, she did not respond.

Dr. Bob informed me after rounds that he restarted Katie's medications. We should have seen some improvement in her tracking. We did not. Katie should have been fighting to pull her ET tube out as she had so many times before. She did not. By Thursday morning, Katie started exhibiting signs of sedative withdrawal. With resignation, the physician increased her sedatives to ease any discomfort.

The test had been a failure insofar as Katie did not emerge from the haze. It succeeded in demonstrating, however unfortunately, that we could not attribute the cause of Katie's inability to track to medications. She all but certainly suffered some degree of neurological damage.

Bad news kept coming. Katie's liver and kidneys continued to improve at a glacial pace, but we were losing ground everywhere else. The sporadic fevers of unknown origin that we chased from late December through early February returned with a vengeance. Her food intake remained a third of the minimum amount needed. The liver, although improving, had yet to resume normal operation. The organ creates enzymes that cause both blood clotting and, counterintuitively, thinning. Its floundering made preventing clots while guarding against unrestrained bleeding extremely difficult. The nurses discovered a clot developing in Katie's femoral line, her only intravenous access. Clots should not have been an issue given her coagulation therapy. If Katie developed a clot in her line, she may have been clotting in other sensitive places. We won the battle of the crisis event, but we were losing the war.

Pat relieved me at the hospital that afternoon, and I returned home to collect some papers. An eerie quiet filled the house. Even when Sam slept, his presence could be felt throughout the house. The sound of my footsteps on the hardwood floor reverberated off the walls. I stopped at the front door before leaving, the sight of our piano sitting in the dark music room catching my eye. The blinds blocked the brightness of the afternoon April sun. The few rays that entered through tiny gaps in the window coverings gave just enough light to turn every item in the room hues of tan and brown. Drawn to the instrument, I crossed the room and sat on the bench.

I stared at the keyboard while searching for some motivation to play. I can play a decent twelve bar blues, but had no heart for an upbeat number. I lifted my fingers to the keys after a long minute. They were cold to the touch. My right hand played a straight "D" chord on a beat while my left thumb played a syncopated low "A." The sound of the piano filled the room and breathed life into the cold house. I transitioned into "God Only Knows" by The Beach Boys, playing the introduction's four measures over and over effortlessly, mindlessly. I smiled with memories of sitting at that very piano while cradling Katie in my left arm as I started the first verse:

> I may not always love you,
> But long as there are stars above you,
> You'll never need to doubt it.
> I'll make you so sure about it.
> God only knows what I'd be without you.

With memories of Katie in my head, my vocal chords began straining, tremulous with emotion, as I started the next verse:

> If you should ever leave me,
> Though life would still go on believe me,
> The world could show nothing to me,
> So what good would living do me?
> God only knows what I'd be without you.

I could not finish. The words cut too deep, were too literal. I pulled my hands from the piano as though the keys were on fire and collected myself. In the past ten months, despite all that happened, I never lost control of my feelings. I never cried a tear. With emotions once again at bay, I pounded out an aggressive instrumental "Surfer Girl," which brought back memories of holding Katie late at night in the NICU.

Ever since the surgical setbacks in early February, I feared to think about the future. Earlier, though, I often imagined the day that Katie would sit beside me at this piano and sing her heart out. I knew the first few songs I would teach Katie, heard her voice soaring over the piano, and pictured her clapping along until she could play the instrument herself. This was my dream for Katie; it would never be anything but a dream. That Katie could no longer appreciate the music she so loved filled me with profound sadness.

I again turned to the piano and started playing yet another Beach Boys song, "Forever." This lesser well-known single, always a personal favorite, meant something much different now:

If every word I said could make you laugh, I'd talk forever.
I asked the sky just what we had, it shone forever.
If the song I sing to you could fill your heart with joy, I'd sing forever.
Forever, forever, I've been so happy loving you.

Let the love I have for you, live in your heart and beat forever.
I've been so happy loving you….

The final verse took a melancholy turn:

So I'm goin' away, but not forever.
I gotta love you anyway … Forever.

Emotions buried and contained for almost a year surfaced as the song progressed, as though each note ticked a tumbler in the lock restraining feelings pining to escape. The heartache of surgeries, catheterizations, extubations, sleepless nights, unabated stress, deaths, and countless vigils conspired to destroy the protective bulwark of denial regarding Katie's condition: Katie was going to die. She would not reach adulthood. She would not learn to drive. She would not go to the prom. She would not go to school. She would not know her sister. She would never attend her own birthday party. Katie was going to die. Surgery could not save her. Medications could not save her. All the love in the world could not save her. Katie was going to die. Sitting alone at our piano, I broke.

I do not know how much time passed before I pulled myself together. I could not save Katie, but I would do everything possible to ensure she died in comfort and dignity. I returned to Peyton Manning Children's Hospital to face the beginning of the end.

CHAPTER 29

Enter the Twilight

KRISTA AND I ARRIVED AT the hospital early Saturday, April 5 to find Katie's condition unchanged. Dr. Halczenko visited us to discuss possible courses of treatment, all quite unimpressive. We either had to push forward with the trach or try extubation. In regards to Katie's inability to track, he posited that she might be suffering from an infection. An e-mail Krista received from a mom of an infant with a similar heart defect supported this hypothesis. This girl had an intestinal issue that sounded very much like Katie's. Months elapsed before she began tracking again. Krista clung to hope, and the three of us agreed to try a 48-hour course of strong antibiotics and then readdress her condition. In the meantime, Krista and I kept a scheduled appointment.

The funeral home was disconcertingly cheerful that morning. Without anyone currently laid out for a viewing, the staff members slipped out of their somber demeanor. A mortician greeted and escorted us into a meeting room off the main hall. He walked us through various options regarding funeral arrangements. I brought the flier for the monastery caskets that I set aside for Krista two months earlier. The mortician promised to procure one if needed. Fearing a low turnout given our families lived so far away, I wanted only one night for a visitation. I did not want Katie to suffer the indignity of a poorly attended viewing. Krista did not interject, which I took as acquiescence.

Krista remained quiet until the mortician offered us a tour. She asked whether we could have an open casket. The mortician hesitated before responding, stating that he could not say definitively. He furrowed his brow while framing his response:

> "Babies don't always hold up well. The skin … it isn't as rugged as an adult's [skin]. It can be, and often is, too discolored."

As the mortician handed her a box of tissues, Krista asked whether he had outfit recommendations. He suggested covering up as much as possible, specifically the arms. He bade us farewell after briefly walking us through the facility, and we left for our next chore.

Krista frequently suggested buying a potential funeral outfit for Katie throughout the previous week. I agreed and suggested she take Laura or her Aunt Pat shopping. Krista neither flatly rejected my advice nor took the initiative to go on her own. She wanted the two of us to go, so I found myself in the toddler department at J.C. Penney after the funeral home visit.

Brightly colored dresses stuffed the racks in anticipation of Easter, just fifteen days away. Excited girls scurried between displays searching for the perfect dress. Their jubilance irritated me somewhat given our purpose, a feeling I knew was selfish. Krista found a couple outfits she liked, and, much to our mutual surprise, so did I. We ultimately chose one of Krista's selections, a pink satin dress. She then found a white shawl to cover Katie's arms. She put the two items together and held them in the air for a final look. "Perfect, I like it" I said. Krista agreed. I walked to the cashier glad I did not delegate this task to someone else.

We stood in line with chirping young girls, moms, and brightly colored dresses. We remained silent as the girls fought over who chose the prettiest dress. When we reached the front of the line, Krista gingerly placed the dress and shawl on the counter. While scanning and bagging our items, a bubbly clerk asked, "Is this for a special occasion?" I bit my inner lip and winced. Krista replied with a simple "yes" and nothing more.

We returned to the hospital to find my mom and Aunt Betty, who arrived that morning, and Pat sitting with Katie. Still reeling from her mother's death not three weeks earlier, Mom now focused her concern on the youngest in the family. I had not a doubt she knew Katie's time was limited, but, like me, she did not say so directly. I suspected my aunt also sensed the eventual outcome, but without my mom's level of certainty. Neither Krista nor I expounded on the morning's events, putting on a happy face instead. Our gratitude to have the Pennsylvania visitors could not overcome the tension we felt.

The intensivist, Dr. Williams, stopped by to check on Katie that evening. The women had gone out for dinner, leaving me to keep an eye on Katie. After his examination, Dr. Williams sat in the very chair in which he told us they could do nothing more for Katie on March 19 and began chatting. Our discussion this night was entirely different. We talked Notre Dame, music, PMCH history, and changes in the medical profession over his decades of practicing. He also told me his story of running into The Beach Boys after a concert in Pittsburgh. Our casual conversation could easily have taken place in a neighborhood bar.

Dr. Williams' two-hour visit evidenced the close relationships we had developed with many members of the staff. Dr. Abraham later expressed surprise that we did not take Katie home as the end neared. Krista and I never considered it. We wanted Katie surrounded by those who cared for and loved her throughout her life, which meant staying at PMCH.

After everyone retired for the night, I returned to the PICU and spoke privately with the night intensivist, Dr. Sichting. She did not camouflage her cynicism regarding Katie's prognosis. The doctor told me that she had expected to see great improvement upon returning from her vacation. If anything, she thought Katie had declined. She did not mention Katie's failure to track. She did not need to. I knew. However, I was not in the PICU that Saturday night to discuss the particulars of Katie's case with a doctor. I wanted some alone time with Katie, and we were certainly alone that night.

For the first time since anyone could remember, the census dropped to one patient, namely Katie. Since Friday afternoon, she had the entire unit to herself. Running with a skeleton crew, the unit felt desolate. With no neighbors to bother, Katie and I threw a little party of our own. I opened the doors to her room, cranked up The Beach Boys, and filled the empty PICU halls with the sounds of Southern California.

Fr. Jim once again asked the parishioners to pray for Katie during mass on Sunday morning. Like all but the immediate family, he did not know the extent of damage the acute infection caused. My periodic e-mail updates were the main source of information for those following Katie's story. I just could not bring myself to write that Katie suffered a neurological injury. I later learned that, to many, no news was good news, which made the events of the upcoming week even more shocking.

Any hope in Dr. Halczenko's antibiotic "Hail Mary" faded with the light of day Sunday evening. We observed no change in Katie's tracking. Defeated, the intensivist discontinued the ineffective drugs.

As Krista and I were leaving the house on Monday, April 7, Krista asked me to arrange a care conference for that afternoon. Anthony scheduled the conference for 4 p.m. My mom planned to leave that morning, but stayed for the conference at my request. Dr. Sichting and Anthony were the only staff members who originally planned to attend. I asked Sarah to join us to refute any notion that Dr. Abraham recommended additional treatment should Krista raise the issue.

I grew increasingly anxious as the meeting approached. My supervisor in the Air National Guard came from Illinois around noon to lend support. Kevin provided a welcome distraction from the unbearable waiting. Having never before met Katie, we welcomed his addition to Katie's normal stable of visitors. She slept for most of his visit. Like so many times before, I stood back and watched Katie charm yet another unsuspecting visitor. Kevin held her hand without the benefit of feeling her grip. He stayed until Krista arrived at 4:00 p.m., at which time Krista, Mom, and I left for the conference room while Aunt Betty sat with Katie.

The empty room in which we held our large care conference less than three weeks before now felt cold and cavernous. Krista and my mom took seats at the far end of the table. I sat immediately to Krista's right. We waited in silence for a few minutes until Dr. Sichting, Anthony, Sarah, and Katie's nurse joined us. The physician sat opposite Krista with the two nurses sitting cattycorner to me. The inadvertent seating arrangement was more fitting for a business negotiation than discussing an infant's medical treatment. Nevertheless, Dr. Sichting pressed forward.

The degree to which Katie had deteriorated surprised Dr. Sichting after a long absence from the hospital. She thought now was our best opportunity to move forward. Katie was not progressing under the current plan. Something needed to change.

The intensivist wanted us to decide whether to proceed with a tracheostomy. Dr. Sichting doubted whether a surgeon would operate on Katie in her current condition, but she could ask if we desired. Tracheostomies are bloody procedures. After weeks of anticoagulation therapy, which thins the blood, bleeding complications presented a major risk. Still terribly deconditioned from weeks of underfeeding, Katie's chest incision had yet to heal. The Wound Team continued to assert Katie needed another "ten to fourteen days." If her tracheostomy incision did not heal, she could very well hemorrhage to death. Krista and I had finally agreed to a tracheostomy after the sternum operation, but the recent developments compelled us to revisit our decision. We concluded days earlier that the tracheostomy risk outweighed the potential benefit, but listened to Dr. Sichting before I relayed our position.

After we took a tracheostomy off the table, Dr. Sichting pivoted to the path forward. The physician explained that Katie's failure to improve troubled her deeply. She then summarized a litany of issues of which we were all too aware:

- Katie's large intestine, ground zero for the crisis event, only tolerated a third of the necessary nutrition after almost three weeks of recuperation. Katie lacked the ability to ingest the nutrition required for recovery.

- Although Katie's kidneys defied the expectations of the medical staff and did not fail, they were very, very slow to resume normal function. This indicated an underlying issue of unknown origin. Dr. Sichting believed the kidneys would be quick to fail under future stress.
- The liver had yet to return to normal operation, making clot prevention while guarding against unrestrained bleeding extremely difficult. Moreover, Katie's poor liver function prevented Katie from receiving TPN nutrition through an IV.
- Katie's heart could not function without significant pharmaceutical assistance, specifically milrinone. Katie must be able to live without it.
- The incision from her March 6 surgery had yet to heal.
- After a prolonged ventilation, the ET tube presented a risk for internal hemorrhage. Moreover, having spent 118 days intubated in total, Katie may be too deconditioned to breathe independently.
- Despite aggressive anticoagulation therapy, Katie developed a clot in her femoral line. This was problematic for two reasons. First, she should not be clotting while undergoing this therapy. Second, the clot would soon block her femoral line, necessitating yet another painful line insertion.
- The lack of nutrition made Katie's skin prone to breakdown. Although fortunate thus far, we recently noticed some red discoloration, a harbinger of things to come.
- Katie still suffered sporadic fevers, possibly neurological in nature.

Even if we could overcome all the above, we did not have a good surgical option. To survive, Katie needed the Glenn procedure or, more drastically, a transplant. With her damaged SVCs, she was not a candidate for either. Dr. Sichting then addressed the dispositive issue:

"Katie isn't moving her eyes."

"She moves her eyes," I corrected her.

"The movement isn't purposeful."

The term of art hung in the air for a moment. "The movement isn't purposeful." Someone had finally stated the fact in the open. No one protested or argued. Everyone knew. Katie's inability to focus, both undeniable and devastating, overshadowed everything else. The doctor then delivered the final blow, echoing Dr. Williams' phraseology of March 19, "I think we've gotten to the point where we're doing things *to* Katie, not *for* Katie."

Having made her point, Dr. Sichting ceased speaking and the room fell silent for a long minute. Anthony broke the silence by asking our thoughts. None of us used terms such as "passing away," let alone the much more definitive words "dead" or "dying." We spoke in generalities prefaced with qualifiers. That the doctor advised us to let Katie go was clear. Finally, nodding slowly in agreement, Krista and I acquiesced without saying a word.

Now that we set the course, my concern turned to the process. I asked, "So how would this work?" Dr. Sichting explained that she would eliminate Katie's non-comfort medications and discontinue the vent. I lacked the expertise to follow Krista's subsequent questions regarding comfort medications and did not ask for an explanation. I did ask, however, how long Katie would have once extubated. Dr. Sichting said she could not say for sure, minutes, maybe longer, but probably minutes. From her tone, she did not expect Katie to last long. Anthony then interjected, stressing the importance of not changing our minds once we committed to palliative care. If we demanded the doctor put Katie back on the ventilator, we risked an emergency tracheostomy if she encountered difficulty. Adamant, Anthony repeated the need for us to abide by our decision multiple times. He fell silent once satisfied we appreciated his concern. Now only one issue remained.

"If we did this, what day are you suggesting?" I asked Anthony.

"Well, there is no set date. Not too much longer, because we're concerned that something else may happen."

"Like a blood clot?"

"Or respiratory infection or another … whatever. Whatever caused her last episode. We don't want something bad to happen, something that would be painful."

"Are we talking tomorrow?"

"No," Krista said with quiet resolve. "Amy and my mom may want to come out."

"Oh, no, you need to give Aunt Elaine time to get here. That's not fair. You need to give her time," mom interjected.

"How about Wednesday?" I proposed.

After Krista nodded in agreement, I turned to Anthony and saw him doing the same. We briefly discussed times, setting extubation for 2 p.m. With that, Dr. Sichting and Anthony left the room. After the door closed, Sarah expressed her sympathies.

"I am so sorry. You need to know that you did everything you could for Katie. Everything. She couldn't have had better parents."

"Thank you," Krista whispered without making eye contact.

"It's so frustrating that, after all of these heart issues, we get knocked out by some abdominal issue. It's so frustrating," I said with resignation.

"I know," said Sarah in her most comforting voice. "If there is anything I can do for you, let me know. We love you guys."

With that, Sarah and Katie's nurse departed. Krista and Mom fought tears. I sat stoically, unable to appreciate fully what just happened. Krista broke the silence, asking whom we needed to contact. We limited our discussions to notification responsibilities and logistics. After establishing a plan, we returned to little Katie.

I soon found myself alone with a nurse at Katie's bedside after the others left to notify family of the new plan. Leaning against the rail on Katie's crib, I watched her sleeping peacefully. Her extremities were mottled. I grasped her right hand, which felt frigid in my palm. I then squeezed each foot and felt similar coldness. I again took her limp hand in mine and squeezed, just as she had done to mine so many times before. My eyes roamed over her body. Wearing only a diaper, scars and wounds from surgeries and countless needle sticks testified to all Katie had endured. Each mark represented pain, whether slight or intense, brief or excruciatingly long. Looking at my little girl, I knew we made the correct decision. I was at peace.

My eyes fell on a score of black and purple puncture marks on Katie's chunky thighs. Katie received her anticoagulation medication via injection at six o'clock in the morning and evening. Even with her current inability to track, she still winced whenever the nurse gave her the shot. I looked over to the clock and saw the big hand at the bottom of the five o'clock hour.

> "Let's not do the six o'clock shot. She doesn't need it," I told the nurse flatly.
>
> "Well, I'll give the shot and then ask the doctor to change the order during tonight's changeover," she replied amicably.
>
> "No," I responded. "No, she is not getting the shot. I withdraw consent for the shot. She's had enough needles in her life. She's done. No more needles."

The nurse nodded in understanding and the conversation ended. I do not know what hoops she jumped through from there, but she did not give Katie the scheduled injection. Katie never suffered through another shot.

CHAPTER 30

No More Needles

THE FAMILY CONVERGED ON INDIANAPOLIS early Tuesday. My dad and Elaine drove up from Jacksonville, Florida. Krista's mom and Amy flew in from Colorado. My Aunt Elaine and sister, Susan, came in from Syracuse, NY and Harrisburg, PA, respectively. Susan, who worked for the Hershey Company, brought bags of her employer's confections. With the census remaining anemic, the staff allowed us to use Room 5 for congregating and storage. The atmosphere had the strange funeral-like combination of joy in seeing relatives gathered in one place tainted by the underlying cause of the assembly.

I sequestered myself in the Family Room that morning to write the final email update during Katie's life. My previous email two weeks earlier described Katie's miraculous recovery from the crisis event, so I started my message by reminding people that Katie faced long odds from the beginning. I then related the numerous difficulties Katie faced, many of which I had not previously disclosed. Once I framed Katie's condition, I crafted the heart of my message:

> Katie has fought the good fight for more than ten months, seizing considerable periods with good quality of life from the jaws of an insidious condition. Any future battles will be fraught with pain in the hopes of a very, very meager reward. Therefore, on Wednesday, April 9, we will transition to a palliative course. Katie will be extubated and mildly sedated until the end. The process may take minutes or weeks. We do not know, but the doctors assure us that she will be comfortable.

Although rambling and lengthy, my message described only a fraction of the drama that unfolded over the last few weeks. I typically tried to capture that drama, but not this time. I just did not have it in me. I closed by asking our supporters to keep us in their prayers.

Katie's vitals remained stable throughout the day. Krista arranged for the Wound Team to discontinue the wound vac. Even with that piece of equipment removed, the ventilator and numerous monitors and tubes confined the rarely awake Katie to the bed. Her trunk remained warm, contrasting sharply with her ice-cold, mottled extremities. By the time night fell, none of the three intensivists on duty that day expected Katie to breathe for more than a few minutes after extubation.

Family members constantly surrounded Katie's crib. As blue skies faded to shades of dark orange, the reality of the next day's events became increasingly unavoidable. Before Krista left for the night, she corralled the family members present to join in Katie's bedtime routine one last time. The family crowded around Katie's crib and placed hands on the sleeping infant. After an "Our Father" and "Hail Mary," we sang Katie's song one final night.

Goodnight, Sweetheart, well, it's time to go....

This marked the 310th time a loved one bid Katie goodnight with this routine.

I spent most of the night staring at my bedroom ceiling. The moment of Katie dying topped my list of concerns. Aside from the occasional spider, I had never seen someone or something die until Sam 23 days earlier. I had no idea what human death looked like and feared not only how I would react, but whether I could be what Krista needed. More than anything, I was scared for Katie. She had endured so much in her brief life. Despite the doctors' assurances, I feared for her. I kept my concerns to myself, even though I knew from Krista's tossing and turning that she also found sleep elusive.

The dreaded room divider once again outside Room 6 Wednesday morning did nothing to quell the surprisingly festive atmosphere. A dark substance on

Katie's lips and ET tube puzzled me when I arrived. Krista admitted that she and her sister had slipped Katie some chocolate. Dr. Steinberg walked in on the scene, had a good laugh, and encouraged our memory-making endeavors. The family held Katie's hands, bathed her, and placed lotion everywhere not covered by bandages, all the while discussing anything other than what was to come. We made the most of our remaining time with Katie, as did the staff.

Many of Katie's doctors, nurses, and therapists stopped to see Katie and offer words of support. This group included one of the hospital chaplains, who administered the Sacrament of Anointing of the Sick. We thanked him for not only this last act of kindness, but also the many prayers and words of encouragement over the past ten months. Not an hour after the priest left, another hospital chaplain arrived to pay his last respects. He finished half of the Anointing of the Sick prayers before I realized he was repeating the sacrament Katie just received. I figured an extra prayer never hurt anyone, so I silently watched the priest bless Katie. I found comfort in the prayers, although I had no doubt Katie had already earned an all-access pass to Heaven.

Just after noon, Krista asked the nurse for help dressing Katie. Everyone left the room to give them privacy and congregated in Room 5 to gorge on chocolate. Krista, Amy, and two nurses placed Katie in a purple knitted dress, an ordeal given the number of tubes and wires present. Katie had not worn an article of clothing since February 12. Krista then sat in the same model of chair she used the first time she held Katie prior to surgery on June 5. The nurses wrestled with a cobweb of tubes and wires and placed Katie in Krista's arms. Another nurse informed me that Krista was ready for us, and I ushered the family back to Room 6.

Any sense of frivolity disappeared by the time we gathered around mother and daughter. Our pastor, Fr. Jim, and associate pastor, Fr. John, joined us. Fr. Jim once again administered Anointing of the Sick, marking the third time she received the Sacrament that day. Little Katie was quite the Catholic.

As the clock ticked down to extubation, Fr. Jim led an impromptu prayer service, including the song "Jesus Loves Me" and one final recitation of Katie's goodnight routine. The group struggled to get through the "Our Father" and "Hail Mary," and fell apart during "Goodnight Sweetheart." Those able to muster something resembling singing struggled to keep their voices from cracking. Emotions overtaking my vocal cords, I fought to get out an occasional word.

Goodnight, sweetheart. Well, it's time to go.
Goodnight, sweetheart. Well, it's time to go.
I hate to leave you, but, I really must say,
"Goodnight, Sweetheart, Goodnight."

Given the situation, the lyric took on an entirely different meaning, and the group barely held it together. Fr. John sobbed on the couch. Once complete, Fr. Jim asked everyone to bless and kiss Katie. One by one, all present approached Krista and Katie to say their final goodbye to my little girl.

The priests left once everyone had finished, and I proceeded to the nurses' station. I had walked that course thousands of times to ask a nurse or respiratory therapist for assistance or an intensivist about Katie's care, but this trip was different. I walked with the dread of a condemned man on the way to the gallows. I told our nurse, "We're ready," and returned to Katie's room. I took a seat on the couch to Krista's left and waited.

Dr. Sichting entered the room flanked by Katie's nurse and Roger, the head respiratory therapist who cared for Katie on her first day in the PICU. The nurse remained at the back of the room while the other two approached Katie in silence. Roger knelt at Krista's feet while Dr. Sichting took a position behind her.

The intensivist and RT worked in tandem, gently removing the tape holding the tube in place. Roger placed a large bandage over Katie's chest to protect her dress and cleaned the adhesive from Katie's porcelain cheeks. For all of the concern and discussion regarding extubations over the past ten months, I never actually saw one. I glanced up at the monitor above Katie's crib and saw Katie's heartrate of 128 beats per minute. My eyes returned to Roger just before, without notice or ceremony, he quickly withdrew the intubation tube. Roger paused a moment and then, concluding Katie was not immediately failing, removed the bandage and equipment. For the first time in six months, Katie finally escaped the oxygen and ventilation tubes.

Thirty seconds passed before Krista broke the silence by requesting music. I hesitated, not wanting to leave Katie. I looked over at the CD player and saw a disc currently playing, but the sound muted. I asked Amy to increase the volume. I knew the song from hearing three base notes leading into the second verse.

Amidst sporadic, muffled sobs, the sound of "Surfer Girl" filled the room. With memories of holding Katie in the NICU, I thought it appropriate that this song be her last. As I stroked Katie's hair, I whispered to her that she could let go. She did not. Her pulse remained rock steady at 128.

The album played so often in Katie's room that I had the track listing committed to memory. The next song, "Dance, Dance, Dance," had no particular significance for us, so I found myself in the surreal position of encouraging Katie to hang on two more minutes for "Fun, Fun, Fun" and then "I Get Around." I suppose one's mind rationalizes to find solace in such a circumstance. Regardless, we spent countless hours exercising and playing to these songs, and I thought either would be fitting. As the latter faded out, Katie continued to breathe effortlessly.

Dr. Sichting and the therapist retreated to the back of the room after a few more songs. Along with the nurse, they quietly left as Katie continued to breathe during "Wouldn't It Be Nice" fifteen minutes later. Krista announced that she felt Katie's unborn sister kicking Katie. The group broke out in laughter as a collective feeling of relief replaced the abject misery pervading the room just thirty minutes before.

No one expected Katie to do so well, which should not have surprised anyone given her penchant for surpassing expectations. Katie looked healthier than she had in weeks, and, for the first time in recent memory, her extremities grew warm. Krista, apparently sharing my confidence that Katie had more time than originally thought, offered to let me hold my daughter. I never imagined that I would have another chance to hold Katie and jumped at the opportunity. The feeling of finally holding Katie without the encumbrance of medical equipment overwhelmed me. Aware of our great fortune of this unexpected time with Katie, the atmosphere turned blissful. I eventually relinquished Katie to my mom. Katie remained stable, and everyone who wanted to hold her had the chance.

Katie held by her dad following her last extubation.

The family held Katie until the nurse told us at 9 p.m. that she needed to rest in her crib. Krista and Katie's grandmothers and aunts bathed and lathered Katie in lotion before putting her to bed. Although her heartrate remained steady at 128, Krista and I decided one of us would stay with her at all times in case she deteriorated quickly. Aunt Elaine volunteered to stay at Katie's bedside, which freed Krista and me to sleep. Krista and Amy checked into one of the PICU sleep rooms while I crashed on the couch in Katie's room. Aunt Elaine stayed at the bedside until early risers relieved her at 5 a.m.

Katie continued to thrive into Thursday morning. Katie's nurse told us that Katie's heartrate would escalate before dropping as she succumbed to heart failure. With Katie's pulse remaining steady at 128, the holding resumed as daylight broke. Katie did so well that I invited friends in Indianapolis via text message to visit her in the hospital.

I returned home late in the morning after more than twenty-four hours in the PICU. The stiff, cool spring air struck me as I left the hospital. Overcast skies blanketed Indianapolis in a sheet of grey. After showering and donning a fresh PMCH shirt, the warmth of the April sun enveloped me when I walked out our front door. We caught another break; the weather had cleared. For the first time in recent memory, Indianapolis experienced a beautiful day. I paused and looked up at the bright blue sky when a thought hit me: Katie had not been outside in more than four months. Katie had enough of her isolated room – she was going on a field trip.

I found Krista holding Katie with Amy at her side when I returned to the PICU. When I told her I wanted to take Katie outside, she said they had been discussing that very thing. I walked down to the nurses' station where Dr. Sichting was tackling paperwork. I asked if we could take Katie for a walk. While not exactly thrilled at my request, she consented, provided Katie's nurse removed the heart monitor first. The nurse appeared just a few minutes later and quickly prepared Katie for her excursion. I lifted Katie from Krista's lap and carried her down to the nurses' station accompanied by family and friends. After saying "hello" to Anthony and a half-dozen doctors and nurses, we left the PICU and rode the elevator to the third floor.

In addition to the pediatric cardiology and oncology beds, the third story also boasts an outdoor playground perched two stories above the PMCH main entrance. The grey cloud hovering above the city earlier had broken into incandescent puffs of white. A light breeze blew gently. The sun shone down on us, raising the temperature to the low sixties.

Katie had never been to a playground. Physicians and residents, many of whom cared for Katie, were eating lunch at two picnic tables when we arrived. I carried Katie to each table so she could visit with them one final time. They welcomed us warmly. Some teared up seeing Katie under the present circumstances. I then passed Katie to Krista, who climbed a brightly colored piece of playground equipment and took Katie down a slide for the first time.

Amy and Krista took turns holding Katie for another ten minutes before we returned to the PICU. With some help from family, Krista bathed and lathered Katie in lotion before putting her in a new outfit. The knit, sleeveless dress transitioned from ivory at the shoulders to a dark pink at her knees. Katie slept peacefully in her new attire for the next two hours. Meanwhile, I visited the nurses' station to report on Katie's adventure. Anthony laughed heartily, saying,

> "I knew it. I knew it. When you left, I told everyone here that Katie was going to go down the slide. I knew it."

I guess we became rather predictable after 149 nights in the PICU.

Laurie, mother of Katie's friend, Kaitlyn, arrived at 4 p.m. after receiving my text invitation. Once again, I stood back and watched someone enjoy Katie, who rested in bed. After a considerable time at the bedside, I asked Laurie if she wanted to hold Katie. Laurie's eyes lit up, and she exclaimed, "Can I?" I nodded my head, saying "Sure" as I directed her to the lone stationary chair in the room. I picked Katie up from the bed and placed her in Laurie's arms. Katie would never again sleep in that bed.

After Laurie left, the family again took turns holding Katie. I had been grazing on the chocolate Susan brought from Hershey all day and needed real food. I asked Amy to join me for a late dinner at one of my favorite restaurants, a Creole hole-in-the-wall a mile from the hospital. Over dinner, Amy, an ICU nurse, told me she did not expect Katie to survive the night. Throughout the day, Katie's pulse increased from 128 to 178 beats per minute before falling back to and stabilizing at 123. Her skin grew increasingly pale and her extremities mottled. Knowing the end approached, fear of watching Katie go dominated my thoughts.

By the time we returned to the hospital at 9:15 p.m., Dad, Elaine, and Krista's mom and aunt had retired for the night. The remaining family members departed two hours later. We repeated the plan from the night before.

Krista and Amy stayed in the sleep room just outside the main PICU doors while Aunt Elaine held Katie and I slept on the couch in Katie's room. Physically and emotionally exhausted, I quickly fell asleep.

An ear-piercing alarm rang out just after midnight, startling me awake. Simultaneously, Aunt Elaine shouted my name and slapped my foot. My eyes locked on a flashing "98" on the heart rate monitor. I ran over to Aunt Elaine and the baby as fast as my body could move. I must have startled Katie, because she opened her eyes wide to seemingly stare at me for a few fleeting seconds. Her eyes closed as her heart rate popped back to the 120s. Not sure what just happened, I called Krista while Aunt Elaine phoned my mom.

Within fifteen minutes, Krista, Amy, Mom, Susan, and my Aunt Betty joined us in Room 6. Krista's friend and coworker, Laura, who had just finished her evening shift at hospice, arrived with her husband, KC minutes later. Katie's heartrate remained fixed at 123, and we apologized for calling everyone back. Assuming the heartrate drop a fluke, those assembled joked lightheartedly over their seemingly unfounded concern. By 12:30 a.m. on Friday, April 11, the newcomers to the room had put on their coats and grabbed their purses. As we hugged each other goodnight, the number on the heartrate monitor changed.

118.

Everyone froze; eyes fixed on the monitor. For a minute, no one moved.

115.

No one said a word, but those already in the hall reentered the room. Purses returned to the floor. Coats came off. We formed a silent, pensive semi-circle around Aunt Elaine and Katie.

110.

Krista asked Aunt Elaine if she could hold her daughter. Amy took Katie from my aunt and, once Krista positioned herself, placed Katie gently in Krista's arms. Katie's head rested on Krista's upper left arm, her legs dangled over Krista's right thigh.

108.

We closed in around Krista and Katie. I sat on the couch to Krista's left, stroking Katie's hair. Mom sat to my left with Aunt Elaine beside her. Amy,

Susan, and Laura sat or knelt on Krista's right. Aunt Betty and KC stood between Aunt Elaine and Laura, completing the circle.

104.

No one had turned on the lights after I turned them off for the night an hour earlier. Only the light from the hallway pierced the darkness of Room 6. Outside, a light rain tapped gently on the windows. Krista asked for music, and I responded with a question.

"What do you want?" I asked.

"How about The Beach Boys? They're her favorite."

"No," I replied. "I think she needs something a little more … classical."

"Okay," Krista agreed.

I asked Amy to play a Bach CD, another frequently played album in Katie's collection. The lush sounds of a piano concerto buried Katie's now labored breathing.

98.

A collective gasp erupted when Katie's heartrate dipped below 100. The nurse must have turned off the alarms since the dark red number on a lighter red background flashed ominously in silence.

95.

My sister gave me a book about the Lincoln assassination back in my grade school days. I remember asking my mom about the unfamiliar term "death rattle," which she explained as a guttural coughing caused by an accumulation of mucus and saliva due to losing the cough reflex and ability to swallow. I immediately recognized the chilling noise. The surprisingly loud "rattle" sound of air passing through Katie's airway sickened me. Katie's sedation prevented any discomfort, but I found the sound grating nonetheless.

83.

Katie's heartrate continued to fall. Those surrounding the little girl gave her whatever comfort they could. I stroked her hair. Many reached out to caress Katie, which reminded me of the biblical stories in which believers laid hands on Jesus. Then and now, they sought a physical intimacy.

77.

We told Katie she was loved, that she was strong, that she could go, and that she did not have to fight anymore. We told Katie she is going to a far better place, and that she will be missed.

68.

At 1:14 a.m., Nurse Kelly quietly snuck into the room and slinked along the wall to the monitor. She had been watching the events unfold on Katie's monitor in the nurses' station. I glanced up to read "63" on the screen just before Kelly turned it away from the family. I continued to stroke Katie's hair. The rattle ended a few minutes before, but otherwise I detected no change. Katie's breathing had grown so shallow as to be almost imperceptible. I watched Kelly watch the monitor. When she discretely pulled a phone out of her pocket, lifted it to her ear, and turned away from the screen, I knew Katie was gone.

The atmosphere could not have been more beautiful. Only words of love and encouragement for Katie interrupted a Bach piano piece and the sound of rain on the windowsills. A warm, gentle darkness embraced the family and staff watching over her.

Dr. Halczenko arrived minutes after Kelly's call. The circle broke to allow the doctor to approach Katie and closed once again behind him. He stopped a few feet before Krista and said, "Mom, Dad, I am truly sorry." He then sat next to me on the couch in respectful silence. We remained quiet and motionless for some time, listening to a melancholy piano piece before I said, "Do what you need to do."

Without saying a word, Dr. Halczenko pressed a stethoscope against Katie's chest with his right hand while holding his cell phone with his left. I watched the numbers on his phone's stopwatch tick upward to one minute. He then returned both items to his pockets. Crouching in front of Katie, he shone a light in Katie's right eye and then the left. With that, he stood, craned his neck to see the monitor, and said, "Let's call it 1:20." He again offered his condolences before leaving with Kelly.

Krista continued to hold Katie while I addressed arrangements. I contacted the funeral home and directed Sue and KC to pack our belongings. A hospital chaplain provided Aunt Elaine some solace. Hours passed before the funeral home representative arrived. In the meantime, Krista asked for some time alone with Katie and me.

After everyone left the room, I took a seat across from Krista with our knees almost touching. I struggled to look at Katie. Her eyes were halfway open. I placed my hand on her forehead and brought it delicately down to her chin to close her eyes. I had seen this technique in movies and on television. Unsuccessful, I tried again. Her eyes remained partly open. I decided against another attempt by the time Krista spoke.

"I want Fr. Jim to perform the funeral."

"Absolutely," I responded. "We can make that happen. Absolutely."

We said nothing else. Maybe we knew what the other thought. Maybe we did not know what to say. Looking back, I cherish that moment. The ever-present fear of Katie in pain that haunted us for more than ten months was gone. Our little family, however damaged and imperfect, was together.

Mom, Amy, and Laura spread out a blanket on the bed. Krista, with Amy's assistance, placed Katie on the blanket. Hands that had squeezed mine countless times rested motionless on the mattress. Her head tilted slightly to her left. Her fancy pink dress contrasted sharply with her ivory skin. She looked like a porcelain doll.

The funeral home representative met the family in Katie's room and expressed his condolences. He was a large man, well over six feet tall in a somewhat rumpled brown suit. Something about the man endeared him to me. Although he gave us the same speech he had delivered to innumerable other families, I did not doubt his sincerity. He told us he would carry Katie out to the car, treating her with the same dignity and respect that he would for his own child. Nurse Kelly interjected, saying that she carried her patients out. With that, she swaddled Katie in the blanket, held Katie against her chest, and left the room with the representative trailing behind.

We exited the PICU for the last time as a family just before 5:00 a.m. A light rain fell as we parted ways in the parking lot. Out of words to say, I drove Krista home in silence.

CHAPTER 31

Goodbyes

AFTER TWO HOURS OF SLEEP, I woke to the sound of my alarm at 8:00 a.m. Friday morning. Dragging myself past the empty nursery to my desk, I started making arrangements. Fr. Jim planned to host a retreat the next day, complicating the scheduling of a funeral mass. When I spoke with the priest that morning, I proposed having the funeral that very afternoon. Clearly, the strain of the last week and sleep deprivation did a number on my thought process. Fr. Jim very kindly pointed out how difficult that would be both emotionally and logistically. We agreed to a Monday service at St. Pius X in Indianapolis. We also needed something in Connellsville preceding the burial on Tuesday so family and friends could pay their last respects. Katie had Anointing of the Sick three times in one day, so I figured two funerals in a week was equally acceptable. I contacted the service coordinator at my hometown parish, Immaculate Conception Church, and requested a funeral mass identical to that of my grandmother's for Tuesday, April 15.

My attention then turned to the obituary. I added the grandparents' names per my mother's request. Otherwise, I submitted my draft unchanged:

> Katherine Elizabeth Murtha, aged 10 months, passed away peacefully in her mother's arms on April 11, 2014 after a heroic struggle against a congenital heart defect. Born on June 3, 2013, Katie touched many lives during her time on Earth. She was always surrounded by the love of her parents, family, pastor, fellow parishioners, caregivers, and friends. Her courage, strength, and determination will forever inspire those who knew her. She will be greatly missed.

> Katie is the daughter of Indianapolis residents John ("Jack") and Krista (Davies) Murtha, formerly of Connellsville, PA and Brush, CO, respectively … In her all-too-brief life, Katie enjoyed playing with her stuffed animals, watching her mobile, visiting with friends and family, and listening to The Beach Boys. She was an accomplished hand holder.
>
> The family would like to thank the staff at St. Vincent Women's Hospital and Peyton Manning Children's Hospital for a year of extraordinary care. Katie's nurses, too numerous to name, are the unsung heroes in her story. The family also expresses their appreciation for the innumerable prayers, cards, gifts, and [expressions of] support from family, friends, and strangers alike … In lieu of flowers, the family suggests contributions toward a memorial for Katie at Peyton Manning Children's Hospital

I realized the mistaken omission of the therapists, equally deserving of recognition as the nurses, when I saw the obituary in the paper.

My mother, sister, and Aunt Betty returned to Pennsylvania that morning. My mom had been silently suffering with a broken tooth since the beginning of the week and needed dental intervention as soon as possible. Meanwhile, Aunt Betty's father-in-law had fallen critically ill with congestive heart failure and was fighting for his life in a hospital outside of Pittsburgh. Dad, his wife Elaine, and my Aunt Elaine remained in Indianapolis for the services. Krista's family arrived from Colorado on Friday and Saturday along with one of my cousins from Pennsylvania.

Krista and I met with a representative at the funeral home at 2:00 p.m. on Friday. We planned the visitation for 5 – 8 p.m. on Saturday so that day and night shift staff could attend. Fearing a low turnout given our cloistered life over the past ten months, I hoped three hours were not too long. After the meeting, Krista went off with Amy to run errands while I crashed back at the house.

I woke to the sounds of Krista's family downstairs in the living room. Not wanting to be social, I feigned sleep in our bedroom. Krista eventually took them to dinner, giving me the opportunity to grab food at a drive-through and eat at home in solitude. I found lots of comfort in lots of comfort food that night. Krista went straight to bed when she returned home, stopping only to wish me goodnight as I succumbed to a food coma on the couch.

Krista and I arrived at the visitation with trepidation. The mortician's caution regarding open caskets and babies rang in my ears. Dad and I ensured Katie looked presentable prior to opening the viewing to the public, a traditional Catholic custom. She was beautiful, and we quickly decided to proceed as scheduled. Dad and Elaine brought a huge bouquet of white roses, which Amy surrounded with picture frames showing off our favorite Katie photos.

Lynne and Erin, Katie's favorite therapists, arrived first. Erin carried a wire bunny sculpture as a gift. I had not realized that others noticed my "Hunny Bunny" nickname for Katie. This metal bunny therefore not only represented Katie, but also the close relationships our family had formed with her many caregivers. The bunny has kept an eye on our family from its vantage point on the mantle ever since.

My fears over a poor turnout were unfounded. Scores of people came to pay their last respects, including Dr. Bob, Katie's three prime NICU nurses, and a handful of our favorite PICU and home nurses. Katie's friend, Kaitlyn, attended with her parents. Dawn, instrumental in helping Krista while I was in Rock Island, paid her final respects along with her husband. Katie's pediatrician, Dr. Stoesz, visited with his wife. A fellow Guardsman drove more than three hours from Chicago. Friends from Legal Aid, St. Pius X, and hospice stopped to say goodbye to Katie. The large crowd forced us to extend the visitation by an hour.

Once the visitors departed, Fr. Jim led the family through an "Our Father" and "Hail Mary" and the song the priest sang during all of his visits, "Jesus Loves Me." He then completed Katie's nighttime routine with the song Krista had sung to Katie during the pregnancy:

Goodnight, Sweetheart, well, it's time to go.
Goodnight, Sweetheart, well, it's time to go.
I hate to leave you but I really must say,
"Goodnight, Sweetheart, Goodnight."

The room fell silent after the song, and Fr. Jim invited those remaining to approach the casket. One by one, family members approached Katie and said their final goodbyes. After everyone departed, Krista and I knelt at the casket for the last time. Before leaving, Krista removed Tracy's rosaries from Katie's wrist, but left the lovie Kat had given Katie on the day she left the NICU. I placed my hand lightly on Katie's chest, told her I loved her, and walked away.

I caught Fr. Jim milling around a throng of people just outside the main parlor. I told him the service coordinator gave us a list of potential gospel readings for the funeral, and I did not want any of them. A few weeks earlier, an old Air Force friend sent me an email with a biblical quote in the signature block that I thought perfect for the occasion:

> As [Jesus] went along, he saw a man blind from birth. His disciples asked him, "Rabbi, who sinned, this man or his parents, that he was born blind?" "Neither this man nor his parents sinned," said Jesus, "it is so that the works of God might be made visible through him." (John 9: 1-3).

I believe that passage captures the reason for Katie's existence. The adversity she faced framed her life; it did not define her life. She inspired many people to be aware of and thankful for the blessings God had given them. Fr. Jim used it as the gospel for Katie's funeral.

Krista and I attended the 11:00 a.m. service at St. Pius X with Dad and Elaine on Sunday morning. Fr. Jim announced Katie's passing before starting mass. A parishioner behind us exclaimed, "Oh, no!" Anonymous amongst the hundreds of people at the service, their collective sadness and love for a little girl they never met touched me profoundly.

We returned to the church the following morning for Katie's funeral. Fr. Jim, Fr. John (the St. Vincent Hospital chaplain), and a parish deacon presided over the mass. My friends John and Micah, who visited Katie a month earlier, served as pallbearers. Each standing well over six-feet-tall, the men towered over the tiny casket they carried through the church. To see so many friends attend the service both comforted and humbled me. Fr. Jim gave a stirring homily and said a beautiful mass. Following the service, John and Micah carried the casket to the hearse while the family followed.

After the funeral, Krista and I changed into comfortable clothes for the trip to Connellsville. Before leaving Indianapolis, we retrieved the tiny casket at the funeral home. We decided to transport it ourselves. I felt it our responsibility. Moreover, the gesture meant a victory against the heart defect that had so controlled our lives. Ebstein's Anomaly prevented us from taking Katie to Connellsville during her lifetime. Now that she was gone, it no longer held that power over us.

A woman at the funeral home carried the casket to our car under one arm. I placed it on a blanket Krista spread out in the back of the SUV. We surrounded the casket with flowers and left for Pennsylvania. By the time we arrived at the Connellsville funeral home seven hours later, a nasty storm was bathing the town in a cold, hard rain. The funeral home owner greeted us in the parking lot. As the rain soaked his clothing, he promised to take good care of Katie.

The funeral at Immaculate Conception on Tuesday morning was every bit as beautiful as that in Indianapolis, another fitting tribute to Katie. Once again, the number of attendees overwhelmed us. Most of Krista's family made the journey from Indiana. My friend, Johanna, who had been instrumental in our selection of Katie's surgeon on the day of her birth, came in from Virginia. My cousin, studying to be a monk, and one of his brothers from St. Francis of Loretto Friary represented the Order. The monks had been praying for Katie throughout her life. Friends and distant family members I had not seen in years turned out to honor Katie.

Less than four years earlier, Krista and I sat in the same pew during our wedding. I never thought we would return under these circumstances. We watched the attendees pass by the casket during communion, many of whom placing their hands on its polished wood.

We proceeded to the chapel at St. Joseph's Cemetery for a brief service following the funeral. Fr. Bob led us in one last "Our Father" and "Hail Mary" before praying that we go in peace. I removed the wooden cross that adorned the casket after everyone paid his or her final respects. Krista, mom, and I were the last to leave. A slight rain fell from the overcast sky as we left the cemetery.

Before departing for Indianapolis the next day, Krista and I stopped by the cemetery. As we walked to the grave, I saw a family friend standing beside a tombstone across the narrow access road from Katie. Harry's twenty-year-old daughter died in her sleep unexpectedly fourteen years earlier. I gave Krista some time alone with Katie and visited Harry. Sharing the unfortunate experience of losing daughters, we commiserated together.

Once Krista returned to the car, I approached Katie's final place of rest. A cold wind blew across the Pennsylvania mountainside as I stood looking at the disturbed ground. Just a few feet over, on the other side of my maternal grandfather, a few blades of grass had emerged from my grandmother's grave. As I thought about the past ten months, I took solace in knowing neither Katie nor my grandmother would again experience pain. More than any other emotion, I felt pride. Fate dealt Katie a terrible hand, but she rose to the challenge. I recalled the words of St. Paul: "I have competed well, I have finished the race, I have kept the faith." (2 Timothy 4:7). She certainly had.

I asked my grandmother to take care of Katie and turned to leave. Out of the corner of my eye, a glint of white caught my attention. In the twenty-seven days since my grandmother's burial, the flowers atop her grave had withered and turned brown. Amongst the decomposing bouquets rested a pristine white carnation, my grandmother's favorite flower. I picked it up and twirled the stem between my fingers as I gazed at the familiar Appalachian Mountain range in the distance. Before leaving them to rest in peace, I placed the carnation on Katie's grave, which Gram would have wanted.

CHAPTER 32

Epilogue

KRISTA AND I RETURNED TO Indianapolis after a weeklong respite in Tennessee. Standing in our kitchen, we paused at the sight of the toys, stuffed animals, and other baby accoutrements strewn about the house. Krista broke the silence, saying, "We have a lot of work to do." Those eight words established our attitude going forward. With another baby less than five months away, we chose to focus on preparing for Katie's sister. The chore proved cathartic, especially for Krista. This is but one example of Krista's pregnancy being a lifeline by which we pulled ourselves up from the despair of losing Katie.

Happiness is a choice, albeit sometimes a difficult choice. People who suffer tragedies must decide whether they will let these events define them. Those who embrace their victimhood condemn themselves to perpetual misery. Ebstein's Anomaly has already cost me more than my share of heartache. I refuse to allow it anymore. Moreover, wearing sackcloth and sitting in ashes would merely accentuate Katie's misfortune at the expense of not celebrating her life.

Countless people have expressed their sympathies since Katie's passing. After stating my appreciation, I always say, "We were lucky to have her as long as we did. We're thankful for that." Framing any further discussion in positive terms, I hope to leave the person inspired instead of saddened.

Having spent the previous ten months singularly focused on Katie, Krista and I struggled in returning to our prior lives. Conditioned to the acute intensity of the hospital, we found our careers mundane by comparison. We slowly acclimated to our newfound normalcy over the next few months. Neither of us, however, returned to our pre-Katie selves. Katie forever changed us; I hope for the better. I certainly have a better appreciation for the gift of life and perspective on what truly matters. My professional ambition has ebbed somewhat, offset by a greater desire to be a good and present father.

We made almost all of Katie's possessions available for her sibling's use; however, we did retire a few items. Katie's faithful stuffed dog, turtle, and zebra now occupy a shelf in our china hutch, forevermore keeping watch over the family. I keep Katie's Supergirl costume and the last dress she wore safely tucked away in my desk. I do not yet know what I will ultimately do with them.

Katie wore Tracy's rosaries during the visitation, and there Tracy intended them to remain. I convinced her that Katie's siblings would want them, so Krista removed the rosaries before the casket closed. They now sit amongst the items formerly decorating Katie's room.

Aside from her stuffed dog, Katie's favorite possession was her mobile. The toy gave out after we left the hospital. With heavy hearts, we bought a replacement for her sister.

I returned to the St. Vincent campus fifteen days after losing Katie. Waking up before dawn on a Saturday morning, I donned a grey PMCH shirt and, after a brief stop, headed to the NICU. I once planned to deliver donuts to the NICU and PICU with Katie monthly to thank those who cared for her and, more importantly, teach Katie the importance of showing appreciation. Now that Katie was gone, I resolved to continue the practice alone until Katie's sibling could join me. After leaving a box of donut holes for the NICU nurses, I drove to the PICU.

Entering PMCH through Door 4, I found the main lobby deserted. The room felt different, foreign. Crossing the expanse towards the elevator, I realized that I, not the room, had changed. I no longer felt the persistent, crushing stress of parenting a critically ill child.

The unit representative buzzed the PICU doors when I held up the donut box in front of the security camera. I delivered them to the nurses' station and chatted briefly with a few nurses. Dr. Abraha gave me a cheerful greeting and hug when he saw me. I did not stay long, but did ask whether one of my favorite nurses was working that day. The charge nurse answered, "yes," and gave me her room number. I passed Katie's last room, now occupied by another patient, on my way to Room 2.

Although close to many nurses, I probably conversed with this nurse more than all others combined. Our personalities just clicked, and we are both more than a little talkative. I stood in the hall for the better part of an hour telling her about Katie's final days and the services. She asked how Krista and I were doing, a question I never quite know how to answer. The visit was very cathartic. Just as one pines for a resolving chord to end a song, I needed this formal conclusion to our PMCH saga.

I leaned against the back wall of the elevator for the brief ride down to the first floor. My head hung low and my shoulders slumped. The car flooded with light when the doors opened. I straightened myself and looked up to see Dr. Bob. After exchanging salutations, Dr. Bob said Krista and I would benefit from seeing a counselor. I told him I would think about it, shook his hand, and went home.

I never spoke with a counselor, instead finding solace in talking with people who cared for or knew Katie. The relationships forged with supporters and caregivers throughout Katie's life became an invaluable resource in coping with her death. Friends and family freely forwarded my messages, exponentially expanding the number of people Katie touched. For more than a year after the funeral, I encountered strangers who followed Katie's story from my e-mails. Hearing so many speak of how Katie inspired and moved them proved to be the best medicine.

I tend to commit to projects without fully appreciating their magnitude. Katie's signature book turned out to be yet another example. Inspired by the message Dr. Abarbanell wrote in the book in which I kept medical notes, I began collecting signatures of Katie's supporters and caregivers. Since few people outside the hospital met Katie because of visitor restrictions or geographical distance, the book is the one item that all these people touched.

Collecting signatures in Indianapolis during Katie's hospitalization gave me something to do. I began the daunting task of gathering the remaining signatures after she was gone: 685 people in 29 states. The signatures are a visceral representation of the wealth of support and love Katie received, with each person supporting Katie in his or her own way.

I added two men to Katie's book during an implausible meeting in Peoria, Illinois. My Guard unit typically trains over the first weekend of the month. In May of 2016, the Commander added another event on the third weekend. To reach the base in Springfield, I drive ninety minutes east to Peoria and then head due south for an hour. As luck would have it, The Beach Boys were playing in Peoria that Friday night. The touring band consists of founder Mike Love and Bruce Johnston, who joined the band in 1965 and whose voice is prominent on "California Girls" and "God Only Knows." Johnston also penned Barry Manilow's "I Write the Songs." Krista could not make the show, and I did not intend to go alone.

Needing one more signature in Springfield, I had Katie's book as well as an early draft of this memoir with me that weekend. On a lark, I searched for the concert venue as I approached Peoria. Seeing it was only a few minutes out of my way, I took the next exit to find two Beach Boys.

I arrived at the Civic Center more than three hours before the concert. The surrounding area was dead at 4:45 on a Friday night. I parked at a Catholic church directly across from the venue and walked to an open door I surmised led to the stage. An elderly man wearing a yellow vest sat alone in a folding chair beside the door. I planned to ask him the best way to get an autograph but wanted to warm him up a little first. I asked him about the building's architecture. Apparently starving for conversation, he was happy to talk.

A van stopped fifty feet from the door within five minutes. The supporting musicians exited along with Bruce Johnston. Carrying a garment bag over his shoulder, he walked directly to us and introduced himself. I asked for an autograph, and he readily obliged. I briefly explained the book's significance and Katie's love of his music. He seemed genuinely touched. Bruce thumbed through the draft of this memoir, which sported a picture of Katie on the front, and said, "I'll give this to Mike [Love] upstairs." I thanked him and rejoined the security guard. Thinking I missed the lead singer, I bid the guard farewell and headed to my car.

I had not taken five steps before another van pulled up and Mike Love exited. I requested an autograph, and he graciously pulled a pen from his pocket. A light mist had started falling and, not wanting to expose Katie's book to the elements, I asked if we could step inside the facility. He agreed, and we entered a small vestibule.

Mike recoiled slightly when I first pulled Katie's book from its protective cover. I imagine he expected an album or some other piece of Beach Boys memorabilia. I gave him a thirty-second description of Katie's story. That was normally more than enough time for Katie to work her charm, and it sufficed for Mike. He asked me about her condition and quality of life. I explained how important music was to her and how much she loved that of his band. He expounded on the healing power of music and said, "You know, Katie's listening to us right now. She's listening." Of that, I had no doubt.

We discussed Katie for a few more minutes before he signed her book. After shaking my hand, he and his assistant walked up a staircase behind the stage. I started to walk back to the door when something stopped me. I returned to the bottom of the stairs and called out, "Mike, one more thing…." He stopped and turned to me as I quickly relayed the story of playing "Good Vibrations" to Katie before her first surgery. He thanked me for sharing that moment with him, and I headed for the door. When out of view, I heard him say to his assistant,

"Wow, what a story. Can you believe that? What a story."

Yes, it is. I returned to the highway after a twenty-five minute detour in which I found two Beach Boys in, of all places, Peoria, Illinois.

The other three surviving Beach Boys rarely tour, but I tracked them down in the three months following the chance Peoria meeting. All five Beach Boys signed the book. Katie would be pleased.

As much as I enjoyed meeting The Beach Boys, those experiences paled in comparison to meeting with Katie's loyal supporters. The book prompted me to seek out and thank them for their support. Many were unaware of how much their email, cards, and texts, which they perceived as insignificant, meant to us. Unquestionably, I benefitted the most from these interactions. The balm of witnessing how Katie affected so many people soothed the ever-present sorrow of missing her.

As of this writing, I have traveled to nineteen states to collect signatures. Upon completing that task, I will add an index of the people within the book along with a description of who they are and how we know them for the benefit of Katie's sisters and future generations. My favorite emails will fill in whatever pages remain. After copying the book, I will preserve the original for Katie's siblings – a gift from their big sister.

I searched for books describing the experience of caring for a critically ill child throughout Katie's life with little success. I found books on spirituality, religion, and grief, but nothing that focused on the day-to-day existence of a parent in such a situation. Fueled by countless people saying, "I can't imagine what that was like," I decided to memorialize Katie's story a few months after losing her.

The writing process, although often a lonely endeavor, proved extremely cathartic. After Krista and the baby were in bed, I sat at the kitchen table going through notes and sketched an outline. Katie's story materialized on paper in coffee shops, fast-food restaurants, greasy spoons, and hotels over the course of a year. I called the countless hours on the computer my "Katie time." Feeling a strong connection with Katie while writing her story, I felt as though I wrote *with*, and not *for*, her. I promised Katie I would proselytize her story. With the memoir complete, I kept my promise.

People often ask me how Krista and I are coping as a couple with all that transpired. I understand the reason for their concern. Relationships certainly crumble from much lesser strain. We grew closer throughout Katie's ordeal. I do not know why exactly and would never claim to be a relationship expert. Although reticent to offer relationship advice, I believe three attributes significantly enhanced our ability to advocate on Katie's behalf:

- We both maintained a positive outlook. Even when depression tore at us, we faked positivity very well.
- We recognized and accepted our strengths and weaknesses. Krista was undoubtedly most qualified to manage Katie's care, while the role of communications manager came naturally to me. We gave each other proper deference and appreciation.
- Most importantly, we forgave each other's failings.

Regarding the last point, I tried in vain to come up with examples of my failings for this chapter. When I asked Krista, she told me that she could write an entire book on that subject alone. I suppose a sense of humor helps, too.

I found my wedding ring hidden amongst the stacks of cards and letters on my desk exactly three months after losing it. I now keep the replacement ring in my dresser as a backup. To the great surprise of family and friends, I have yet to need it.

Although a doctor and technician failed to diagnose Katie's defect during her ultrasound, we never filed a malpractice claim. On principle, we were reticent to drag someone to court for making an honest mistake. Moreover, as a hospital employee, Krista was reluctant to sue her employer. The big concern, however, was how litigation would affect Katie's continued care in the hospital. Krista directed me to hold off on any malpractice considerations until Katie came home.

Krista asked me to explore our options a year after losing Katie. She hoped a lawsuit would increase the diligence of the doctor who missed Katie's defect after a cursory reading of her films. A successful malpractice claim requires establishing a breach of the standard of care and damages. I felt confident that I could establish the former, but not the latter. Early intervention may not have improved Katie's prognosis, but, at the very least, she would have been born during a scheduled C-Section. One could reasonably argue that may have prevented the cerebral bleed. After receiving advice from a few attorneys who lacked my emotional involvement, I concluded that establishing damages would be too difficult to justify the emotional and financial investment. Thus, Krista and I knowingly watched the statute of limitations pass.

Krista and I continued to attend St. Pius X Catholic Church in Indianapolis for the remainder of our time in Indiana. Katie's passing did not sever the bonds formed with the congregation that followed Katie throughout her journey. Although he did not know our family, Fr. Jim joined us on the day of Katie's birth and stood by us through the end. We were truly blessed to have such a priest. Likewise, the support of Fr. John from St. Pius X, Frs. John and Ben of St. Vincent, and the St. Pius X community not only aided us in coping with our situation, but rekindled a spirituality too long neglected. Not until this trial did I appreciate the strength of a parish community.

Prior to Katie's diagnosis, I never truly felt a visceral connection with God. The prospect of losing Katie made worldly concerns meaningless. Nothing else mattered as long as Katie did not have her health. No longer blinded by distractions, I felt an intense and tangible spiritual presence. The distractions returned and subdued that connection after losing Katie, but I know now what I am missing. I liken it to a shipwreck hidden under the sea. For years, elders tell you it is there. You believe them, but doubt lingers. One day, a prolonged drought causes the waters to recede, revealing a shipwreck on the seabed. The sky opens up not long thereafter and the sea again covers the wreck. You can no longer see it, but now you *know* it is there.

With thoughts of Katie's undiagnosed heart defect looming large in Krista's second pregnancy, we sought every test available to rule out any problems. The highlight occurred two months after the funerals. Krista's obstetrician ordered a fetal echocardiogram to ensure proper heart development. Krista and I waited in an examination room on the first floor of St. Vincent Women's Hospital, hoping one of Katie's cardiologists would perform the procedure. We were not disappointed. I jumped up to greet Dr. Parikh when he entered. The elation from seeing the doctor paled in comparison to his report that the baby's heart looked normal. Another physician performed a more holistic examination immediately afterward. With two assurances that the baby appeared healthy, Krista and I allowed ourselves to dispel caution and celebrate the gift of another child.

Elizabeth Anne was born on September 12, 2014 at St. Vincent Women's Hospital. Unlike the chaos of Katie's birth, Beth's birth was textbook perfect. Hospital policy requires a NICU nurse to examine babies born under a C-section. Since Katie left the NICU, one of her primary nurses had moved into management. The position had its privileges. When Cindy learned the delivery date, she scheduled herself for the procedure. The doctor who delivered Beth handed her directly to Cindy.

After finishing her examination, Cindy invited me to the bassinet to meet my daughter. Beth squirmed on the mattress as Cindy explained her twelve-point inspection. She pronounced Beth both beautiful and healthy. I nodded in agreement before a feeling of dread struck me. I flashed back to Katie's birth, remembering the fear of losing both mother and daughter. Leaning down closer to Beth to prevent Cindy from seeing my eyes, I struggled for the right words.

> "Before … you know, Krista couldn't see Katie. Before we put [Beth] on the [heart] monitor, can we take her over to Krista so she can see her?"
> Cindy replied in a near-whisper, "There is no monitor."

My eyes locked on those of Cindy. I just assumed all babies wore heart monitors. I never knew anything different.

Dr. Bob often reminded me to bring Katie back for a visit after her discharge, and I always promised I would. I sensed a twinge of sadness in his plea. He and others in the PICU bonded with their patients, but never saw many again after discharge. Although on a smaller scale, I could relate. Seeing many kids come and go throughout Katie's 238 days in the hospital, I often wondered how they fared. Even with Katie gone, I tried to make good on my promise.

Although desperately wanting to introduce Beth to our PICU friends, we feared her catching something at the hospital. After battling repeated infections with Katie, I was more than a little cautious. Krista, on the other hand, was adamant: Beth would not see the inside of PMCH. We came up with an alternate plan.

I invited Dr. Bob to meet us at a coffee shop near St. Vincent seven months after losing Katie. Although tired after a long day, his face brightened upon seeing Beth. I immediately handed the two-month-old over after he took a seat across from Krista and me. Watching this doctor, who had fought so hard to save Katie's life, cradle her healthy sister was bittersweet. For all the time Dr. Bob spent with Katie, he never held her. That most basic human interaction was so rare for Katie, yet natural for Beth.

Our conversation with Dr. Bob differed significantly from our previous interactions. No longer living under the shadow of Katie's illness, we were normal people living typical lives under ordinary circumstances. We sat at that table as three friends, simply enjoying each other's company.

Krista made an exception to Beth visiting the hospital the next month. The hospital chaplain's office hosted a memorial service at the main hospital for deceased PMCH kids. Krista and I attended with Beth. Since we were already in the hospital, I convinced Krista to walk over to the PMCH lobby. A few people broke free from the PICU long enough to come down and see Beth. Before leaving, we sought out two small memorial tiles bearing Katie's name in the hallway connecting the lobby to the emergency department. I find a measure of solace in these reminders of Katie.

The St. Vincent Foundation, the charitable arm of St. Vincent Hospital, raises funds in part by offering naming rights to various objects and places. Aside from the tiles, the only naming opportunities at PMCH were PICU or Peds rooms. Rooms 8-10 in the PICU sported large plaques in the hall with pictures of their namesake kids. I want Katie to have Room 6, her picture forever preserving her memory in the facility. The price tag was and is far above our means, but I hope that, over time, we can give Katie her room.

Many of Katie's supporters made donations in her name following her death. Some gave to the Foundation, while others sent their gifts directly to the family. Before my conversation with a family friend during Katie's final week, I would have simply written a check to the Foundation. He made an off-hand comment that donated money was fungible and, once donated, the donor had no control. I recoiled at the thought of Katie's donations paying for a pothole or some executive's furniture. That conversation planted the seed for what would become *The Hunny Bunny Project.*[11]

11 www.hunnybunnyproject.org

Krista and I founded *The Hunny Bunny Project* (HBP) to provide the kids at St. Vincent Women's Hospital and Peyton Manning Children's Hospital at St. Vincent with items to improve their quality of life. Nine months after transferring to the NICU, I still could not get over the unit lacking a single working mobile. I thought of the tremendous joy the toy gave Katie and wondered how many sick infants missed this simple pleasure. The generosity of Katie's supporters enabled us to right that wrong, to make these struggling kids' lives a little better.

The HBP made its first purchase three months after Katie's passing. Katie's favorite therapists, Lynne and Erin, and one of her primes, Karrie, joined Krista, Laura, and me at a chain baby store to select items. The shopping spree resulted in the purchase of hundreds of items, including mobiles, costumes, bouncers, and sports equipment. Not wanting to burden the hospital, we had a kick-off party soon thereafter where the attendees assembled the items prior to giving them to the hospital. Many of Katie's supporters turned out to help, including some special guests from Ohio. Three-year-old Mia Wilson, who also has Ebstein's Anomaly, traveled from Ohio with her parents and three older sisters. Our families had been following each other's stories since we discovered each other on-line the previous December. Clad in pink or blue HBP shirts, the Wilsons joined Katie's other supporters in celebrating her life.

The HBP continues to raise funds to purchase items deemed most needed by the nurses and therapists at the facilities wherein Katie spent so much of her life. Neither Krista nor I are involved with selecting items to procure. We rely solely on nurses and therapists, who know the need better than anyone, to determine what to purchase. The Foundation graciously covers any transaction fees; therefore, every penny the HBP collects goes to the kids – 100 percent. As you read this, no matter the time of day or year, kids at St. Vincent campus are benefiting from gifts made in Katie's memory. I can think of no better tribute.

ACKNOWLEDGEMENTS

I FIRST OWE A DEBT of gratitude to those who gave me the ability to memorialize Katie's story: My parents, who provided a quality education, and my sister and grandparents, who ensured I took advantage of it; the congregation of Immaculate Conception Church in Connellsville, Pennsylvania who underwrote my elementary and high school education; my English teachers at Conn-Area Catholic School and Geibel Catholic High School, Terry Kopec, Dee Manack, Linda Mongell, John Riley, and Arlene Severin; my composition professors at the University of Pittsburgh – Johnstown, Dr. Patty Derrick and Dr. David Ward; and Jimmy Gurulé at the Notre Dame Law School, whose mantra "words have meaning" is forever etched in my mind after a semester of criminal law.

This book would not have been possible without the assistance of Katie's many supporters, especially those who reviewed early versions of the memoir: Betty Anne Barberich, Dr. Patty Derrick, Teresa "T" Harrison, Laurie Goggins, Geraldine Hensel, David Huebner, Elaine Huebner, Matthew King, Patrice Livingston, Sharon Loftus, Tracy Manning, Sr. Mary Margaret McDonnell, Amy Miller, Sylvia Murtha, Aleta Nims, Gregory Field Price, Meghann Salamasick, Amanda Schneider, Wendy Wilson, and Johanna Wolf. I also want to acknowledge the tremendous support I received from Katheryn Lumsden, who not only reviewed multiple drafts, but also guided me through the writing and publishing processes.

I benefitted from the expertise and assistance of many in designing and publishing the book, especially Tom Geagan, Susan Hampton, Sarah Hollowood, and Sheldon Siegel.

I want to thank the following nurses and therapists for their assistance in explaining the care they provided Katie: Karrie Cottington, Katherine "Kat" MacKenzie, Erin Patterson, Lynne Steffus, and Cindy Syrek.

I also want to acknowledge Wildie "Bud" Richter, the former Scoutmaster of Troop 111. In all my travels, I never met anyone who could tell a story like Bud. I hope I learned a little from his example.

Reliving some of the experiences in this book was difficult. Remembering the many wonderful people at St. Vincent Hospital lifted my spirits, just as they had during our journey with Katie. I thought of two people on the environmental staff often while writing, Bobby Wilson and Niecey White. I never saw Mr. Wilson when he did not have a smile on his face. No matter how busy he was, Mr. Wilson always asked about Katie whenever he saw me. Ms. White left little notecards for Katie with a handwritten prayer whenever she cleaned Katie's room and many days when she did not. These small tokens of kindness did not go unnoticed. I want to take this opportunity to express my appreciation.

Finally, I offer my deepest gratitude to my wife, Krista, who was also my editor, technical advisor, and cheerleader.

ABOUT THE AUTHOR

JACK MURTHA JOINED THE FRATERNITY of parents with kids enduring congenital heart defects upon the diagnosis of his first child, Katie. With no medical background, he learned as much as he could about Katie's condition and, perhaps more importantly, caring for an acutely sick child. He chronicled his daughter's life as he experienced it in his first book, "The Hunny Bunny: A Memoir."

Born and raised in Connellsville, a small town on the Youghiogheny River in southwestern Pennsylvania, Jack joined the Air Force after graduating from the University of Pittsburgh - Johnstown. He subsequently earned an MBA from Auburn University, an ALM from Harvard University, and a law degree from the University of Notre Dame.

Jack, his wife, Krista, and their daughters, Elizabeth and Hannah, live in Rock Island, Illinois, where they belong to Sacred Heart Catholic Church. He currently serves in the Air National Guard. Jack can be contacted at jack@hunnybunny.org.

CREDITS

Forever
Words and Music by Dennis Wilson and Gregg Jakobson

God Only Knows
Words and Music by Brian Wilson and Tony Asher

Good Vibrations
Words and Music by Brian Wilson and Mike Love

Goodnight, Sweetheart, Goodnight (Goodnight, It's Time To Go)
Words and Music by James Hudson and Calvin Carter

Cover Photo: Jan Van Velse
The Hunny Bunny Project Logo: Jennah Johnson

Made in USA - Kendallville, IN
36445_9781544630571
12.26.2024 2045